Lessons from the Bible

VOLUME 1: GENESIS-MALACHI

THE REV. DEBRA MOODY BASS, PH.D

WestBow
PRESS®
A DIVISION OF THOMAS NELSON
& ZONDERVAN

WestBow Press books may be ordered through booksellers or by contacting:

WestBow Press
A Division of Thomas Nelson & Zondervan
1663 Liberty Drive
Bloomington, IN 47403
www.westbowpress.com
1 (866) 928-1240

ISBN: 978-1-9736-7553-2 (sc)
ISBN: 978-1-9736-7552-5 (e)

Print information available on the last page.

WestBow Press rev. date: 9/25/2019

This book is dedicated

To My son

Joshua D. Bass

And my Late Mother

Mrs. Lillie Bell Douglas Moody

CONTENTS

INTRODUCTION

*L*essons from the Bible is a two-volume book of 66 meditations. The first volume will consists of books from the Old Testament of the Bible – Genesis through Malachi. The second volume will begin with the Gospel of Matthew and end with the book of Revelation. Each meditation is written with a congregation in mind. The goal is to encourage the reader – both laity and clergy – to examine the books of the Bible more closely. The result is to apply the scriptures to their everyday life situations.

Each book of the Bible is unique in its own way. The books are meant to not only address the situation the writers found themselves in and the original audience, but to advise future generations who may experience similar situations and circumstances. Authors of the books were redacted throughout the centuries in order to make them relevant to every new congregation. This allows the Bible to be called *The Living Word*.

The inspiration for the book is to teach, by example, the art of biblical writing and research. Sermons should not go from the newspaper or TV straight to the congregation. Study of the text and its history is paramount to extracting *"What thus says the Lord"*. The Old Testament question was asked, *"Is There a Word from the Lord?"* People come to church seeking an answer to this question. It is my hope that reading these meditations will inspire sermon writers to do their homework before mounting the pulpit on Sunday mornings.

May the reading of each meditation bring a word from the Lord into your life as you to walk this Christian journey. AMEN!

THE TORAH

Genesis to Deuteronomy

THE BOOK OF GENESIS

The Reconciliation of
Two Brothers

IN THE SPIRIT OF RECONCILIATION

Genesis 33:1-4, "Now Jacob looked up and saw Esau coming, and 400 men with him. So he divided the children among Leah and Rachel and the two maids. He put the maids with their children in front, then Leah with her children, and Rachel and Joseph last of all. He himself went on ahead of them, bowing himself to the ground seven times until he came near his brother. But Esau ran to meet him, and embraced him, and fell on his neck and kissed him, and they wept."

INTRODUCTION

The story of Jacob and Esau comes to a climax with the reconciliation of twin brothers, whose feud started when they were still in their mother's womb. The story endorses reconciliation rather than violence and anger; as the proper resolution of conflict.

You know the story. When Rachel was pregnant with the twin boys, Jacob and Esau wrestled trying to come out first. Rebekah was convinced that God told her Jacob was the chosen one, not Esau the firstborn. Then later, Jacob and his mother tricked his father Isaac and brother Esau, out of his birthright and tribal blessing. So angry was Esau that he vowed to kill his brother Jacob after his father's death.

Rebekah was so afraid for her favorite son, that she sent him to Haran to live with her brother Laban and his family. While there, Jacob was the recipient of his uncle Laban's tricks. You see, *"what goes around, comes around."*

Then Jacob fell in love with his first cousin Rachel. He worked 7 years for the love of his life – Rachel – only to learn later that Haran's tradition stated that the youngest could not marry before the eldest. Leah was Laban's eldest daughter and Rachel's big sister. So on the wedding night, the sisters were switched in the dark of the night, and Jacob was too drunk to tell the difference.

When he awakened the next morning, he went into a fit of rage, when he realized it was Leah lying next to him, not Rachel. He threatened to leave Laban's camp without his "new bride" Leah. In shock by Jacob's reaction to his trick, Laban offered Jacob his beloved Rachel at the end of the wedding week, if he would work another 7 years for him.

You know love makes you do strange things. Jacob accepted his uncle's offer and worked another 7 years for his soul mate and the love of his life – Rachel. Under Jacob's administration, Laban prospered greatly because Jacob had the blessing of Isaac on his life. Yet Laban continued to play tricks on his nephew. However, God blessed Jacob despite the tricks of Laban. This is why the Bible says, *"No weapon formed against us shall prosper." (Isa 54:17)*

After 20 years of separation from his family back in Canaan, God told Jacob it was time to go back home, make amends with his brother, and settle in the land promised to his grandfather, Abraham. When he left Canaan, his name was Jacob, which means *trickster*. But on his return home, his new name is Israel. Israel means *He wrestled with God and prevailed.* His new name gave him a new outlook on life. Jacob wanted to make amends for his past mistakes. So he left Haran and headed towards Canaan, the Promised Land, in the spirit of reconciliation.

There are some people today who need the spirit of reconciliation in their lives. Some need to be reconciled with someone in your life, or may need to be reconciled with God. The prescription for reconciliation is found in our text. So let us listen now for a word from the Lord.

_____

2)

In order to achieve true reconciliation ***ONE MUST FIRST BE HUMBLED.*** Read v 3, *"He himself went on ahead of them, bowing himself to the ground 7 times until he came near his brother."* Jacob was on his way back home to make amends for his past sins, when he is brought news by one of his servants in the front of the group, that Esau, along with 400 men, were heading in his direction. I can imagine great fear must have come over Jacob, and out of fear, he began to plot in his mind, how he could appease his brother's anger and save his family from total destruction. You know it's not easy to teach an old dog, new tricks.

But because a change had come over Jacob while away those 20 years, he realized the best approach was a direct approach. He would first admit he was wrong and then ask his brother for forgiveness. There was no need to pretend that his actions were vindicated or justified. He tricked his brother! He kicked him when he was down! He stole his identity!

You remember in one incident, Esau returned home starving after a long hunting trip, where he killed nothing. Jacob took advantage of that situation. He only agreed to give his starving brother food, if he sold him his birthright! The consequences of Esau selling his birthright to Jacob meant that now Jacob would be considered the firstborn son of Isaac and Rebekah. He would then inherit all that goes with that title. Jacob would now be considered the priest of the family. He was also allotted a double portion of their father's inheritance.

But Esau knew he still had a blessing from his father as the eldest child on his side. This blessing guaranteed protection and prosperity for his life and the lives of his children. It gave him honor among the community. It promised those who bless you, will be blessed, and those who curse you will be cursed. It gave Esau authority over his brother. Esau did not know that later, his mother would also plot with Jacob to steal that blessing as well.

There was nothing Jacob could say accept "I'm sorry! Forgive me brother." A humble and contrite heart was the order of the day. Not arrogance or excuses (*It was mom's idea*). Not an attitude of superiority, (*although the blessing he received from his father entitled him to have such a disposition*). Not confusion or trickery, just humility, with a spirit of reconciliation.

When we have disagreements with our families, at work, or in God's house, the first step towards reconciliation is humility. We have all sinned and fallen short of God's glory. We have all said some things we should not have said, and done some things we should not have done. Paul says, "*When I would do good, evil is always present*". *(Rom 7:19)*

So let us go to one another, not with 20-year grudges, or attitudes of jealousy and anger, but in a spirit of reconciliation. That is the only way we as Christians can survive the evil darts of the devil. For John 10 tells us, "*The thief comes to steal, kill, and destroy, but I came that you may have life and have it more abundantly.*" Therefore, let us live in the spirit of reconciliation, and not division, or character assassination.

_____

2)

After we have reached a state of humility, **_RECONCILIATION IS NOW LEFT UP TO THE ONE WHOM WE HAVE OFFENDED_**. Read v 4. "*But Esau ran to meet him, and embraced him, and fell on his neck and kissed him, and they wept.*" Jacob approached his brother with humility and in the spirit of reconciliation. His attitude affected the outcome of the situation. For surely Esau and his 400 men could have wiped out Jacob and his whole family, taken all his herds, servants and wealth, and gotten the revenge he was due.

But that is not how the story ends! You see Jacob sent gifts ahead by way of his servants, hoping to soften Esau's heart. Whether or not the gifts made a difference, we don't know. However, when the two brothers finally met face to face, to Jacob's surprise Esau responded with an embrace of forgiveness and a spirit of reconciliation. He even invited Jacob and his family to stay with him in his camp. Because of his suspicious nature, Jacob decided to move on instead, just in case Esau was faking a reconciling spirit, and had plans to hurt him in some way. His trickster reasoning had not yet completely left his spirit.

All the times Jacob had wronged him were melted away from Esau's heart. The feud had gone on for too long! It was time to forgive. By this time both his parents were probably deceased. It was now time to reunite the family, embrace the present realities and blessings of the day, and let go of the hurt of the past.

So Esau took the high road. When he saw his brother coming towards him, like the father in the prodigal son story, all he felt was love and forgiveness. They embraced and wept together.

You know sometimes people don't realize they have offended you. Some people don't care! Yet, if we are going to wear the title "*Christian*" we, like Jesus, must say, "*Father forgive them, for they know not what they do.*" *(Lk 23:34)* Then like Esau, when the person who has offended us comes to us in humility, seeking forgiveness, don't bite their heads off! Don't throw up past mistakes in their face! Don't dismiss them or ignore their attempt to make amends! No, no! Be the bigger and better person. Show the love of God that is in your heart.

The spirit of reconciliation is a two-way street. Let us treat one another with love, respect, and appreciation. Let us not wound each other with words or actions. Instead, whatever has happened in the past *"let go and let God!"* God will fix it. For the word says, *"Vengeance is mine saith the Lord." (Rom 12:19)* Just love each other *"For love covers a multitude of sins." (1 Pet 4:8)*

In the spirit of reconciliation let us worship God as one family, not divided by names, gender, race, or creed, sexuality. For we are all united through the blood of Jesus. Jesus died to reconcile us back to God. The sin of Adam and Eve caused a great rift to exist between the spiritual and the physical worlds. So let us be thankful for what God has done for us through his Son Jesus the Christ. Let us live and love and be reconciled with one another. For united we stand firm against the evil one, but divided we fall for the divisive tricks of the world. In the spirit of reconciliation we claim power and the victory.

—————————————

3)

The final element to complete the process of reconciliation is **_GRATITUDE._** Read vv 9-10, *"But Esau said, 'I have enough, my brother; keep what you have for yourself.' Jacob said, 'No please, if I find favor with you, then accept my present from my hand; for truly to see your face is like seeing the face of God – since you have received me with such favor.'"*

Back in ch 32, Jacob sent gifts of livestock and servants to his brother Esau in preparation for their meeting after 20 long years. Admittedly, Jacob was afraid of what his big brother Esau might do to him, when Jacob learned Esau was approaching him with 400 men. That's a whole army! All Jacob had were a few servants, 2 wives, and 12 children *(or so he thought, God had his back all the time).*

Yet in the spirit of reconciliation, he offered gifts as restitution for his earlier theft of Esau's blessing and birthright. The Old Testament is very clear about the practice of restitution *(Exo 22)*. If a person takes something from someone else or violates a family member, they must repay 2-fold, depending on the nature of the crime. This practice continued into the New Testament. Remember Zacchaeus and the sycamore tree? *(Lk 19)*

By Jacob's receiving his father's blessing of prosperity instead of Esau, it allowed Jacob to receive great wealth, protection from his enemies, and blessings of every kind. His attempt at paying restitution through gifts he received, because of the blessing on his life, was his way of completing the cycle of his relationship with his brother. For he realized all he had was the result of him stealing the firstborn blessing from Esau. Jacob thus felt the need to share from his bounty for the Bible says, *"To much is given, much is required." (Lk 12:48).*

But Esau told Jacob it was no longer necessary, that he had enough. His curse was only temporary, because he was still a grandson of Abraham. So having heard that he had found forgiveness and favor in his brother's eyes, Jacob's gifts of restitution became gifts of gratitude.

Like many people today, Jacob thought material things would win his brother's love and forgiveness. But in reality, Esau had already forgiven him. Surely he knew his brother was living in Haran for protection from him. Had Esau wanted to do his brother in, he could have done so before 20 years had passed! Somewhere through the years, Esau realized that hate and anger only hurt the person doing the hating. Forgiveness frees the soul from the prison of hate and anger.

So grateful was Jacob that he compared his brother's face to the face of God, for God had forgiven him with the same gracious spirit of reconciliation. Therefore, gratitude is the proper response to reconciliation. Jacob was grateful that his brother had forgiven him. He was grateful that he approached his brother in the spirit of humility. He was grateful that God blessed him with the means to offer restitution. He was grateful that no harm would come to his family.

When we are grateful to God for all that God has done for us, we cannot help but respond to others with a spirit of reconciliation. So in that spirit, let us be humble; let us receive the apologies of those who have offended us, for the Bible says not to let the sun go down on our anger *(Eph 4:26)*.

Then let us be grateful that we too, have received the gift of forgiveness and reconciliation through the life, death, and resurrection of our Lord and Savior, Jesus the Christ. God bless you!

THE BOOK OF EXODUS

The Genocide of our Children

WOMEN EMPOWERED TO DO THE RIGHT THING

Exodus 1:15-17, *"The king of Egypt said to the Hebrew midwives, whose names were Shiphrah and Pual, 'When you help the Hebrew women in childbirth and observe them on the delivery stool, if it is a boy, kill him; but if it is a girl, let her live.' The midwives, however, feared God and did not do what the king of Egypt had told them to do; they let the boys live."*

INTRODUCTION

In the Old Testament, the book of Exodus had a role comparable to that of the four Gospels in the New Testament. Its focus is the historic event on which the community of Israel was built. Exodus is a book of faith, displaying God's great power and authority over nature. Exodus therefore, assumed that Israel's escape from slavery and her establishment as a people on Mt. Sinai is the event of God's revelation to God's people. It is God who stands at the heart of the book, not Moses or Israel. It is God's power that overcomes the Pharaoh and gives Israel the victory.

The book of Exodus belongs to the category of the five books of Moses, the other four being *Genesis, Leviticus, Numbers and Deuteronomy*. These five books are known in the Jewish tradition as the *Torah*. Our text takes place in the 13th century B.C.E. (*before common era*), on the continent of Africa. In Exodus 1:8-22, we learn about the condition of the Hebrews after their ancestor, Joseph, died and a new Pharaoh or king over Egypt, takes the throne.

The Hebrew people reside in Egypt because of a famine in their own country of Canaan. Jacob's sons sold their brother Joseph to a caravan of merchants heading to Egypt, because they were jealous of his close relationship with their father, Jacob. They did not know that Joseph had the favor of God on his life so he eventually rose through the ranks because of his ability to interpret dreams. Only Joseph could interpret the Pharaoh's dream and because of his foresight and correct interpretation of the dream, he saved Egypt and the surrounding lands from a devastating famine that lasted for 7 years. He was promoted to second in command of Egypt's agriculture as his reward.

The Hebrew people experienced much prosperity and wealth in Egypt. They held good positions and lived in fine houses in the best section of Egypt – Gosen. God blessed them tremendously and they were as numerous as the stars in the sky (*One of the promises God made to Abraham if he would follow Him -Gen 12*).

But as the old cliché says, *"All good things must come to an end."* After Joseph died, a new king arose in the land, and did not know of Joseph or how he saved Egypt and the whole region from starvation. Eventually, Joseph and his generation died off and the new Pharaoh was unaware of the important role the Hebrew people played in the success of making Egypt a great and powerful nation.

Either this Pharaoh was too young when Joseph's dream went down, or there were no accurate records kept for historical purposes. So he overreacted to the large population of immigrants now living on Egyptian soil. Acting out of fear, the Pharaoh tried to limit Hebrew reproduction by first limiting their male birth rate, and then finally resulting to outright genocide of all male babies. But these midwives were having no part in this "collusion of genocide."

We will learn three lessons that will empower us to do the right thing no matter the unforeseen dangers and consequences to our personal situation.

_____

1)

The first lesson we learn as people of faith empowered to do the right thing, is that ***THE POWERS THAT BE DO NOT CARE ABOUT THE CHILDREN.*** Read vv 14-16, *"The King of Egypt said to the Hebrew midwives, whose names were Shiprah and Puah, 'When you help the Hebrew women in childbirth and observe them on the delivery stool, if it is a boy, kill him; but if it is a girl, let her live.'"*

The Pharaoh was disgusted that his attempts to curtail the Hebrew population had failed up to this point. He had given orders for the taskmasters to literally work the Hebrew people until they were too tired to think about sleeping with their wives in a sexual way. This Pharaoh obviously is not learned in the human physiology. Some things just happen beyond one's bodily control, no matter how tired one might be! In other words, the Hebrew women kept on having babies.

So the Pharaoh launched another plot. This time he was going to get help from two midwives, - Shiprah and Puah, women who were educated in the art of childbirth. He summoned them to his palace and told them what he wanted them to do. He ordered them to kill all male Hebrew baby boys at the moment of their birth. His thinking was that if you kill the male children, there would be no adult males to reproduce! But this strategy again reveals the naivety of this young Pharaoh. As most genealogists would agree, one's ethnicity is determined by the mother's lineage, not the father's.

But these women knew that what Pharaoh was asking them to do was wrong and an abomination to God. Yet, it goes to show you just how far the oppressor will go to get rid of an ethnic group that is viewed as a threat to their security. Pharaoh did not care about the Hebrew children dying. Pharaoh did not care that he would be breaking the hearts of mothers and fathers throughout the land. Pharaoh did not give a hoot about how he would be destroying families. All the Pharaoh had on his mind was self-preservation and how can he keep the Egyptian people secure as the majority ethnic group in his country.

This kind of ethnic cleansing continues throughout the world. We have had a great surge of attacks on people of all ethnicities and religious practices due to immigration across national borders. Unfortunately, many Christians forget that under God's banner, we are all one family. For Paul reminds us in Galatians 3:28, *"In Christ there is no Greek or Jew, no male or female, no slave or free; for all are one in Christ."* If we could all practice this what a wonderful world this would be.

_____

2)

The second lesson we as faithful people of God empowered to do the right thing can learn is that ___WE MUST DEVELOP STRATEGIES TO OUTSMART THE OPPRESSOR.___ Read vv 17-19, *"The midwives however, feared God and did not do what the king of Egypt told them to do; they let the boys live. Then the king of Egypt summoned the midwives and asked them, 'Why have you done this?...The midwives said to Pharaoh, 'Hebrew women are not like Egyptian women. They are vigorous and give birth before the midwives arrive.'"*

Now the midwives obviously are smarter than the Pharaoh in the story. They are women who feared God rather than man when told that they were to kill the male babies born to the Hebrew women. They felt empowered by their reverence for God to save the children instead. In other words, their reverence for God took precedence over their fear of Pharaoh and their own lives. Remember Jesus' words, *"Those who find their life will lose it, and those who lose their life for my sake will find it"* (Mt 10:39).

So the midwives made a decision. "We will not kill the male babies and we will create a story to cover up our actions." This was brilliant on their parts. They developed a strategy on how to outsmart their oppressors. They knew Pharaoh was ignorant about childbirth, so they told him that the Hebrew women gave birth without their assistance. By the time they arrived, the babies were already born and nursing and they could not kill them and blame it on some medical complications. Pharaoh had no choice but to believe the midwives. This, however, only made him the more determined to commit genocide.

As faithful followers of Christ, we too are empowered to do the right thing. We must prevent ways that are being devised to kill our children. Suicide, drug addiction, bullying, promiscuity, all lead our children down the wrong paths of life. But we cannot stop at birth. Our children need safe and educational childcare. They need proper immunization shots and regular visits to the dentist and the doctor. We can teach them reading and writing skills early so they will succeed in school and not become statistics and drop out before high school.

The oppressor wants us to drop the ball and allow our children to wander away from our knees and get involved with the dangerous lifestyles of the streets. We must find ways to outsmart the oppressor! Seeking God's guidance and revering God's word is the best strategy to preserve our children from extinction. If we have too, let us do as our parents did with us – drag them to church. Read the Bible aloud. Pray with them before you go to work and they go to school. Say grace over the meals you consume throughout the day. We are empowered because of our Lord and Savior, Jesus the Christ. He is our role model. We are empowered through faith in him! So now let us empower our offspring so they too will realize that *"Greater is He that is within me, than he that is in the world." (I Jn 4:4)*

---

3)

The third lesson we learn as believers empowered to do the right thing is that __OUR EFFORTS WILL BE REWARDED BY GOD.__ Read vv 20-21, *"So God was kind to the midwives and the people increased and became even more numerous. And because the midwives feared God, He gave them families of their own."*

The midwives received their orders, but could not bring themselves to carry them out. Good will, mercy, and kindness, always finds a way even in the most brutal scheme of power. This is true of Schlinder's List, which saved thousands of Jews from Hitler's gas chambers. The Underground Railroad saved thousands of African Americans from slavery, torture, and recapture. The Civil Rights Movement saved thousands of poor people of all races from economic exploitation.

The midwives' compassion for the male babies was for them an obligation that outranked any orders from an evil Pharaoh. They made the king look like a fool and saved as many male babies as they could before their strategy was discovered and Pharaoh caught on to what was really going on. Yet, their faith and courage kept them safe and under the protection of God. The reverence they had for God helped them make the right decision, do the right thing, when it really mattered the most. They risked their own lives. How ironic for saving the children was their life's work. After all, they were midwives, trained and experienced in bringing new life into the world.

Our text tells us that their deeds of mercy did not go unnoticed by God. God rewarded the midwives and was kind to them. The text said that God gave them families as a reward, which suggests that the midwives were probably barren and had been unable to have children on their own.

As faithful believers, God will reward us too in His own time. Our rewards may come in the form of good health, financial prosperity, good friends, happy families, or just peace of mind. But however you are rewarded, you must give God the praise and glory.

Saving children is not an easy task. In today's society the odds are against us with social media, Internet bullying on the rise, a murder every day on TV, and teen-age suicide. Yet when the "*odds*" are against us, it means the "*evens*" are for us. These "*evens*" include God's power and love. So as faithful believers of God, we know that *"all things work together for good for them that love the Lord and are called according to His purpose"* (Rom 8:28)

No matter the cost, just do the right thing and God will bless you. AMEN!!

THE BOOK OF LEVITICUS

Guilty or not guilty?

GUILTY AS CHARGED!

LEVITICUS 5:17-19, *"If any of you sin without knowing it, doing any of the things that by the Lord's commandments ought not to be done, you have incurred guilt, and are subject to punishment." (v 17)*

INTRODUCTION

The book of Leviticus forms the center of the Torah – the first 5 books of Moses – *Genesis, Exodus, Leviticus, Numbers, and Deuteronomy.* It is used to introduce Jewish children to the basic elements of the Jewish faith. It gets its name from the Levite priests. However, the Levites are only mentioned in one passage in the book (25:32-39). Most of the book's contents address the people as a whole.

A dominant theme in the book is the presence of God in the midst of the community. It always addresses opposites such as clean/unclean; holy/unholy; life/death. The book's primary focus is to make clear to Israel how to stay holy in the eyesight of God, and what to do if one finds oneself unclean and subject to either expulsion from the community or death.

Our text highlights one particular ritual and offering that eliminates the guilt of one who has unintentionally sinned against God. Surely this is inevitable, no matter how hard we try to do the right thing. Because we are made of flesh, we fall, we make mistakes, and we hurt somebody's feelings with an unkind word or deed. Therefore, we are guilty as charged. But God has provided a way for us to stand guiltless before his throne.

Let us now examine the word of God more closely as we too, stand guilty as charged.

---

1)

The first lesson we learn from our text is that **_SOMETIMES WE ARE GUILTY WITHOUT INTENT._** Read v 17, *"If any of you sin without knowing it, doing any of the things that by the Lord's commandment ought not to be done, you have incurred guilt, and are subject to punishment."*

In chapters 1-6, we find the fifth and final offering – the guilt offering. The central issue with this offering is the problem of lying, especially in religious matters.

Verses 17-19 are a description of the ritual that dealt with cases of suspected sins that were unknowingly committed. An example would be to misuse an item dedicated to God for another use.

The expression in our text deliberately speaks to those whose sins are committed "in error" or "mistakenly" but not with an attempt to mock God or commit blasphemy. However the reparation has to be paid for the unintentional wrong that was committed by the individual because the guilt offering is personal.

When we wake up in the morning, each of us has 24 hours to come and go as we please. Within those 24 hours, we will unintentionally commit a mistake. It can be a word taken the wrong way or out of context. It can be an action or deed left undone or a promise to someone broken because of our too busy schedules. It can be an angry exchange of words due to frustration, exhaustion, or gossip.

Yet because we are human, unless we stay on top of everything we do and say, inevitably an unintentional mistake will occur! So God gave the Israelites a way to recover from their unintentional mistakes so they would not be held against their souls. The way out was the guilt offering. All one had to do was admit the mistake and come before God with a contrite heart and a right spirit.

That is all God asks of us. If we have offended anyone, the Bible says that we must first go to that person with a guilty conscience. Jesus then says God wants us to come to him in humility and receive the forgiveness that comes only from a merciful God. We cannot be too proud to admit our mistakes! Can I get a witness? Isaiah stood in the presence of God and when he was exposed to all the holiness in his midst, he cried out, 'Woe is me for I am a man of unclean lips and I dwell in the midst of a people with unclean lips." (Isa 6)

Therefore, like Isaiah, let us not make excuses for our innate state of sin, but instead let us stand in the presence of a holy God and declare, "Guilty as charged!"

_____

2)

The second lesson from our text ***PROVIDES US WITH A RECIPE FOR FORGIVENESS.*** Read v 18, *"He is to bring to the priest as a guilt offering a ram from the flock, one without defect and of the proper value. In this way the priest will make atonement for him for the wrong he has committed unintentionally, and he will be forgiven."*

One of the distinctive features of the guilt offering is the restriction imposed on the animal used. Only one animal was acceptable, "a ram from the flock, one without defect and of the proper value."*(v 18)* Now the proper value was a silver shekel. This guilt offering was no respecter of persons – rich or poor; high or lowly, it did not matter. Guilt was guilt in the eyes of God. The debt attached to the guilty act had to be paid by the offender of God's commandment.

No other offering makes it clear as this one that sin is treated as a debt. In the ancient world livestock – particularly sheep and rams – were used as a means of payment for debts. This fact reinforces the concept that the guilt offering is given because sin places the sinner under an obligation of debt.

In our text, the guilt offering is provided to give relief. It deals with instances where the conscience troubles the individual, but for some reason the sinner cannot say precisely why, or put their finger on what they did wrong. When you have the Holy Spirit within, your spirit cannot rest when you are out of sync with God's righteousness.

The sinner's conscience begins to experience a sense of guilt and feels responsible for what has been done. The person knows the law and somehow feels they have crossed the line in some way although they did not so with malicious intent. So they go to the temple to be on the safe side of the law, and to honor the presence of the Almighty God.

What do you do when in your heart and spirit you know something is not right? We live in a society today where people blame others for their mistakes and no one wants to take responsibility for sin. When I was in seminary, in the 1980s, there was a popular book called, "What ever happened to sin?" The book's premise was that whatever you did wrong, if you dug deep enough into your past, there was somebody to blame. It was not your fault!

But God wants us to come to him when we mess up. God wants us to own up to our mistakes and make restitution through an apology or financial restitution. The Bible has given us a recipe for forgiveness. Today we do not have to buy a ram and offer it as a guilt offering. Instead we just need to believe in Jesus as the Son of God and our guilt will be blotted out. Today we have the communion meal to remind us of our guilt and forgiveness.

All we have to do is acknowledge our sin. For the Bible says *"We have all sinned and fallen short of God's glory." (Rom 3:23)* So let us not pretend we are perfect. Rather seek forgiveness through the guilt offering which is the cross. For though we are guilty as charged, it was Jesus who became our ram in the bush.

It was Jesus who became our sacrificial lamb who takes away the sins of the world. Yes, we are guilty as charged! But our guilt has been redeemed and our salvation has been secured, for Jesus paid it all through his death and resurrection. That's why the songwriter wrote, *"But drops of grief can never repay the debt of love I owe. Here Lord, I give myself away Tis all that I can do!"*

---

3)

The final lesson teaches us that ***GOD IS THE OBJECT OF OUR GUILT***. Read v 19, *"It is a guilt offering; he has been guilty of wrongdoing against the Lord."* There are intentional sins that we commit that bring about feelings of guilt. However, there is also a condition of guilt before God caused by both sins known and unknown, intentional and unintentional. But ignorance is no excuse of the law. Ignorance cannot directly affect the condition of guilt or that our sin has caused a rift between God and his creation.

In the law of the guilt offering only a ram is accepted. The guilty person, with a confession of the sin, brings the ram to the priest. Then the priest kills the animal. But unlike the sin offering, where the blood is then applied to the horns of the altar, the blood in the guilt offering is sprinkled on the common courtyard altar on all sides as a testimony to the individual's remorse.

The reason for this difference in how the blood is dispersed is that the guilt offering represents the need for satisfaction for the sin committed. Again, it gives relief to the one who unknowingly committed the sin against God.

Even when we sin against one another, we have sinned against God. Jesus tells us in Mt 25:40, *"I was hungry, and you gave me food; I was sick and you visited me; I was lonely and you comforted me; I was in prison and you visited me. Truly I tell you as you did for the least of these, you have done unto me."*

Whatever we say or do God should always be the object of our praise and given all the glory. When we behave in a way that is not pleasing in God's sight, we knowingly and unknowing incur guilt. If our lights do not shine so others will see our good works and glorify our Father in heaven, then we are guilty of living less than we agreed to when we accepted Christ into our lives. We have broken our contract with God as his children. Yes, we are guilty as charged!

But God is faithful and has given us a way out through faith in his precious Son, our Lord and Savior, Jesus the Christ. We only have access to this forgiveness because one day Jesus hung on a cross and died for our sins. Through his blood, not the blood of a ram, Jesus became the Lamb of God that takes away our guilt as well as the sins of the world. All of this was done so that we can now stand guiltless before his throne.

Yes, before Jesus' death and resurrection we were all guilty as charged. But today through faith in a resurrected Savior, we are free from sin. God will not see "sinner" stamped on our foreheads on Judgment Day. God will only see our faith, our obedience, and our forgiveness, secured by the sacrifice of his beloved Son.

We will continue to sin as long as we are in the flesh. But do not allow our salvation to give us a license to sin. Rather bring your guilt to the altar, to the communion table knowing that when you get up, as Christ got up from the grave, you too are guilt-free.

As the songwriter said, *"I was guilty of all the charges, doomed and disgraced. But Jesus with his special love, saved me by his grace… Jesus dropped the charges and now I'm saved through grace and faith."* God bless you!

THE BOOK OF NUMBERS

When Faith contradicts our Vision

DO YOU SEE WHAT I SEE?

NUMBERS 13:30-14:10, *"There we saw the Nephilim...; and to ourselves we seemed like grasshoppers, and so we seemed to them." (v 33)*

INTRODUCTION

The book of Numbers got its title because Moses is told to count those who have come out of Egyptian slavery, and later a second count is taken before they enter into the Promised Land. The total official count included only men 20 and older who would be able to join an army. This count was 603,550 able bodied men. Women and children were not counted, so the real total is about 4 times as much.

Out of the many memorable accounts found in the book of Numbers, the central and defining narrative of Numbers is the spy story in chapters 13-14. It is a lesson learned in regards to seeing with the physical eye, which negates the power of God, instead of seeing with our spiritual eyes, eyes fixed on one's experience and relationship with God.

This relationship in the past demonstrates God's power to do whatever it takes to protect, provide, and sustain God's people. The spiritual eyes see more positive possibilities than those using only their physical eyes. For we are told in Hab 2:4, *"The righteous live by faith."*

So let us now examine our text and then ask ourselves the question: *Do you see what I see?*

---

1)

The first lesson we learn from our text is **<u>WHEN WE SEE WITH SPIRITUAL EYES, ALL THINGS LOOK POSSIBLE.</u>** Read 13:30, *"But Caleb quieted the people before Moses, and said, 'Let us go up at once and occupy it, for we are well able to overcome it.'"*

In chapter 13, Caleb, Joshua, and 10 representatives from the tribes, went to Canaan to spy on the land they were about to inhabit. They were told by Moses in v 17, *"Go up into the Negeb, and go up into the hill country and see what the land is like; and whether the people who live in it are strong or weak; few or many; whether the land is good or bad; whether the towns were walled or unwalled; whether the land is rich, or poor; if there are trees or not."* Then as proof of the fertility of the land, they were told to bring back some fruit because it was the season of the first ripe grapes.

The 12 spies studied the lay of the land for 40 days. Then they returned to the wilderness of Paran, at Kadesh, and gave a full report before Moses and all the people assembled. The 10 representatives of the tribes gave their report first. They reported that, Yes, the land flowed with milk and honey, and before them is evidence of some of its fruits. They brought back grapes, promgranates, and figs. The months of July and August were their harvest time. Yes, the towns were walled and fortified. We also saw descendants of the Anak – who were giants from the lineage of Goliath.

The people who lived in the Negeb were the Amalekites. The people living in the hill country were the Hittites, Jebusites, and Amorites. The people living by the sea, near the Jordan River, were the Canaanites.

The tone of the 10 Elder spies was full of fear and doubt. The audience was immediately afraid that they could not defeat and capture the land for themselves. In their hearts they forgot that this was to become the Promise Land for their descendants to inhabit throughout all generations; a promise God made to their ancestors – Abraham, Isaac, and Jacob.

Now Caleb could hear and see the discomfort and fear in their faces. Therefore, he stepped up to the plate and put a positive spin on the report given by the 10 Elders. Caleb first had to quiet the people in order to get their attention. Then he spoke from the vision and victory that comes from seeing with one's spiritual eyes.

Caleb declared that they should immediately go up against the people of Canaan in an element of surprise. Caleb, seeing the same situation that the 10 Elder spies saw, proclaimed through his spiritual eyes, *"We are well able to overcome it."* Now Caleb did not just say, *"able"*, but he said *"well able."* These words were packed with a sense of knowing that God had their back. When God has your back, all things are possible if you believe and see with your spiritual eyes. Caleb saw the size of those men. Caleb saw the walled cities. But Caleb looked through his spiritual eyes and boldly declared *"We are well able to overcome it!"*

With God all things are possible. Caleb said Canaan cannot come up against the God of Israel! See what El Shaddai did to Pharaoh of Egypt.! See what El Shalom did at the Red Sea! See how Jehovah Jirah fed us in the wilderness with both manna and quail meat! Our God is an awesome God and our God is able to provide for us according to his riches in glory.

That is a word for us today. If we believe God will make a way out of no way, then keep the faith and hold on to God's unchanging hand. Stop seeing through your physical eyes. Nothing is too hard for God! Just turn it over to God. Then stand still and see the salvation of God at work in your life and in our church. **DO YOU SEE WHAT I SEE?**

2)

The second lesson we learn teaches us that ***WHEN WE SEE WITH OUR PHYSICAL EYES, THE FLESH DWELLS ON THE IMPOSSIBLE.*** Read vv 31-33, *"Then the men, who had gone up with him said, 'We are not able to go up against this people, for they are stronger than we.' So they brought to the Israelites an unfavorable report of the land that they had spied out saying, 'The land that we have gone through as spies is a land that devours its inhabitants; and all the people that we saw in it are of great size. There we saw the Nephilim; and to ourselves we seemed like grasshoppers.'"*

The 10 Elders spies took an opposite position from Caleb and Joshua, the leaders of the mission. Through their physical eyes, everything looked impossible to achieve. Everybody was bigger, for the Nephilim were the offspring of the semi-divine beings and human women *(Gen 6)*. The challenge was too great; failure was the only outcome; the land is not even hospitable to its own inhabitants! How can we, with only 600,000 men take on this vast land and its mighty army of giants? Surely we will all perish, our wives and children will be taken into captivity, and our men killed by the sword.

Wow, can you get more negative than that! The physical eye is always deceiving. An old cliché says, *"Believe half of what you see and none of what you hear."* The reason is because we tend to allow our preconceived notions to influence what we think and see. Again, that is why eyewitness testimony in court is not enough without some physical evidence to back it up and convict a person of a crime. *(Of course that is not always true if you are a person of color or female)*

In the Bible days, two witnesses had to testify before something could even be brought to court! The judicial system understood that the physical eye is not 100% reliable and can sometimes play tricks on you. That does not even take into consideration wearing glasses or contacts.

But the 10 Elders spies felt the need to be realists, to give a literal account and interpretation to what they saw with their own eyes. They never thought to take into consideration what a mighty God they served. They allowed the physical situation to blind their hearts and minds to the point that they interpreted what they saw outside of the framework and perimeter of faith.

Sometimes life throws us a curveball and we are temporarily knocked off our feet of faith. We then become consumed with negative feelings and thoughts about our situation and want to blame God. The 10 Elder spies lived by their physical sight! That is why the people in the wilderness constantly challenged and threatened Moses and Aaron. They could not see pass their physical eyes.

No matter how many times God made a way out of no way, when they felt in lack or tired or sick or desperate, their physical eyes would fuel their doubt and magnify their fears. Their next thought was to return to Egypt and go back into slavery, a life they had become accustomed to, and knew very well.

If the Elder spies of the tribes – whose role was to inspire and comfort the people – lacked faith in Israel's God surely their negative physical sight was transferred to the people. For after they gave witness to what they saw, the people were ready to stone both Caleb and Joshua.

Sometimes we feel that God has not heard our prayers. We see bills that can cause us to feel overwhelmed and give up. We ask the questions: How? Why? When? Who? But do not allow the questions asked by our physical eyes undermine our faith in a God who created the heavens and the earth. Do not allow the physical eyes of frustration, despair, doubt and fear, to blind our spiritual eyes. God has been too good to us for us to turn our backs on him now! We may not understand right now the move of God in our personal lives. But rest assured God is greater than anything we can imagine.

God's plan for us goes beyond our understanding with the physical eye. Yet we know what God has done for us in the past. We know that *"All things work together for good for them that love the Lord and are called according to his purpose." (Rom 8:28)* Therefore, let us not grow weary or become filled with fear and doubt like the 10 Elder spies. Instead, let us speak the words of the songwriter, *"Courage my soul, and let us journey on. Though the night is dark, it won't be very long. Praise be to God, the morning light appears. The storm is passing over Hallelujah!*

Remember, what is impossible for humans, is possible for God.

_____

3)

Our final lesson from our text that addresses how we see God's mighty hand at work in our lives is that **_SEEING IS NOT ALWAYS BELIEVING._** Read vv 8-9, *"If the Lord is pleased with us, he will bring us into this land and give it to us, a land that flows with milk and honey. Only do not rebel against the Lord; and do not fear the people of the land, for they are no more than bread for us; their protection is removed from them, and the Lord is with us; do not fear them."*

The people's response of fear and doubt was fueled by the report of the 10 Elder spies. Caleb and Joshua tore off their clothes in response to the people's decision to choose a new leader and go back to Egypt. Moses and Aaron fell to the ground before the congregation in anticipation of God's wrath against these rebellious people.

Caleb and Joshua repeat their positive reports to the congregation in an attempt to cancel the reports of the Elder spies. What they saw that the 10 Elder spies did not see was beyond their physical eyesight. For God spoke to Caleb and Joshua and tried to give them a hint of how God had already given them the victory over the inhabitants of the land.

Caleb told the people not to rebel against the Lord God of Israel because of their present situation. Yes, those currently living in the land appear to be mightier than us. Their fortified walls look stronger than any weapon we can carve out of stone. But that is what we see today, in this moment. Just like they could not see their way clear out of Egypt or through the Red Sea.

Caleb and Joshua declared that God was about to do a new thing. Those living in the Negeb, the hill country, and by the sea, were in for a rude awakening. They thought they were protected by their location, their size, and their walled cities. But God can do anything but fail. Caleb told them that, *"seeing is not always believing."* Right now as we speak to you, God has already begun to remove the physical protection from them. We shall consume them as we do our daily bread.

So do not fear what you see with the naked eye. Trust in God's mighty and powerful hand to do what needs to be done on behalf of his people in order to fulfill his promises. For God is not a man that he should lie. Just trust God. He has never failed me yet! He has said no, yes, and wait. However, the few times God has said no it was for my own protection and good.

Seeing is not always believing! It does not matter what you're going through in life. It does not matter who you are or where you come from. God is still in control! God is still in charge! God can make your enemies your footstool. Just do not rebel against him. Just do not doubt him. Instead believe the words of the songwriter, *"I trust in God, wherever I may be. Upon the land or on the rolling sea. For come what may, from day to day. My heavenly Father watches over me."*

Because of the 10 Elder spies' report and the people's rebellion, Israel's punishment was to wander in the wilderness for the next 40 years, 1 year for every day they spied on Canaan. Not trusting in God's power to handle our situations will always result in negative consequences. That was the problem with the Pharisees and the Sadducees in Jesus' day. They would not believe Jesus was the Promised Messiah. They refused to believe that he was the Son of God and that God raised him from the dead in just 3 days. So Israel was no longer the first nation under God. Now every nation has the privilege of standing before God in righteousness and declare that Jesus saves, and whosoever will let them come.

That's God's invitation to all of us. Believe and you shall be saved! For Jesus said to Thomas, *"Blessed are they who believe and have not seen."* (Jn 20:29) We are they. Do you see what I see? I hope so because where you spend eternity depends on it. God bless you and keep you is my prayer.

THE BOOK OF DEUTERONOMY

Making Right Decisions

CHOOSE LIFE!

DEUTORONOMY 30:15-20, *"See I set before you today life and prosperity, death and destruction. For I command you today to love the Lord your God, to walk in his ways, and to keep his commands, decrees, and laws: then you will live and increase, and the Lord your God will bless you in the land you are entering to possess."*

INTRODUCTION

The book of Deuteronomy is the last of the five books attributed to Moses, known as the Torah to the Jews. It contains many of Moses' speeches to those who had escaped Egyptian slavery and had lived in the wilderness for 40 long years. In the wilderness the people were constantly challenged both physically and spiritually. They had no homeland. They were totally dependent on God for survival.

Scholars believe this book was written when they were living in Babylonian Exile. Now once again Israel is facing homelessness, this time spiritual homelessness. She is in Babylonian Exile far away from home. Jerusalem was in ruins; the people were politically divided, and spiritually demoralized. After all they once believed no one and nothing could ever penetrate the walls around Jerusalem or destroy the holy city of God!

The author of Deuteronomy sees the similarities between the past and the present and invokes the former speeches of Moses as a source of encouragement and inspiration to the people now living in Exile. For many wanted to give up on God and serve the idol gods of their captors – Babylon. They asked their religious leaders, *"Where is God? Can God help us now?"* When their captors requested a song they stated in Ps 137, *"By the rivers of Babylon, we sat down and wept, when we remembered Zion. How can we sing the Lord's song in a strange land?"*

Realizing that something drastic needed to happen, the author began to read the speeches Moses gave to their ancestors just before they crossed the Jordan River and entered the Promised Land. Moses' reputation was solid and his relationship with God was a role model for every Israelite.

So when Moses called the people together and offered them the deal of a lifetime – choose life and be blessed or choose death and destruction – the author of Deuteronomy knew that it was time again for the people of God to make the same decision in lieu of their current situation in Exile. Making this choice is the focus of this text.

_____

1)

When the Deuteronomist reiterated the words of Moses to an unbelieving audience, it was obvious, first of all, that there were ***BENEFITS TO CHOOSING LIFE.*** Read vv 15-16, *"See, I set before you today life and prosperity, death and destruction. For I command you today to love the Lord your God, to walk in his ways, and to keep his commands, decrees, and laws; then you will live and increase, and the Lord your God will bless you in the land you are entering to possess."*

Israel's current situation placed her in Babylonian Exile where the upper classes were taken after the destruction of the city of Jerusalem. King Nebuchadrezzer and his army burned down the temple, smashed the walls surrounding the city, and destroyed the homes of its inhabitants. Israel was spiritually confused about why things turned out like they did. Was not Israel's God more powerful than the Babylonian god Marduk?

Was not Jerusalem supposed to be the "footstool of God?" What about the royal theology of the court prophets and priests that said no enemy could ever penetrate the city walls because God was their protector? Was it all just a bunch of junk, lies, and myths? Where is God now and what has God done for us lately?

This was the mindset of many of the people. The religious leaders had to do some serious damage control in order to bring the people back to the place where they trusted God again and become loyal to God alone. So they read the same speech that Moses read to their ancestors on the brink of entering the Promised Land. Moses' audience was 20 and under because the older generation was allowed to die out because of their sins against Moses and their lack of faith in the power of God.

So Moses tells these young people to choose life, not death like your parents did. Choose life, for if you choose life you choose prosperity. When you choose life, you choose to love God because serving God means loving God and your neighbor. Then if you love God you will be anointed to walk in his ways, to keep his commands, decrees, and laws. You will live and increase, and your land will be blessed. These are the benefits of choosing life.

Every day we wake up we have to make that same choice. Do I choose to be blessed today and bless others, or will I choose to be obnoxious, uncaring, annoying, unloving, gossiping, and backstabbing? What choice did you make this morning? Did you come prepared to give unto the Lord your all in worship: time, tithes, and talents? The Bible says *"You will know a tree by the fruit that it bears."* Choose life and it will be obvious to everyone around you. Just choose life and wait on the blessings of God to fall freely in your life. Whatever you need, God's got it! These are the benefits of choosing life in God.

2)

Moses knew that not all who heard his speech would choose life and all the benefits it brings. So Moses also warns us about ***THE CONSEQUENCES FOR REJECTING LIFE.*** Read vv 17-18, *"But if your heart turns away and you are not obedient, and if you are drawn away to bow down to other gods and worship them, I declare to you this day that you will not live long in the land you are crossing the Jordan to enter and possess."*

The theology of the author of the book of Deuteronomy is that *"Bad things happen to bad people."* Therefore, by placing emphasis on the curses of disobedience, the author gives a spiritual explanation for why they are in exile, why Jerusalem lay in ruins. It was not about God breaking his covenant with them, but instead it was about their infidelity to God.

The author tried to get the exiled audience to look back on what had happened, take stock in the present situation, and ask themselves the question, "How did we get here?" No one could plead ignorance to the law for Jeremiah prophesied that it would one day be written on the people's hearts. They had no excuse for disobeying God's covenant laws. Disobedience is the action that releases God's curses upon your life. These curses are not to be taken lightly.

In addition, if they chose other gods in the land of their captors, that would only make matters worse for them. Moses said, *"I declare to you this day that you will certainly be destroyed."* It is plain and simple as that! Do not let the forgiveness and salvation we find in Jesus fool you into thinking that God does not expect loyalty from us. God is watching us, 24/7. You may be able to pull the wool over some people's eyes some of the time, but you can never fool God.

God sees everything we do and hears everything we say. What words come out of your mouth? What kind deeds and actions are you performing from Monday-Saturday? If we fail his word, death and destruction is our destiny. Nobody has to go to hell. Going to hell is a choice we make every day of our life when we do not choose obedience to God's word.

Anything that we put before God is considered an idol in his eyes: work, play, family, and friends. Nothing comes before God. Do not make the mistake believing hell does not exist. The consequences will be eternal death. So choose life today while you still have a choice.

3)

The author understood that Israel was suffering from despair and needed something to renew their faith, loyalty and hope in God. So we find one last attempt to rally the exiles in faith: ***THE PROMISE OF RESTORATION.*** Read vv 19-20, *"This day I call heaven and earth as witnesses against you that I have set before you, life and death, blessings and curses. Now choose life, so that you and your children may live and that you may love the Lord your God, listen to his voice, and hold fast to him. For the Lord is your life, and he will give you many years in the land he swore to give to your fathers, Abraham, Isaac, and Jacob."*

Many of the early prophets, like Isaiah of Jerusalem, Amos, Hosea, and Jeremiah, all prophesied impending doom because of Israel's idolatry and sins against her neighbor and God. They were known as "prophets of doom." But now the prophesied catastrophe has happened and was behind them. All the curses came true. The author sees no need then to dwell on the negative. Yes, they were in Babylonian captivity. Yes, Jerusalem was in ruins. However, the worst was over.

What they now had to look forward to was the promise of restoration. God always made his prophets aware that a remnant, a small elect group of faithful followers, would return and restore the land of their ancestors. This remnant would return to Jerusalem, rebuild the temple, rebuild the city, replant the vineyards, and reestablish God's covenant laws. The promise of restoration was never in jeopardy. God will never give up on those who love and trust in him.

Moses called on heaven and earth to be witnesses to this promise of restoration. If you choose life, you and your children will live. If you choose life, you will love the Lord your God with all your heart, mind, body and soul, and your neighbor as yourself.

If you choose life, you will listen to God's voice and God's voice only. If you choose life, you will hold fast to God, even when the storms of life are raging. If you choose life, you will receive all that God has promised you and your descendants. It is a promise that you can take to the bank.

What have you lost because you made some bad choices in life? It is not too late to turn your life around and choose life. God is waiting to restore you fourfold. God is ready to restore your health, your family, your relationships, your job, and your finances. Do not allow hard times to come between you and God. Paul said it right in Rom 8:28-31, *"What can separate me from the love of God...hardships, distress, persecution, famine, nakedness, peril or sword? No, in all these things we are more than conquerors through him who loved us."*

But you must choose life in order to receive the benefits, avoid the consequences, and accept the promise of restoration. Choose life and let us get on with living for God! However, there was a man over 2000 years ago who chose death on a cross. But he chose death so that you and I can choose life and through his precious blood receive eternal life as part of the family of God. Now your name, and my name can be entered into the Book of Life. Choose life and be blessed!

THE HISTORICAL BOOKS

Joshua to 2 Kings

THE BOOK OF JOSHUA

Receiving the Promise

COMING OUT OF THE WILDERNESS

JOSHUA 1:10-16, *"Then Joshua commanded the officers of the people, 'Pass through the camp, and command the people: Prepare your provisions; for in 3 days you are to cross over the Jordan, to go in to take possession of the land that the Lord your God gives you to possess.'"*

INTRODUCTION

The book of Joshua opens with God announcing to Joshua that his servant, Moses, is dead. The people are still in the wilderness and God chooses Joshua as Moses' successor. Just as Moses led the people out of Egypt, Joshua's task was to lead them out of the wilderness and into the Promised Land of Canaan.

Joshua assumes the command in the place of Moses and preparations are made to cross the Jordan River. Victory is assured if only Israel is obedient to all the commands of God. Moses, and the 21 and over crowd, all died in the wilderness. Only Joshua and Caleb were spared the death sentence because of their obedience to God and their support of God's chosen servant – Moses.

The children of Israel were in the wilderness for 40 years and all the time they were there, all they did was grumble and complain, grumble and complain. Everything Moses did or said somebody took issue with, when all Moses tried to do was to communicate what *"Thus says the Lord!"* Moses lost his chance at making it to the Promised Land because he allowed the complainers to aggravate him to the point that he mistook God's power for his own. So he was not allowed to finish his task.

Instead, God took Moses up on the mountaintop and let him view all the land that was about to be given to the people 20 and younger. There he died and was buried by God. Joshua would finish the journey and complete Moses' assignment. After 40 years, the people were allowed to come out of the wilderness and enter the Promised Land. That is why the songwriter asked the question, *"Tell me how did you feel when you come out the wilderness leaning on the Lord?"*

Life sometimes feels like a wilderness journey. Our wilderness experiences can affect us spiritually and emotionally. The Book of Joshua helps us break out of the wilderness and cross over into the promises God has in store for us. So let us listen now for a word from the Lord.

_____

1)

The first lesson we hear from the Lord is the command to **_GET UP AND GO!_** Read vv 10-11, *"Then Joshua commanded the officers of the people, 'Pass through the camp, and command the people: Prepare your provisions; for in 3 days you are to cross over the Jordan, to go in to take possession of the land that the Lord your God gives you to possess.'"*

The journey from Egypt to Canaan was less than a two-week journey. But because of the people's disobedience to the laws of Moses and their constant grumbling and complaining and lack of faith in the miraculous power of God, God caused them to go around in circles for 40 long years. They were not ready to receive the promises and blessings of God.

But now it was time. Now everything that Moses had taught the generation born in the wilderness about God's Promised Land flowing with milk and honey, was about to become a reality. It was just across the Jordan River. It was within their reach. Their walk by faith was about to become a sight to behold with their own eyes.

They had to get ready. They had to perform an act of ritual cleansing. The day was finally here. Soon the wilderness would be a thing of the past, behind them, a story to tell their children and grandchildren.

When one thinks about the wilderness, it usually conjures up negative images in our minds such as: dryness, death, loneliness, solitude, danger, challenges, hunger, heat, thirst, barrenness, hopelessness and drought. Not a positive place or a place you would willingly go or want to remain in for 40 years.

Yet whenever we have come to a point in our lives that we call *"a wilderness experience,"* God has always been there. Our wilderness experiences are designed to teach us a lesson and until the lesson is learned, we remain in the wilderness. But God is speaking to us loud and clear every morning. God is telling us to *"Get up!"* Prepare yourselves for the journey ahead. Get ready, get ready, get ready! For in God's time you will depart from your wilderness and cross over into the promises of God for your life situation and circumstance.

I do not know what your wilderness experience is today. Maybe it's your marriage; maybe your children or the workplace. Maybe you have health challenges or financial shortages. But whatever your wilderness experience, God says it is over! Accept it! Believe it! Come out of your wilderness now! Step out on faith and know that God has you in his hands. He is holding on to you. God has your back! You only need to keep holding on to him and do not let go. Get up and go forth in faith and God's power. That is our command from God today. Your wilderness experience has come to an end. You only need to claim it and start living it!

2)

The second lesson from the Lord is that **_ENTRANCE INTO THE PROMISED LAND REQUIRES WORKING TOGETHER._** Read vv 14-15, *"Your wives, your little ones, and your livestock shall remain in the land that Moses gave you beyond the Jordan. But all the warriors among you shall cross over, armed before your kindred and shall help them, until the Lord gives rest to our kindred as well as to you, and they too take possession of the land that the Lord your God is giving them."*

While in the wilderness, Moses and the Israelites encountered hostile peoples who refused to let them pass through their land. Two such cities – Sihon and Og – were handed over by God to Moses and the Israelites. These lands were located east of the Jordan and Moses gave these two cities, for an inheritance, to the tribes of Reuben – Jacob's firstborn, Gad and the half-tribe of Manasseh.

So now these 2 ½ tribes are told by Joshua that their help is needed to insure the military victory of their relatives who were crossing over the river. They could not do it alone. They needed to work together so that all of the family members, on both sides of the river, could find rest and settle in the land promised to them by God.

Joshua realized a major element in his ministry – in order to lead God's people, you have to work together – not one group, not one tribe, not one family, but all who were a part of the chosen people of God. For Joshua, there was only one common goal – to inhabit the Promised Land. Whatever differences existed between the tribes should be left in the wilderness.

As a new day approaches, and new opportunities to serve God are revealed to us, we should leave our differences in the wilderness of the past. We must work together under the banner of *One Lord, One Faith, and One Baptism.* If we focus on the "I" in every situation, we will die and God will not be glorified. When we argue and complain, the result is conflict and a lack of communication. One songwriter wrote, *"The struggle is over."* That should be our attitude. Just keep focusing on Jesus, the author and finisher of our faith. Then one day we too will enter our Promised Land, Heaven.

Come out of the wilderness even if you have to leave family and friends behind. Yet God prefers we work together as one unit for him. However, each of us has to answer for our own actions. We can choose to enter the Promised Land and live together, or we can remain in the wilderness and die together. Get ready, get set, let go!

3)

The third and final lesson from the Lord is **_BE OBEDIENT!_** Read vv 16-18, *"All that you have commanded us we will do, and wherever you send us we will go. Just as we obeyed Moses in all things, so we will obey you. Only may the Lord your God be with you, as he was with Moses!*

Whoever rebels against your orders and disobeys your words, whatever you command, shall be put to death. Only be strong and courageous."

The eastern tribes again pledged their full obedience, this time to Joshua. They will obey Joshua as they had Moses. Anyone who disobeys in the smallest way will be executed. They made only one condition in exchange for their loyalty – *"Only may the Lord your God be with you, as he was with Moses."* The Israelites only followed the leader upon whom the spirit of the Lord rested.

We live in a society today where leadership comes in all shapes, sizes, genders, ethnicities, and from every geographical location. In secular and worldly arenas of life, qualifications for leadership range from educational experiences to nepotism. But when it comes to the sacred arena, none of these qualifications come before an anointing by God upon the leader's life. God chooses whom he wills to serve and lead his people. Then God anoints the chosen one with his Holy Spirit as evidence that the person is under contract with God. For only then is God's protection guaranteed. Only then can the leader say get ready, get set, go and the people willingly follow.

When we look through the pages of the Bible, we sometimes question God's choice of leadership because we use human standards and qualifications that we do not even hold ourselves to:

- *Noah got drunk*
- *Abraham lied about his wife being his sister*
- *Jacob stole his brother's birthright and blessing*
- *Jacob's sons sold their brother into slavery*
- *Moses killed an Egyptian soldier*
- *Samson slept with Delilah*
- *Saul broke the rules of Holy War so God sent an evil spirit upon him*
- *David committed adultery and had his mistress's husband killed*
- *Solomon bankrupted Israel and had to sell some of the land to pay off his debts*
- *His son Rehoboam's greed caused the nation to split in two – Northern Kingdom and Southern Kingdom*
- *Kings in both kingdoms continuously committed idolatry and led the people away from the teachings and laws of God*
- *But it does not stop in the Old Testament. In the New Testament, Peter denied Jesus and Judas betrayed him*
- *Paul persecuted the Christians and witnessed the stoning of Stephen*

So who are we to place judgment on God's leaders? We only need to pray for them and support them according to the word of God. All these persons had character flaws, just like you and me. Yet God placed his Spirit in them and called them to do his work. As God's people we are called to *followship* and to be obedient to God's chosen leader.

If the leader is wrong, and lacks obedience to God's word, God will deal with them. It is not your responsibility. You will only bring a curse upon your own life. For the bible says, "*Touch not my anointed one and do my servant no harm.*" Get ready, get set, go!

Coming out of the wilderness was a big step for the Israelites. They did not know what was before them. They did not know if they were up for the challenge. Yet, they did know God had not brought them this far to leave them. So let us come out of the wilderness spaces in our lives, and walk with God and God's leaders, into the Promised Land. God bless you!

THE BOOK OF JUDGES

Too Many to Count!

/

GOD MAKES UP THE DIFFERENCE!

JUDGES 7:2-7, *"The Lord said to Gideon, 'The troops with you are too many for me to give the Midianites into their hand. Israel would only take the credit away from me,' saying, 'My own hand has delivered me.'"*

INTRODUCTION

The man I want to talk about is a man by the name of Gideon. His birth name is Jerubbaal. Gideon was a man who learned that if God was on his side, it did not matter how many were against him. He had the victory.

Our story takes place during the period of the Judges. The book of Judges is a cyclical account of Israel's constant failure to follow God's laws and turn away from the worship of idol gods. The people would fall into sin. Then God allowed her enemies to capture or punish her. Israel would then cry out to the Lord for deliverance. God would have mercy on them and anoint a military warrior (judge) to deliver Israel from the situation.

But Israel never learned her lesson. This scenario went on for 14 more episodes in the book of Judges. Israel sinned against God; God allowed her enemies to oppress her; she cried out to God for deliverance; God sent an anointed judge to deliver them, and they lived in peace for the life of the judge. As soon as that particular judge died, Israel would return to her sinful ways and the scenario would repeat itself. There seemed to be a generational difference between each episode.

We meet Gideon during one of these episodes of Israel in distress. The people were being held by the Midianites, who were at one time allies of Israel. That is where Moses escaped to when he ran away from Egypt and married the daughter of a Midianite priest – Zephorah. The purpose of this conflict was to show Israel that God is in control and not the people of Israel. Let us now review the situation and learn that God is always in the majority.

1)

The first lesson we learn from the text is that **_GOD DOES THE SEPARATING._** Read vv 2-3, *"The Lord said to Gideon, 'The troops with you are too many for me to give the Midianites into their hand. Israel would only take the credit away from me. Now therefore proclaim this in the hearing of the troops, whoever is fearful and trembling let him return home.' Thus Gideon sifted them out; 22,000 returned, and 10,000 remained."*

God once again heard the people's cries for help. God sent an angel to Gideon with instructions that he was to be the next judge over Israel. Gideon, being a humble man, said, *"Lord with what shall I save Israel? My family is poor in Manasseh and I am the least in my father's house."*

The people that God chooses to use to his glory are never proud or think too highly of themselves. God knew that Gideon was only the human vessel that he was going to use to free his people Israel from the Midianites.

Now earlier in chapter 6, God told Gideon to go and destroy the baal idol god and build an altar to him. Gideon obeyed God's command. This action caused the people to call him "Jerubbaal, which means, *"Let Baal contend against him."* But when the people discovered it was Gideon who destroyed the idol god of baal, they wanted to kill him! God sent his spirit to dwell in Gideon and he sounded the trumpet to call the people to battle. Many of the tribes responded and eventually there were 32,000 troops. This number was too big, so through two tests, God brought the number down to 300. The people would then know that their large numbers did not win this battle, but the mighty hand of God.

Sometimes along this Christian journey, we feel alone or that God is not with us. Our enemies come up against us for no reason at all, causing fear to rise up in our spirits. But God does not want cowards in his army. God wants us to trust him and know that he is working things out on our behalf and to our advantage. It may not look like we are winning, but rest assured that we have the victory in Jesus. For in the words of the prophet Habakkuk 2:4, *"The just shall live by faith."*

Jesus tells his disciples to let the wheat and the chaff grow together. Jesus said he would do the separating at the end of time. Everybody in God's house is not there for the right reasons or even to worship God! Some are agents of the Satan! Yet, God knows our hearts and our minds. God connects to our spirits and let us know that he knows just how much we can bear.

Friends come and go; family members turn against us. This may be God separating us from people who mean us no good. So hold on for the race is not given to the swift, neither is it given to the strong, but to those who hold out until the end. You and God are always in the majority. God will bring his people into your life to sustain you and allow you to complete the mission he has assigned to your hands.

2)

The second lesson we learn from this text is that **_GOD DOES THE DELIVERING._** Read vv 9, *"That same night the Lord said to him, 'Get up, attack the camp; for I have given it into your hand.'"*

Now once Gideon had his army he gave them instructions. Each man was given a trumpet to blow and an empty pitcher with a torch. Gideon was to be the first to blow his trumpet and they were all to follow his lead. God only calls one leader and success is guaranteed when we follow God's leader.

So Gideon and his men surrounded the Midianite camp and Gideon blew his horn and broke his pitcher and all 300 men did likewise. The Midianite camp was thrown off guard into total confusion and the Lord set every man's sword against his own army. In other words, they were killing their own people! Gideon and his men had no weapons, only the power of the Lord God Almighty.

The Midianite army was defeated and they ran in fear, with the Israelite army in hot pursuit after them. But Gideon learned his second lesson while dealing with God. God is the deliverer! That is why God only wanted 300 men to fight against the Midianites! As the songwriter says, *"The battle is not yours, it's the Lord's."*

Gideon's men never lifted a single hand against the enemy. All they did was blow trumpets and broke pitchers. God did all the delivering. God is still today in the delivery business. If you have faith God will deliver you from your bondage to sin. Some of us may be bound by fear, sickness, anxiety, or financial difficulties. But whatever may have you in bondage today, remember that God is a mighty deliverer!

If you ask him with a repentant heart, God will hear you and come to your rescue. Do not worry about the situation of our country or our world. Do what you can to help, and leave the rest up to God.

So often there are dangers that we encounter day by day. Dangers we do not even see. But God is there with his angels delivering us. Many of us can remember the times in our lives when we had close calls, but somehow we overcame them. We did not do it on our own, but God was there, pulling for us, encouraging us, and strengthening us. God reassures us that weeping may endure for a night, but joy comes in the morning.

3)

Our third lesson is that **_GOD MAKES UP THE DIFFERENCE._** Read v 14, *"And his comrade answered, 'This is no other than the sword of Gideon son of Joash, a man of Israel; into his hand God has given Midian and all the army."*

A man was telling a dream to his comrade and predicted that Gideon was going to destroy the Midian camp because God has given the enemy into their hands. Gideon and his army were victorious and all the days of Gideon's life the people lived in harmony with God. Gideon learned his third and last lesson from God, a lesson that we all can benefit from. That lesson is that God makes up the difference for us in any and all areas of our lives.

Gideon's purpose was to lead his people out from under the Midianite yoke of oppression. He knew he could not do it alone, but he also knew that where he and his army were lacking, God would make up the difference. Our purpose is to witness and proclaim Christ as Lord and Savior over our lies. We are to be about our Father's business telling others about the goodness of the Lord and bring others to Christ. We may not feel eloquent or even adequate to share our faith with others, but when we run short, God makes us the difference by sending his Holy Spirit to speak on our behalf.

Once we have realized our purpose, then we can accomplish our goal. Gideon possessed loyalty to the God of his fathers. He did not worship the Baal gods but remained loyal to the one and true living God. Gideon had the faith he needed to complete the job assigned to his hands. He tested God, but God allowed it to happen in order to solidify Gideon's courage and faith in his power and might. He learned that God does make up the difference. What the Midianites failed to realize was that their arms were too short to box with God.

God makes up the difference in our lives if we let him. If we do not allow God in our lives, we will be found wanting on the balance when we face God on Judgment Day. When we encounter people who try to steer us away from God's ways, allow God to do the separating. When we find ourselves in trouble, know that God will deliver us. Then finally when we find ourselves short of the mark, believe that God makes up the difference. God bless you!

THE BOOK OF 1 SAMUEL

What Happens when Women Pray?

WOMEN IN PRAYER

I SAMUEL 1:9-19, "*After they had eaten and drunk at Shiloh, Hannah rose and presented herself before the Lord. Now Eli the priest was sitting on the seat beside the doorpost of the temple of the Lord. She was deeply distressed and prayed to the Lord, and wept bitterly.*" *(v 9-10)*

INTRODUCTION

The two books of Samuel and the two books of Kings were originally one book. Over the centuries it has been divided up into these 4 volumes: I and II Samuel and I and II Kings. When the Hebrew Bible (Old Testament) was translated into the Greek (the Septuagint), because the Greek vocabulary is much more verbose than the Hebrew, the two books were divided into two.

The stories in Samuel are some of the best known in the Old Testament: Israel wants to be like the other nations so she demands that God give her a king. Saul becomes Israel's first king. David, a mere shepherd boy, is hired to play the harp for Saul who was given an evil spirit as punishment for his violation of the rules of Holy War. The story of David and Goliath is also found in the books of Samuel.

Hannah's story is a story of victory over life's trials and tribulations. It is a story about what happens when women pray. Hannah has three lessons to teach us as women who pray to God for strength and direction. Let us now hear a word from the Lord.

---

1)

The first lesson of our story is that **PRAYER IS THE CORRECT RESPONSE TO OUR PAIN AND FEAR.** Read v 10, "*She was deeply distressed and prayed to the Lord and wept bitterly.*"

In the ancient Hebrew religion there was something known as corporate personality. The nation, the community, and the family, were all a part of one unit. That is why the sins of the parents were passed on to their children. There were no individuals. Therefore, a man believed that he could live on with a more substantial immortality through his children. So it was important for a wife to give him children.

But Hannah was barren. In her tradition it was thought to be a curse from God. A barren woman had no status in society and was often looked down upon by her husband and other wives who lived in the house. This is where Hannah's pain began. Hannah was very fortunate, however, for her husband Elkinah, loved her very much. He added another wife to his house in order to have children to pass on his inheritance and his name. This second wife was named Peninah.

Now Peninah was jealous of Hannah because she knew that her husband loved Hannah. Her jealously led her to anger and she would tease and bully Hannah until poor Hannah was in tears. Peninah had many children for Elkinah and Hannah had none. This is the pain of Hannah and why she went to the temple to pray to the Lord.

Women in today's society face many pains, encounter so many obstacles and internalize so much anger that we too come to God's house looking for a word of hope and encouragement from the Lord. We know from whence our help comes.

Our pains and disappointments often stem from childhood – daddy wanted a boy, abuse, incest, rape, through adolescence – I'm too fat, not pretty enough, not popular; through college – I'm not smart enough, teachers cater to the male students; through adulthood – why can't I find somebody to love me, why can't I get a loan with out a husband, why was I not hired when I am the most qualified. Even worse is to get the job and nobody gives you any respect because you are a woman!

As women, our pains are real and our disappointments must be acknowledged, voiced, and heard. We must not allow anyone to silence our pain. We must not allow anyone to deny our experiences and call us crazy or suggest, "It must be that time of the month" or "she must be going through the change."

Yet, unlike Peninah, we do not have to turn against one another for the attention of a man! Sisterhood is a connection, a bonding. We need to support one another to survive in a hostile male environment. Do not turn on your sister, whatever the situation. Life is always in flux – everything changes, people are here today and gone tomorrow. Therefore, the need for sisters to connect and remain connected is essential. We need to pray together, cry together, work together, shop together, study together, and share one another's stories of survival and victory.

I can learn from you and you can learn from me. We need not be jealous of each other's accomplishments. Let us not be petty, when we can be loving and kind towards one another. Peninah did not have to persecute and ridicule Hannah year after year, after year. And sisters, we do not have to behave that way either. Let us go to God in prayer when we face a difficult situation in our lives. For it is only through prayer and sometimes fasting, that we find strength and guidance for the journey. For God's grace is sufficient.

2)

The second lesson of our story is that **_PRAYING WOMEN HAVE NO PROBLEM ASKING GOD FOR WHAT THEY WANT._** Read v 11, _"And she vowed a vow and said, O Lord of hosts, if you will indeed look on the affliction of your maidservant and remember me, and not forget your maidservant, but will give to her a son, then I will give him to the Lord all the days of his life..."_

Hannah had enough of Peninah's verbal abuse. The text tells us that this happened year after year, until finally Hannah was not going to take it any longer. So she decided she was going to take it to the Lord in prayer. Hannah got up from the place where they were feasting with food and wine, and went to the temple. This time she was not going to pray in a broad and general sense for everybody else. This time Hannah was going to God on her own behalf. You know sometimes you have to stop depending on other people praying for you and pray for yourself!

The text seems to imply that Hannah had not prayed on her own behalf before now. She just accepted her fate as God's will and nothing could be done about her infertility. Is not that just like women? We take beatings from our boyfriends, our husbands, and just accept it as normal and that somehow we deserved it. The devil is a liar!

But on this particular religious pilgrimage, Hannah was going to do something about her situation. God was going to hear from her directly and she began to pray a vow: _"Lord, if you will look on my afflictions and remember me... and will give me a son, I will give him back to you for service."_

Now some people call that bargaining with God. But Hannah was going to God, and whatever she had to say, or do, to have God make her fertile, she was willing to do it. Anything was better than facing Peninah again and her brutal teasing. So she prays and tells God the desires of her heart. As women we cannot be afraid to ask God for what we want. God answers prayer in three ways: yes, no, and wait. But whatever the answer God will send you away with strength and joy just from the conversation with him.

It was customary to pray aloud. But Hannah was only concerned about God hearing her prayer request, nobody else. She was praying from the pain deep down in her heart and words were not coming out of her mouth, but her lips were frantically moving.

Now when the priest saw this, moving lips with no words spoken, he immediately assumed she must be drunk from the day's festivities. Eli insulted her and called her a _worthless_ woman. The word used here is also used in the post biblical period as a name for Satan. Surely this priest was out of touch if he could not discern between praying and drunkenness.

Hannah explained her behavior to the priest disputing his claim that she was drunk off of wine. Instead she told him she had been pouring out her soul before the Lord. When he realized his mistake, he told her to go in peace and the God of Israel will grant your petition. Hannah got up and was sad no more.

When women go to God in prayer, it is our time with the Lord. Although God already knows all about us, God still wants us to come to him and make our requests known. Whatever it is, tell God about it. Whatever you need, or want, claim it in Jesus' name. Prayer is still the key to the kingdom. All you need is the faith to unlock the door.

_____

3)

Our third and final lesson from our text is that ***PERSISTANT PRAYER ALWAYS GETS RESULTS.*** Read vv 19-20, *"And they rose up in the morning early and worshipped before the Lord, and returned and came to their house to Ramah; and Elkanah knew Hannah his wife and the Lord remembered her. Therefore, it came to pass when the time was come about, after Hannah had conceived, that she bore a son, and called his name Samuel, saying 'because I have asked him of the Lord.'"*

Hannah took charge of her own life. She did not depend on her husband's prayers and love to get her through her pain. She went to the source that she knew had the power to make something happen and change her life. God had compassion on Hannah. There is no pain that exists that God does not know about it. If God's eye is on the sparrow, I know God watches me.

The very next time Hannah and Elkinah were intimate, God stimulated Hannah's ovaries causing them to release an egg. A healthy egg traveled through those now unblocked fallopian tubes and rested in her womb. In God's miraculous time, Elkinah's sperm fertilized that egg and finally Hannah was pregnant. In her heart she remembered, *"With God all things are possible."*

Hannah's persistent prayer paid off! God heard her prayer and said, "Yes!" Therefore, we need only take it to the Lord in prayer. We need to fall down on our knees and pray until somebody thinks we are drunk! Remind God that you are his child and do not stop praying until your change comes. Listen to what Job said, *"Though he slay me, yet will I trust him. I'm going to wait until my change comes." (Job 13:15)*

If you need help, get a prayer partner or organize a praying network. Agree to pray at the same time every day. Flood heaven with your prayer requests. God's nature demands that he pays attention and listens to our supplications. So keep praying! Then like Hannah we can sing, *"My heart exults in the Lord, my mouth derides my enemies, because I rejoice in your salvation."*

THE BOOK OF 2 SAMUEL

Ashes to Ashes, Dust to Dust

WHEN ONLY THE ASHES ARE LEFT

II SAMUEL 13:19, *"But Tamar put ashes on her head, and tore the long robe that she was wearing; she put her hand on her head, and went away crying aloud as she went."*

INTRODUCTION

II Samuel explores this theme: How do the personal relationships of public figures affect the nation? II Samuel begins with David learning of the death of King Saul. It seems that the demands of kingship were too much for Saul, but David felt comfortable in a position of power. When he was anointed King over first Hebron then all of Judea, he ruled his kingdom with an iron fist. II Samuel deals more with ruling and less with the form of government.

When one thinks about ashes, what comes to mind first is that something has been burned or used up. Ashes are usually discarded once the object of the burning has been totally consumed and its worth and purpose are no longer in view. Ashes are remnants of what use to be but is no more and is categorized and labeled as trash. Yet, what was put on the fire to be burned was at one time considered a necessary sacrifice for the welfare of the living.

This is why in Leviticus many sacrifices are required to promote and maintain a right relationship with God: the burnt offering used for celebrations and festivals; the grain offering, a substitute for the poor to use; the offerings of well-being and a peace offering. Then there's the sin offering and the guilt offering used for both intentional and unintentional sins. So there was a whole lot of burning going on resulting in large piles of ashes that had to be taken outside of the camp and disposed of properly.

Our text talks about a different use of ashes and the symbolic meaning behind putting ashes on one's head as a way to denote violation, rejection and suffering. So now let us examine the text more closely and listen for a word from the Lord.

1)

The first lesson we receive from our text is that **_ASHES THAT ARE LEFT BEHIND SOMETIMES REPRESENT OUR VIOLATION._** Read vv 11-12, *"But when she brought them near him to eat, he took hold of her, and said to her, 'Come, lie with me, my sister.' She answered him 'No, my brother, do not force me; for such a thing is not done in Israel; do not do anything so vile!"*

Amnon and Tamar were half sister and brother. They both had the same father, King David, but different mothers, since David had a harem full of many beautiful wives. However, Amnon had erotic feelings for his half-sister Tamar that were not the kind of feelings a brother should have for his sister.

Amnon watched her every day, lusting after her and plotting in his mind how he was going to set up a situation that would bring her to his bedchamber. So he faked an illness and convinced his father, King David, to send Tamar to his bedchamber with food for him to eat. Now mind you, there were many servants to do this task, but because David was unaware of Amnon's feelings towards Tamar, he saw nothing inappropriate or suspicious about Amnon's request. After all, Tamar was a virgin and wore special clothing, which identified her as pure and available for marriage.

As the story goes, Tamar obeys her father and unsuspectingly enters her brother's trap with food to help Amnon feel better. When Amnon saw Tamar, his lust for her overcame him and he sent his servant away. Then he grabbed Tamar and forced himself on her. Tamar tried to reason with him by using logic. This terrible act on his part would label him as a fool in the eyes of the community and she would be defiled and put to shame. He refused to listen to her reasoning, and her identity as a virgin woman was taken away. Any future hope of becoming somebody's wife and mother was dashed forever.

Many women (and men) have been violated in some way or another. It may or may not be sexual, as was Tamar's experience. It may be a lack of respect on the job, at home, in a relationship. It may be bullying or intense teasing at school because of your sexual preference or how you dress, speak or act differently.

Yet, when we are violated in any way, shape or form, our personhood feels as if it has been sacrificed and burned up, and the only thing left are the smoldering ashes of who we were before the violation made against us. We are lost, disoriented, saddened, despondent, depressed, suicidal, not caring if we live or if we die.

But I have come to bring you good news! When only the ashes are left, do not be discouraged. Do not give up. Know that it is from the ashes that the Sphinx rises to soar another day in victory. Your ashes of suffering do not have to lead to death or defeat. Just call on the Lord and wait for your answer. Isaiah 40: 31 declares, *"They that wait on the Lord shall renew their strength, they shall mount up on wings as an eagle, they shall run and not grow weary, they shall walk and not faint."*

If you trust God and believe in his Son, Jesus the Christ, then our ashes of violation will lead us one day to our resurrection. *When Only the Ashes are left.*

2)

The drama continues in the text and reveals the next lesson for us: ***ASHES THAT ARE LEFT BEHIND SOMETIMES REPRESENT OUR REJECTION.*** Read vv 15-16, *"Then Amnon was seized with a hatred for her. In fact, he hated her more than he had loved her. Amnon said to her, 'Get up and get out!' 'No!' she said to him. 'Sending me away would be a greater wrong than what you have already done to me.' But he refused to listen to her. He called his personal servant and said, 'Get this woman out of here and bolt the door after her.'"*

Even though her brother Amnon had violated her in the worst way possible, she realized that he was the only man who would marry her because she was no longer a virgin. In the Jewish tradition she could be stoned to death for not being a virgin or sold off as a prostitute. She was considered "damaged goods," worthless to her father because he could not get a dowry for her hand in marriage.

But now that he had his way with her, Amnon wanted nothing else to do with Tamar. The text says his hate for her was now greater than the lust he had for her earlier! Tamar begged him not to throw her away like the trash, even suggesting that he go to their father and ask for her hand in marriage. Imagine the level of desperation and shame on Tamar's part to want to marry her rapist.

His response was the worst kind of rejection. He called his personal servant to throw her out and lock the door behind her! Can you imagine the physical and mental condition Tamar must have been in? She was bruised and left bleeding from the attack and there was no compassion towards her at all from her attacker, her own brother!

In just a few hours Tamar went physically and emotionally from a virgin with a bright future ahead of her, to a woman who was used, violated and rejected. A woman hated, disrespected, and cast out. In her heart and mind only the ashes of what used to be a good life were left behind.

We have all grown up experiencing rejection of some kind: rejection from a parent, a teacher, a sibling, a friend, a spouse, a colleague, or a boss. Rejection does not feel good no matter how you serve it up. The ashes of rejection can be found at the feet of each of us at some point in our life.

Therefore, when and if rejection shows up where you live, just remember that our Lord and Savior was rejected. He came down 42 generations from the right hand of God to save us from a dying hell. Yet he too was rejected. God Himself was rejected by the very people he created to worship him! *"He was despised and rejected by others; a man of suffering and acquainted with infirmity. He was despised and we held him of no account! Surely he has borne our infirmities and carried our diseases. He was wounded for our transgressions, crushed for our iniquities; upon him was the punishment that made us whole, and by his stripes we are healed." (Isa 53:6)*

Yes, sometimes the ashes that are left are ashes of rejection. Just remember if we are to live like Jesus, we will experience rejection as his followers. *When only the Ashes are left.*

3)

The final message from our text is that ***GOD ALWAYS SENDS SOMEONE TO TAKE CARE OF THE ASHES.*** Read vv 18b-20, *"She was wearing a richly ornamental robe, for this was the kind of garment the virgin daughters of the king wore. Tamar put ashes on her head and tore the ornamental robe she was wearing. She put her hand on her head and went away, weeping aloud as she went. Her brother Absalom said to her, 'Has Amnon, your brother, been with you? Be quite my sister, he is your brother. Don't take this to heart.' And Tamar lived in her brother Absalom's house as a desolate woman."*

Tamar could not believe what had just gone down in her life. Twenty-four hours ago she was a happy virgin with all kinds of future possibilities – husband, children, status, and honor. After all she was a princess, a daughter of King David. Now in a twinkling of an eye her whole world was turned upside down. She was only trying to do a good deed towards her so-called sick brother. But as the saying goes, *"No good deed goes unpunished!"*

What was she to do! Where was she to go? Who would save her from the dismal fate that was ahead of her? In her mourning and despair, Tamar did the only thing she knew to do. She officially mourned the loss of her virginity and future by putting ashes on her head as a sign of humility and suffering before the Lord.

Next she tore off the clothing that characterized her as a "virgin," which she was no more. In this way she was taking control of her own destiny. Finally, she breaks down and cries out aloud in her emotional turmoil. Her full brother, Absalom, hears her crying and immediately suspects what happened to her. Then he saw the torn virgin garment. He saw the ashes on her forehead. After putting two and two together, he figured out what had happened to his beloved and innocent sister. He also knew that Amnon was the culprit.

Absalom did not judge her, how could he? It was not her fault! He did not blame her in any way for her situation (as some people do today to victims of rape and incest). No, Absalom became Tamar's savior that day. He took charge of the situation and welcomed her to live with him in his house, safe and cared for, for the rest of her life.

Absalom knew in his heart that he would make Amnon pay one day for what he had done to his sister. It was just a matter of time. Absalom believed *"You shall reap what you sow."* For the law said a life for a life. Absalom was more than happy to fulfill this law on behalf of his sister's honor.

I can imagine Absalom bought her a new outfit to replace the torn garment and then washed the ashes right out of her hair and off her face. As her big brother, he wiped away the tears from her eyes and comforted her. He reminded her that she was more than a rape victim, using ashes to give her a new identity. She was still a child of the king!

Church it does not matter where the ashes of your past came from, violation or rejection. It does not matter how they ended up a part of your everyday life, holding you down, preventing you from being your best. Just remember you are still a child of the King and, King Jesus is his name. That's why the songwriter wrote, *"Ride on King Jesus, no man can a hinder me."*

Your big brother Jesus is waiting to wipe your tears away. Like the father of the Prodigal Son, God has a new robe for you to wear to replace the torn garments of sin and shame in your life.

Do not allow your ashes to come between you and God. The words of the Apostle Paul ask the question, *"Who will separate us from the love of God? Will hardship, or distress, or persecution, or famine, or nakedness, or peril, or sword? ...For I am convinced that nothing will be able to separate us from the love of God in Christ Jesus our Lord."* (Rom 8:35)

Remember, God loves you, ashes and all! When only the ashes of our past mistakes are left, know and believe that God sent His Son to collect the ashes of your life, so that you will live again with him throughout all eternity. *When only the Ashes are left.* God bless you!

THE BOOK OF 1 KINGS

Jehovah Jira, Our Provider

GOD WILL PROVIDE

I KINGS 17:8-16, *"Then the word of the Lord came to him, saying, Go now to Zarephath, which belongs to Sidon, and live there; for I have commanded a widow there to feed you.*

INTRODUCTION

When our needs arise, so do our doubts! The devil and the flesh whisper to our hearts, *"Can God really meet all of my needs?* Sometimes our needs are physical; sometimes they are emotional or financial; other times they are spiritual in nature.

Now most of the time, we can provide for our needs. It is those times when we've tried everything and are at the end of our rope, having exhausted every resource, that we turn to God for provision, for help, and when we need God the most. When chaos and turmoil are all around us, we must stop and hear that still small voice inside us saying **GOD WILL PROVIDE!**

This blessed assurance comes from our experience with God in the past and in the present. Our faith will take us into the future. So let us venture now into Elijah's world and hear firsthand how God will provide.

---

1)

Our first lesson is **_WE FIND PROVISION IN GOD'S WORD._** We find evidence for this in I Kings 17: 2-3, *"The Word of the Lord came to him, saying 'Go from here and turn eastward, and hide yourself by the Wadi Cherith, which is east of the Jordan. You shall drink from the wadi and I have commanded the ravens to feed you there.'"* God provides for Elijah in the face of starvation, drought, and even the threat of death. Elijah knows firsthand that God's promises to him, have provided for him in the past. Elijah is situated by the Wadi or brook Cherith, east of the Jordan River. He was running for his life because King Ahab and Queen Jezebel wanted to kill him. He went to them and prophesied that there would be no rain for the next few years. This was God's way of showing Israel that He and He alone was the God of the storm and rain, not the idol god baal.

This punishment came to Israel because of the sins of King Ahab and Queen Jezebel. God told Elijah to arise and leave the city. Because Elijah was obedient, he was able to face a situation that might have jeopardized his own life.

But before he could panic and find fault in God's calling him to do the right thing, faith reminded him of God's provisions for him in the past. He remembered when he faced the 400 prophets of Baal in a competition on Mt. Carmel and how God rained down fire. Then when he fled for his life because Jezebel swore she would kill him, God again provided for his security and refuge in a cave. Now again, in vv 1-7, God sent ravens to feed Elijah and a brook to provide water to drink. So Elijah had a history with God making a way out of no way.

When we encounter adversity in our lives, our first reaction is to question, to fear, and to run away from God's presence. Our text today tells us not to resort to any of those options. Elijah knew he was being obedient to God's word. So whatever the consequences he was ready to face them in faith, knowing that God would provide.

We too as Christians, must face our fears and our trials and tribulations in faith and obedience, knowing that God will provide. It does not matter what you are going through. Did God not bring you out before? Was God not there when you needed him the most? Did God not make a way for you to escape? Will God not open doors that no one can close? Can God open up a window of heaven and pour out a blessing that will wipe out all your debt?

Then trust him now! He will not forsake you. He may choose to lead you down a different path, but wherever he leads you, like Elijah, just go! For God will provide!

---

2)

Our second lesson from the text teaches us to **_GO FORWARD EVEN IF YOU DO NOT KNOW YOUR DESTINATION._** Read v 11, "_As she was going to bring it, he called to her and said, 'Bring me a morsel of bread in your hand,' But she said 'As the Lord your God lives, I have nothing baked, only a handful of meal in a jar, and a little oil in a jug; I am now gathering a couple of sticks, so that I may go home and prepare it for myself and my son, that we may eat it and die,'_"

Elijah had a history with God so he knew where to turn in his hour of need. He knew God had been there for him in the past. God was again telling Elijah to go forward, leave town. So Elijah had to trust that God would provide for him in the present, and move forward in the direction of his destination.

Due to the sin of King Ahab and Queen Jezebel and the nation of Israel, God sent a drought that affected the area where this widow lived as well. The widow was an innocent bystander and the victim of an unfortunate situation. There were many widows in Israel in the days of Elijah. Yet, he was sent to honor and bless with his presence a widow in a city in Sidon – Zarephath – a Gentile city. He became the first prophet to the Gentiles.

The person who would host his presence in Zarephath is not a rich landowner, or a member of the religious community, but a poor widow who had nothing extra to offer him to eat. She and her son were about to eat their last meal and lay down to die.

The drought must have caused her garden to fail or the market place was bare because farmers had nothing to bring. Their crops had failed for the lack of rain. So food began to run low throughout the region. There was no supermarket to drive to and pick up what you need. Farming was the primary means for food in that day. The question the reader asks is **"WILL GOD PROVIDE?"**

So here comes Elijah. He had just left one situation where he had to depend on the ravens to feed him and a brook to provide him with water, which eventually dried up. Perhaps he thought going to Zarephath would be an upgrade, things were going to get better, and food would be readily available, plentiful and abundant.

However, that was not the case. When he arrived at Zaraphath and found the widow struggling to feed herself and her son, he was perplexed. What is God doing now? He thought, "I was obedient. I risked my life confronting the King and Queen about their idolatry and sins against you. Am I now to die in Zarephath, a Gentile city, with this widow and her son? You said the drought would last several years and this woman does not even have enough food for one day! How will you provide for me in this situation?"

As far as this woman was concerned, her life and her son's life were about to come to an end. She was going to fry up her last meal cake in the last bit of oil, share it with her son, and they both would lie down, never to rise again. This was her moment, her present, her today. She did not believe there would be a tomorrow.

Yet Elijah asked her for something to eat and out of obedience to the prophet of God, she did as he asked of her. She shared her situation with the prophet, expecting probably for him to change his mind about eating her last morsel of food and leave without blessing her and her son. Elijah assured her that the God of Israel would provide for her now, right this minute. All she had to do was cook in faith and feed the prophet of God, which showed she had faith in the God of Elijah. She recognized him as a man of God and obeyed his every word. His words gave her the faith to believe God would provide for her after her provisions were exhausted.

There have been times in our lives when the now was just too much to bear. Our burdens had us so wrapped up that death seemed like the only deliverance we could look forward to. Yesterday is gone, tomorrow seems hopeless, so the now closes in on us and we want to end it all! We have convinced ourselves that God does not care. God does not love me. I am unlovable. But God is saying to us, "Get up and move forward!"

Do not remain stuck in your situation. See beyond your situation and trust God no matter what it looks like today. There is a new relationship, a new job, a new city, in a new state, with a new company. Obedience is the key to receiving our blessings! It is the voice of the devil that tells us to stay put and die.

But the devil is a liar! God loves you! God proved it one day when he sent his Son to die on a cross for our redemption. God did not leave you alone, no, no. When Jesus returned to the Father, God sent the Holy Spirit, the Comforter, to keep you day by day. We sing the song,

"Lord keep me day by day." God keeps us every day, week by week, month by month, and year by year.

Sure life gets tough sometimes. Sure money is short and the bills are long. Sure pain is a frequent visitor to your body, but whatever your condition, do not allow today's struggles to cause you to give up, cook your last meal and die! God will provide! God will answer your prayers! God will supply all your needs according to his riches in glory. Like our ancestors used to say in the midst of their trials and tribulations, *"God will make a way somehow!"* The gospel singer Shirley Caesar says it this way, *"You're next in line for a miracle. Today is your day for a miracle."* If you get out of the line, you might miss your breakthrough.

---

3)

As we move to the end of the story, we read our final lesson, **_"GOD'S PROMISES ARE REAL._** Read vv 14-15, *"For thus says the Lord the God of Israel: 'The jar of meal will not be emptied and the jug of oil will not fail until the day that the Lord sends rain on the earth.' She went and did as Elijah said, so that she as well as Elijah and her household, ate for many days."*

Elijah sensed that the widow was a little skeptical about sharing her last meal with him. However, she was obedient. She obeyed his command not knowing what was about to occur and that God had already provided for her future needs. Widows were among the poorest class in Israel, along with the orphan. She had become accustomed to doing without, feeling hungry more than full. Today's rations were all she could muster up to eat, tomorrow had to take care of itself.

So imagine to her surprise, even shock, when this man of God prophesied to her that her jar of meal and her jar of oil would not become empty until the God of Israel once again allowed rain to fall upon the earth. Now remember this woman was a Baal worshiper, like Queen Jezebel who was trying to kill Elijah! Baal was the Canaanite god of storm and rain. Elijah prophesied there would be no rain for several years! This widow was unaware of the curse placed on the earth by the God Israel!

Yet there was something about Elijah that made a believer out of her. She went into her cooking room and began to measure out the last bit of flour in the jar. But when she thought that was the last of it, she looked into the jar and miraculously, the flour continued to pour out. Then she reached for the jar of oil to fry the cake and hoping to get enough oil to fry the meal crispy, the oil kept pouring out. She set the jar of oil down and it was filled to the brim. This did not just happen on that one day, no, no, the miracle repeated itself every time she went to the jars, until the rain returned, just like Elijah said.

What jars are empty in your life? What jars need a prophecy from the servant of God? What situations seem hopeless? What sickness goes undetected? Believe today Church that God will provide for your tomorrow and tomorrow's tomorrow, and tomorrow's, tomorrow's tomorrow.

The future is God's business. Stop worrying about it. Let your faith lead you to obedience to God's word. The songwriter said it so well, *"Many things about tomorrow, I don't seem to understand. But I know who holds tomorrow, and I know who holds my hand."*

So let us keep our hands in the hands of the man from Galilee. Hold on to God's unchanging hand. For God's almighty hand was the same yesterday, is the same today, and will be the same forever more. God will provide! And when looking at tomorrow gets you down, just sing the words of this songwriter, *"Because He lives, I can face tomorrow. Because He lives, all fear is gone. For I know who holds the future, and life is worth the living just because he lives."*

THE BOOK OF 2 KINGS

Trusting the Healing Process

FINDING HEALING IN STRANGE PLACES

2 KINGS 5:1-14 (1-4), *"Naaman, commander of the army of the king of Aram, was a great man and in high favor with his master, because by him the Lord had given victory to Aram. The man, though a mighty warrior, suffered from leprosy. Now the Arameans on one of their raids had taken a young girl captive from the land of Israel, and she served Naaman's wife. She said to her mistress, 'If only my lord were with the prophet who is in Samaria! He would cure him of his leprosy.'"*

INTRODUCTION

The book of Kings was divided into two books when it was translated from the Hebrew language into the Greek. The book of Kings begins with the death of King David and ends with Israel being destroyed by the Babylonians and the people carted off into exile for the next 70 years. It covers more than 400 years of Israel's history – the good, the bad and the ugly.

The kings and the religious leaders were supposed to make sure the people stayed faithful to God's covenant laws. Yet, in the end, they were the very ones that led Israel astray and into destruction because of their disobedience to the covenant laws.

Our text is found in 2 Kings 5:1-14. The king of Israel during this time was King Jehoram and the prophet was Elisha, the successor to Elijah. Israel is at odds with the kingdom of Aram, the home of the Arameans, who defeated them recently in battle. Ironically the story begins with two enemies needing each other in order for a miracle to happen! Let us listen now for a message from God telling us how we too can find healing in strange places.

1)

The first message from our text tells us that ***SOMETIMES INFORMATION ABOUT OUR HEALING COMES FROM A STRANGER.*** Read vv 2-5, *"Now the Arameans on one of their raids had taken a young girl captive from the land of Israel, and she served Naaman's wife. She said to her mistress, 'If only my lord were with the prophet who is in Samaria! He would cure him* *of his leprosy.' So Naaman went in and told his lord just what the girl from the land of Israel had said. And the king of Aram said, 'Go then, and I will send along a letter to the king of Israel.'"*

Our story begins with a man named Naaman who was a general in the Aramean army. He had a skin condition called leprosy. To have leprosy in the Ancient Near East, is like having Aids 30 years ago – it had a social stigma attached to it, and the prognosis was death. Yet Naaman is described as a great man because of his victory over Israel.

Now, on one such military raid, they captured a young girl and made her the servant of Naaman's wife. However, at the time, Naaman did not realize his healing was connected to this young slave girl, a stranger living in Aram.

Church, God always put people in our path to offer healing, restoration, and salvation. Sometimes it is a co-worker. Sometimes it is someone you meet on vacation or at the grocery story. It may be a strange encounter at the post office, the bank, yes, even in the doctor's waiting room! You may be in need of a financial, physical, emotional or spiritual healing. But whatever you have prayed about know that God's help is on the way.

The servant girl could have kept quiet and resented her captivity. She could have interpreted her master's illness as karma for her captivity and Israel's defeat. But God put his Spirit in her and she became a witness for him in a strange land. Can I get a witness! Joseph was sold as a slave by his own brothers and taken to Egypt, a strange land, as a slave. There with his gift of interpretation of dreams, God saved the whole geographical region from famine and starvation. Queen Esther lived in Persia, as its queen although she was a displaced Jew. As a stranger she was able to foil the plot to kill her people by the native Persians.

Church, expect your healing, but do not just limit it to the people you know! Trust that God can heal you in his own way and in his own time. God can use anybody to restore you to wholeness. The songwriter said it in these words, *"Any ole way you bless me Lord, I'll be satisfied."*

_____

2)

The second message coming from our text says **_SOMETIMES YOU HAVE TO LEAVE HOME TO GET YOUR HEALING._** Read v 5, *"And the king of Aram said, 'Go then, and I will send along a letter to the king of Israel.' He went taking with him 10 talents of silver, 6000 shekels of gold, and 10 sets of garments."*

Naaman was not in position to ignore any possible cure for his skin condition. So he brought the servant girl's information to the king of Aram. The king could see the hope in Naaman's eyes and because he had favor for Naaman, he supported him in this quest to find healing for his leprosy. To show his support, the king wrote a diplomatic letter to the king of Israel for Naaman to carry with him so the king of Israel would know he comes in peace.

Naaman set out towards Samaria, the capital city of the Northern Kingdom of Israel. He did not come empty handed, because he knew he was coming seeking a service from the king.

He brought 10 talents of silver, 6000 shekels of gold, 10 sets of garments in order to show how serious he was about his healing from the dreaded leprosy.

It is obvious that Naaman was a rich man back in Aram. But at home, no amount of money or fame could buy his healing. He had to leave the comforts of his home, his family, even his country, to receive healing. The spiritual climate in his home country was not conducive to his restoration.

When we are in need of a healing sometimes God has to send us away from our comfort zones so we can depend solely on him. Being home means we are in control and can predict what is going to happen. We have tunnel vision and see only what we want to see, sometimes totally missing the blessing that is right in front of our eyes!

Leaving home in search of healing allows us to be totally open and available to God's touch. Sometimes financial healing is tied to a job out of state or oversees. Go and receive your healing! Sometimes your emotional healing is tied to a different relationship outside your community, ethnicity, away from your family, leaving your current employment or position. Let go and let God!

Depending on the status of your physical illness, God may be telling you to get a second opinion, a third opinion, read a medical journal, go to a support group and share information, or watch Dr. Oz on TV. In other words, do not just accept your condition! Trust that God hears the prayers of the righteous and that *"There is a balm in Gilead, to heal your sin sick soul."*

Whatever your need this morning *"God can supply your needs according to his riches in glory." (Philippians 4:19)* If your soul is sick and your body is racked with pain, let me recommend Dr. Jesus. His blood can heal every manner of disease. Isaiah tells us *"By his stripes we are healed. For he was wounded for our transgression, bruised for our iniquities." (53:5)*

Yes, Jesus left his home – he came down 42 generations. He left his Father's right hand to offer salvation to a dying world. Do not sit still and accept your condition of eternal death. Today salvation has come to this house. You need only say "Yes" to the Lord then stand still and see the salvation of the Lord work miracles in your life. Finding healing in strange places.

---

3)

Finally, the last message we need to hear from our text is that ***OBEDIENCE BRINGS ABOUT HEALING.*** Read vv 9-10, *"So Naaman came with his horses and chariots, and stopped at the entrance of Elisha's house. Elisha sent a messenger to him saying, 'Go wash in the Jordan seven times, and your flesh shall be restored and you shall be clean.'"*

When Naaman first arrived in Samaria, he went straight to the king with all his gifts and his diplomatic letter. He forgot to mention to his king that the servant girl told him that there was a prophet of God who could heal him, not the king of Israel! Therefore, the letter made no mention of a prophet and when the king of Israel received the letter he panicked because he knew he had no healing powers. He thought the king of Aram was trying to pick a fight and provoke him into battle again.

The king got so upset that he ripped his clothes as a sign of despair and great anguish. When this action was told to the prophet Elisha, he sent word to the king to send Naaman to his house. He would handle the situation. So Naaman left the king's palace and showed up at Elisha's door with horses and chariots. Elisha was neither afraid nor impressed by Naaman's status. As a matter of fact, Elisha did not even answer the door! He sent his messenger out with Naaman's prescription for healing. The prescription said: *"Go wash in the Jordan seven times, and your flesh shall be restored and you shall be clean."*

Now this prescription was simple, but true. It is like when you go to the doctor with the flu or a cold and the doctor says, rest and drink plenty of fluids. You get upset because you are convinced you need an antibiotic, a shot or something more. This was the attitude of Naaman. First he was angry because Elisha did not come before him with some magic potion or ritual using his hands and sending prayers up to his God. He wanted something more dramatic; after all, he had leprosy!

So rather than saying thank you to the messenger for bringing the prescription to him, he turns around and leaves. He thought he could have stayed home and washed in the rivers in Aram, surely they were cleaner than the Jordan River!

But you know sometimes we are our worse enemy. Naaman was about to lose his blessing through healing because of his arrogance. So God intervened again through another servant. This servant said to Naaman, *"If the prophet told you to do something difficult, you would have done it! So why can't you do this simple, easy task and be healed? What do you have to lose?*

At that moment Naaman remembered he was in Israel because of a servant, so now another servant was trying to give him good advice and save his life. He allowed his anger and his arrogance to fade away and became obedient to the word of Elisha. He went to the Jordan and dipped down 7 times.

I can imagine he went down one time and did not see any immediate change. Then he went down a second time and he noticed the itching of the leprosy had stopped. He went down a third time and the pain affiliated with leprosy stopped. He went down a fourth time and the blisters started growing scabs. He went down a fifth time and the scales began to fall from his body. He went down a sixth time and the discoloration from picking his soars cleared up.

When Naaman went down the last and 7th time, he came up out of that dirty Jordan River with skin as soft as a baby's behind. The skin was younger than his current age. Naaman was converted on that day and gave his allegiance to the God of Israel.

Church, obedience was the key to Naaman's healing, and obedience will bring God's healing blessings into your life. He requires us to give of our tithes, talents, and time. Until we are completely obedient to him, we will not be made whole. We will go through life only partly healed. Salvation comes when we submit to God's prescription and not our own.

You can find healing in a strange place if and when, you trust God's word and are obedient to his will for your life. God bless you and keep you is my prayer.

THE BOOK OF I CHRONICLES

When Numbers Are Misleading

NOT COUNTING THE COST

I CHRONICLES 21:1-2, "*Satan stood up against Israel, and incited David to count the people of Israel. So David said to Joab and the commander of his army, 'Go, number Israel, from Beer-sheba to Dan, and bring me a report so that I may know their number.'*"

INTRODUCTION

The two books known as 1 and 2 Chronicles were composed as one, entitled, "The Events of the Days," by the Chronicler, whose name we do not know. The Greek translators divided the book of Chronicles into two books from Hebrew. They assumed it was a supplement to the books of Samuel and Kings. The Chronicler used both the books of Samuel and Kings as his primary resources.

In the Greek, it was titled "The Things Omitted." The title "1 and 2 Chronicles of all of sacred History" came from the Catholic priest Jerome, who wrote the Latin translation of the Bible known as the Vulgate, in the 4th century. It spans from Adam to Cyrus the Great, who freed Israel from Babylonian Exile. Chronicles is listed as part of the historical books in the English Bible, although scholars place it in the Writings section.

The Chronicler focused on three theological themes: 1) continuity with the past, 2) a concern for "all Israel", and 3) the concept of retributive justice. The Chronicler seeks to encourage his struggling post-exilic community to seek and serve God. God is a loving God who hears their prayers despite their current reality.

What does this mean for the reader today? Let us listen to the words of our text and receive the faithfulness of God as we *count the cost*.

---

1)

Our first lesson teaches us that ***THE SATAN ALWAYS TRIES TO INFLUENCE OUR DECISIONS.*** Read v 1, "*Satan stood up against Israel and incited David to count the people of*

Israel. So David said to Joab and the commanders of the army, 'Go number Israel from Beer-sheba to Dan and bring me a report so that I may know their number.'"

At the end of chapter 20, David and his army had just defeated the Philistines, including the relatives of Goliath. David was feeling proud and victorious as if the victory was because of his military might, instead of God's power, mercy, and grace.

Satan knows who are God's chosen servants, and goes after them more aggressively than other believers. After all, David was *"a man after God's own heart!" (1 Sam 13:14)* Controlling David's emotions again – would be seen as a victory for Satan. Remember his affair with Bathsheba and the "murder" David sanctioned for her husband, Uriah. So David did not have clean hands, but he did have a clean heart.

The Chronicler's account differs from 2 Sam 24:1, which says God put his anger in David to cause David to do a census count. I Chronicles credits Satan for inciting the thought in David's mind, not God. We find Satan in this same role in the book of Job and Zechariah 3, where he stood to accuse the high priest. In this text, for the first time, Satan appears as a name for God's nemesis and not a descriptive noun.

Satan has a mysterious role in God's purposes for his creation. Whether Satan is functioning as a prosecutor as in Job, or an evil tempter here in I Chronicle 21, he is allowed by God to test God's people. However, do not get it twisted. God is still in charge and has it under control.

David did not pass the test. Rather than resisting the temptation to count his army, David allows Satan to pump up his pride and arrogance. This leads David to order a census count so he would personally know how large and how mighty a military force was at his deposal. This was a sin because its purpose was to show human might, not God's intervention in history. God has never needed large numbers of people to get his will done. So for David to want to have this human assurance in his back pocket was a slap in God's face. It was an insult to the theological statement, *"There's nothing too hard for God!" (Gen 18:14)*

We have to make decisions every day of our lives, sometimes multiple times in a day. It is in our best interest to consult with God beforehand and to make sure we are in the will of God. It is so easy to do what we want to do and take no thought for how it affects anybody else.

However, usually that does not work out very well. If we pray and read God's word, God will order our steps and then we cannot go wrong. Challenges may still come our way, but at least we know we are influenced by God, and not by some other entity, either human or demonic. The Bible says, *"pride comes before a fall." (Prov 16:18)* David let his pride rule over his heart and mind, and suffered the consequences. David did not Count the Cost!

————————————————

2)

Our second lesson teaches us that ***GOD SENDS PEOPLE TO BLOCK SATAN'S INFLUENCE IN OUR LIVES.*** Read vv 3-5, *"But Joab said, 'May the Lord increase the number of his people a hundredfold! Are they not my lord the king, all of them my lord's servants? Why then should my lord require this? Why should he bring guilt on Israel?'"* In our text Joab, David's military general, seemed more in touch with God's will and purpose for Israel than David! Joab expressed his concern that David's request was an act of presumption against the Lord as the giver of national blessing and ultimately Israel's Protector.

Joab asked David, *"Are they not all your servants?"* Why then would David bring an act of sin on Israel that will invoke the wrath of God? David thought he was totally in charge. We would say in the slang, *"David got a big head!"* Joab began to question David to see if he could determine the motive behind David's request for a census count. Was he insecure over the loyalty of his soldiers? Was David on some power trip and unaware of the consequences this count would have on all of Israel? Did he care? After all David was the shepherd boy who singlehandedly killed Goliath!

Joab tried to shape David's thinking by reassuring him that the count does not matter. They are all a part of the Israelite army and subject to his commands. A census would only bring the wrath of God upon all Israel, and for what reason, to stroke David's ego? Joab objected and told David he is trespassing on God's prerogatives. If he wanted to count something, count the many blessings God has bestowed upon his chosen people Israel. Do not do something that will knowingly invoke the wrath of God! David's request was repulsive in Joab's eyes and he excluded both the tribes of Levi and Benjamin in the count.

How many times have our parents and friends tried to prevent us from making mistakes and bad decisions? From touching a hot stove at the age of 2, to trusting a so-called friend who only wants to use you, to marrying the bad boy of the neighborhood or the loose girl, ending up in divorce and everybody saying, "I told you so!"

Sometimes like David, we have to learn things the hard way. Although we know the word of God and it's written on our hearts, we still allow negative outside voices to try and direct our steps. But the good news is that God puts positive people in our lives, people willing to step in and counter our corrupt and ungodly thinking before we ruin our lives.

We often refer to this counter intelligence as the *"voice of reason."* However, it is this very phrase that causes some of us to go off half-cocked or to the dark side first to prove we can handle the consequences. Young people like to live life on the edge, taking unnecessary risks to give their lives more excitement and a broader list of adventures.

Yet, so many people, young and old, are in the graveyard because they were hard headed and nobody could tell them to avoid the danger or the thrill. There is no temptation that God allows in our lives where God does not provide an escape. Just listen and hear that still small voice inside of you. Then remember that the *"steps of a righteous person, are ordered by the Lord." (Ps 37:23)*

——————————————

3)

Our final lesson learned from this text is ***NOT COUNTING THE COST CAN RESULT IN PROVOKING GOD'S WRATH.*** Read v 7, *"This command was also evil in the sight of God; so he punished Israel."* David was the king over Israel. It was his job to keep the people operating under the laws and statutes of God. It was not Joab's job, but Joab was David's general. It was his job to protect Israel against any threat from human enemies when under attack. So why not sound the alarm when divine vengeance was on the horizon? An attack against Israel was an attack no matter the source.

Joab tried to warn David of the possible consequences from such arrogance, but he would not listen and ordered General Joab to count the soldiers from Beer-sheeba to Dan, a geographical area spanning hundreds of miles. The total count was over 1 million able-bodied soldiers, excluding the 2 tribes of Levi and Benjamin.

If the report was meant to give David peace of mind, it was short lived. David's actions stirred the divine hornet's nest. God's anger was provoked and God set out to punish Israel as a consequence for the census. You see, the chosen people of God were seen as a corporate unit. If one sinned, all were held accountable, not just the one individual. Can I get a witness! Remember when Achan took a souvenir of Jericho, which was against the rules of Holy War? When Joshua and Israel tried to conquer the next city, *Ai*, they failed miserably and many lives were lost. When the Lord told Joshua that it was Achan's fault they were not victorious the second time, Achan and his whole family were taken outside the camp and stoned to death.

So David was not bringing wrath only upon himself, but all of Israel! This was what Joab was trying to get the king to understand. But now it was too late! God's anger was kindled. Yet, because God is a gracious and merciful God, he did give David 3 options of punishment to choose from. David chose the third option of punishment – a plague in the land with the angel of the Lord ravaging every part of Israel.

Seventy thousand fell dead. The devastation was so great that God called the angel back and said, "ENOUGH!" The punishment was too great for David to bear. He asked God to punish him and his family only for his sin. David wanted God to stop punishing the people who had nothing to do with his act of sin.

The angel responded and David was told to build an altar to the Lord. David obeyed and the punishment was subsided. David quickly learned that his *"arms were too short to box with God."* God sometimes has to turn his back to our sinful behavior and leave us to our own devices. When God turns away all manner of evil and sickness are allowed to confront us – just ask Job!

But the good news is that God does not stay angry forever. Eventually his anger subsides and we are once again in his favor. The Bible was written and preserved as our example and alarm system to warn against behaviors that provoke God's anger. Yet we tend to ignore, rationalize, excuse, negate the words in the Bible, and do whatever we feel we are big and bad enough to do.

As the prophets of old were sent to warn the people to avoid God's wrath, as preachers, pastors and laity, we too are assigned the task of warning others to stay out of the path of God's wrath. God expects us to be true to his word. God expects us to worship him in his sanctuary. God expects us to tithe and give of our time and talents in order to advance the coming of the kingdom.

If we choose to do it our own way, even though God has blessed us, God has healed us, God has made a way out of no way, God has made our enemies our footstools, then we have not counted the consequences of disobedience to God's word and God's will in our lives.

You can convince yourself like David, that you can do what you want to do, but just be ready to accept the consequences for not counting the cost. Not counting the cost of sin can be devastating to you and your family. Instead count the cost every day and in every way. Ask God for forgiveness and restoration for your soul. We do not want to hear on Judgment Day the Lord say, "*I know you not!*" That will happen if we do not realize that "*99 ½ won't do!*" Are you counting the cost? God bless you!

THE BOOK OF II CHRONICLES

Taking Steps to Remain in God's Favor

THE FOUR CONDITIONS TO
RECEIVING DELIVERANCE

II CHRONICLES 7:14, *"If my people, who are called by my name humble themselves, pray, seek my face, and turn from their wicked ways, then I will hear from heaven, and will forgive their sin and heal their land."*

INTRODUCTION

In II Chronicles, David's son Solomon is king. Solomon successfully built the temple his father David so wanted for God's presence to dwell on earth, and in Jerusalem. Unfortunately, after Solomon's death, the United Kingdom divided because of his son, Rehoboam's greed. Rehoboam refused to lessen the financial and physical burden placed on the people when Solomon was building the temple. But now that the temple was completed, the Elders requested that the people's load be reduced. Rehoboam refused and the nation split – 10 tribes went north and claimed Samaria as their capitol city, and 2 tribes remained in the south, taking the name Judah, showing loyalty to the person of David.

The Chronicler records the behavior of several kings in both kingdoms. Their behavior led the people away from the laws and statutes of God. God allowed the curse side of the covenant agreement to come into play against the people of Israel. The curses are recorded in Lev 26:14 ff:

> *But if you will not obey me, and do not observe all these commandments; if you spurn my statutes, and abhor my ordinances, so that you will not observe all my commandments, and you break my covenant; I in turn will do this to you: I will bring terror on you; consumption and fever that waste the eyes and cause life to pine away. You will sow your seed in vain, for your enemies shall eat it. I will set my face against you, and you shall be struck down by your enemies...*

So the book of Leviticus goes into great detail about the negative consequences of disobedience to God's laws. Israel knew the deal and boldly chose to disobey God and worship the idol gods of her neighbors. Yet, God's grace and mercy is everlasting. God again gives Israel an opportunity to turn away from their wicked ways and turn back to him. This is where our text begins. God proposed four conditions to Solomon in order for Israel to receive healing from the devastation of the land and the peoples return to their homeland.

Let us read God's word and learn how we can avoid invoking God's curses upon our lives by embracing the four conditions of deliverance.

---

1)

The first condition for deliverance in the text tells us **_TO HUMBLE OURSELVES._** Read v 14-A, *"If my people, who are called by my name humble themselves..."* Chapter 7 begins with Solomon ending his prayer of dedication of the temple he completed. The finished temple was a dream of his father David. But David was not allowed to build the temple because he had blood on his hands. So the responsibility and the assignment were given to his son Solomon.

In his prayer, Solomon invited God's glory to dwell in the temple. He and all the people offered sacrifices before the Lord. It was a grand celebration with music played by the priests, 22,000 oxen and 120,000 sheep sacrificed to God. Solomon held the festival for seven days along with all of Israel.

Then later, after Solomon sent the people home, that night the Lord appeared a second time to Solomon. He told Solomon that he had indeed heard Solomon's prayer of dedication. God decided to choose this temple as a place to store his glory and as a house of sacrifice. At last the promise made in Deut 12:4, 5, 11 was coming to pass:

> *You shall not worship the Lord your God in such ways. But you shall seek the place that the Lord your God will choose out of all your tribes as his habitation to put his name there...then you shall bring everything that I command you to the place that the Lord your God will choose as a dwelling for his name...*

However, there were four conditions that God imposed on Israel if God was to agree to dwell in this temple. One such condition was that the people of God must humble themselves before the Lord. This was a necessary condition in order for the people to remain safe whenever God sent his wrath on the land in the form of drought, pestilence, and locusts.

Solomon referred to Israel as "God's people" a claim that God committed to in his response to Solomon. Israel was still the object of God's care and possession. God warned Israel not to become haughty and arrogant, not to turn to idol gods but submit herself to God's will. However, the kings of Israel, both the northern and southern kingdoms, led the people into a false sense of security and turned them away from their first love. The prophets tried to bring the people back to God, but they would not listen. Eventually it ended with the holy city and the temple destroyed and the elite of Israel carted off to exile.

Humility is viewed in today's society, as a form of weakness by many people. People try to take advantage of you or even bully you into thinking and behaving their way. But God wants us to remain humble so he can use us in his service to do his will. If we loose our humility we can become self-righteous and lean on our own understanding. This then leads to our thinking that we are self-sufficient and do not need to consult God before we make decisions.

Self-sufficiency was a goal of Adam and Eve. Satan made them an offer they could not refuse – to be like God! It is a temptation that we must resist every day of our lives. We are nothing without God! For in God we live, move, dwell and have our being.

God requires his people to be humble. Whenever we loose our humility, we become susceptible to the temptations of the world.

---

2)

The second condition for our deliverance is **_TO PRAY!_** Read 14-b, *"If my people who are called by my name humble themselves and pray..."* The temple had two functions: 1) a place to offer sacrifices in order to have one's guilt forgiven, and 2) a place of prayer. Solomon's prayer invoked the presence of God to reside in the temple, for his generation and every new generation to come. Solomon emphasized humble prayer in his dedication speech. Humble prayer triggers God's divine love. Humble prayer is an expression of seeking God's face. Humble prayer was an idiom for worship at the temple.

God promised to honor humble prayers and accept them as evidence to wipe the slate clean in forgiveness as Solomon had asked. Ernest prayer removed all the curses that were connected to the land. God responded to Solomon's prayer through worship at the temple as a way of ending guilt and the spiritual and material crises it caused. Solomon's prayer moved primarily from a situation of existential crisis caused by human sinning to temple centered prayer.

The bible is filled with prayers of major biblical characters. These prayers have prevented many catastrophes over the period of Israel's existence as God's chosen people. Prayer has held back the hand of an angry God. Prayer caused the dead to rise, the sick to be healed, the hungry to be filled and battles to be won. Therefore, when God listed prayer as one of the four conditions for deliverance, it is no surprise. Prayer has been God's primary line of communication with his creation.

There is more power in prayer than all the nuclear bombs in the world. That is why God says "pray." Prayer is a form of praise, worship, and honor. For we pray to the One who can give us assistance in our time of need. Prayer reminds us that we belong to God and that *"It is he that made us, and not we ourselves." (Ps 100:3)* Prayer keeps us humble because it is our spiritual evidence that we can do nothing without God, but with God all things are possible! Prayer remains the key to the kingdom, but it takes faith to unlock the door.

3)

Our third condition of deliverance is **_TO SEEK GOD'S FACE._** Read 14-c, *"If my people who are called by my name humble themselves, pray, and seek my face…"* In the biblical tradition, it was sudden death to look on the face of God and in some cases, God's emissaries as well. When God wrote the 10 Commandments on the mountain, Moses' face was hidden and he was allowed only to see the back of God.

So why would God now list "seeking his face" as a condition for the peoples' deliverance? Well the definition of seeking is to "attempt to find something or someone; the attempt or desire to obtain or achieve something; in search of the truth; seek the solution to a problem." All of these definitions fit for Israel's situation. The Chronicler is addressing a people in exile who are devastated and in despair over their identity and location. Will they ever return to their homeland Israel, the Promised Land? Where is God in all their misery?

The Chronicler realized there was a faith crisis going on and that a solution was needed to turn this situation around. The people had assimilated into the Babylonian culture and were beginning to worship the idol gods of their newly found home away from home. The Chronicler's message was that now Israel must seek God's face. Israel must vehemently go after God's favor, mercy, and deliverance. The situation was dire! Time was of the essence! It was now or never!

The Chronicler then reverses the tradition of not looking on God's face to seeking the very face of God. Seeking God's face means returning to their special status as God's chosen people. Seeking God's face means to try and persuade God to see Israel in her plight as he did in the book of Judges, and deliver them from ultimate genocide. Seeking God's face is to ask God for another chance to be all that Israel was created to be.

However, before they seek God's face, they must humble themselves, and pray. These prior conditions allow Israel to qualify to seek God's face and in return, invoke God's glory and presence to dwell in their temple.

How do you seek God's face? Do you fast and pray? Do you ask for forgiveness and come to Church with a bow down head and humble heart? Do you kneel at the altar to confess your sins and ask God to restore your faith in his power? How you seek God's face is a personal decision, but a decision each of us has made in our time of trials and tribulations.

We have learned from experience God does not move away from us; we move away from God in our thoughts, and through our words and deeds. But God is never too far away that God cannot or will not hear our prayers and turn his face towards those who earnestly seek him with a clean heart and a contrite spirit.

4)

The final condition for deliverance is to **_TURN FROM YOUR WICKED WAYS._** Read v 14-d, *"If my people who are called by my name, humble themselves, pray, seek my face, and turn* *from their wicked ways, then I will hear from heaven, and will forgive their sin and heal their land.*" Now the rubber is about to hit the road! This condition is at the heart of why Israel is in her current situation – exile! The Chronicler takes Israel back to a happier time, when Solomon has just finished building a magnificent temple to the glory of God. Yes, it was a happier time, invoked for the purpose of reminding the exiles of a time when they were serving God and Israel was in a great place.

But it was also meant to remind the audience of God's four conditions to insure the temple and God's people would continue to be in the Promised Land and prosper. Living in exile caused many of them to forget "the good ole days" of festivals and celebrations in the presence of the Almighty God.

It was their wicked ways that brought them to this place, this period of time in their history. Israel's God was not defeated by the Babylonian god Marduk as some speculated. No the people's personal sins and wickedness activated the curse side of the covenant God made with Moses and their ancestors at Mt. Sinai. Some blamed the fore-parents for the destruction of Jerusalem, and their captivity. But Jeremiah and Ezekiel quickly put that lie to rest. It is because of their generation's sins against the poor, the widow and the orphan, and their poor record on social and economic justice that caused this drastic punishment to occur. They have no one but themselves to blame.

Yet, God is a gracious God and in his conversation with Solomon, God assures their restoration "I will hear from heaven, and I will forgive their sin and heal their land."

This is a promise of hope for the future. As we say in the Black Church, "*Trouble don't last always!*" Israel needed only to wait until her change became a reality. When her penance is over, God will be right there to embrace them, as any father of a prodigal child would do.

What ways do you have about you that are an insult to God and to others? How convicted are you when you read God's word knowing that, "*We have all sinned and fallen short of his glory." (Rom 3:23)* Yet even in our worse conditions, even at our lowest point, we have a Savior who will not leave us, nor forsake us. The only catch is that we humble ourselves, pray, seek God's face, and turn from our wicked ways. Once we have fulfilled this prescription, our deliverance is on the way. God bless you!

THE WRITINGS

Israel responds to life after Exile

(Books of Poetry, Wisdom Literature, Short Fiction, and Sacred History)

THE BOOK OF RUTH

(Festival Scroll – the Harvest Festival of Pentecost)

A WOMAN OF WORTH

RUTH 3:11, *"And now, my daughter, do not be afraid, I will do for you all that you ask, for all the assembly of my people know that you are a woman of worth."*

INTRODUCTION

When one usually thinks about worth, it is usually connected with a sum of money, or to describe how many possessions a person has accumulated in life. However, when we use the term "worth" in relation to a person's character, many people fall short of this adjective.

The book of Ruth is a parable-like form of a story that encourages us to be more like Ruth, and less like Naomi who submits to bitterness over the loss of her husband and two sons – Chilion and Mahlon. Ruth refuses to allow her mother-in-law to succumb to total depression and maintains her commitment to her in order to see her through this difficult time.

Naomi was not happy for long because after only 10 years of living with her family in Moab, her husband and her two sons die, leaving her with two daughters-in-law. She was living in a foreign country without any male heir, which placed her in a bad situation. Her family moved to Moab because there was a famine in Bethlehem. Now she was vulnerable to foreign traditions, and practices, that may have well threatened her well-being. Her two daughters-in-law – Orpah and Ruth, were natives of Moab. They still had family they could return to and survive. The main characters of the book are Ruth and Naomi. After all, the book is name in her honor.

Ruth is our woman of worth. She possessed three qualities that distinguished her in the eyes of the wealthy landowner, Boaz, and the biblical writers as well. Let us now examine the story about a *woman of worth*.

1)

The first lesson we learn about a woman of worth is that she must possess **_A SENSE OF LOYALTY._** Read v 16, *"Entreat me not to leave you or to return from following you; for where* *you go I will go, and where you lodge, I will lodge; your people shall be my people and your God, my God.*" When you suddenly find yourself single again it is so easy to forget the needs of others and think it is time for you to have a little fun. When Ruth's husband died, her mother-in-law gave her freedom from any obligation she might feel towards her or her lineage. Naomi told her two daughters-in-law to go back to their own mother's house and perhaps find another husband. Orpah resisted at first, but eventually took Naomi's advice and returned to her ancestral home.

Ruth on the other hand, felt a deep sense of love and loyalty to the woman who gave birth to her late husband. She felt her past was behind her, and that when she married she took on a new life with a new family. Naomi was her family now. Naomi tried to convince Ruth to leave for her own good, for she was still young and had not yet produced children. She had no more sons to give her as the levirate law allowed (*If a husband dies without heirs, his brother must marry the widow and give her children that would be considered the children of the deceased brother – Deut 25:5-10*). But Ruth knew that Naomi needed her and she needed Naomi. A great bond had grown between the two women that Ruth was not about to let go.

Loyalty is one of life's greatest assets. A person who is loyal to nothing is not much good for anything. A *woman of worth* is loyal first to her God and then to her family and friends. For in verse 16, Ruth exclaims to Naomi her total commitment to spending the rest of her life at her side. For a woman to have any worth, she must first demonstrate loyalty.

---

2)

Secondly, a *woman of worth* **STRIVES FOR EXCELLENCE.** Read 2:12, "*May the Lord reward you for your deeds, and may you have a full reward from the Lord, the God of Israel, under whose wings you have come for refuge.*" A *woman of worth* is not satisfied with a mediocre performance or a job half done, or doing just enough to get by. She puts her best effort forward always. This is the case with Ruth. It was up to Ruth to acquire food for her and her mother-in-law. So after following Naomi's instructions on where to glean, Ruth went and found work in the field of Boaz, a wealthy landowner who just so happened to also be a distant relative.

Ruth worked very hard to gather food left on the vines in the field in order to provide food for her and her mother-in-law. When she finished one field, she worked on another, from sun up to sun down, never taking time to rest. She wanted to be sure there was enough food for both her and Naomi to eat. Her work ethic (as well as her beauty) gained the attention of the owner, Boaz. He inquired from the field manager about her identity.

Boaz was told about Ruth's sacrifice to leave her home country in order to take care of her mother-in-law. This impressed Boaz and he instructed the manager to watch over Ruth and make sure she got plenty of food for her and Naomi. In addition he was told to see that no harm or harassment come to her.

Striving for excellence never goes unnoticed. Women of worth are often honored for great contributions to their Church, their community, and their family. Great women of faith and action have moved our country in ways that only a women's touch can do. Such women as *Harriet Tubman, Sojourner Truth, Mary McCloud Bethune, Elenore Roosevelt, Rosa Parks, Susan B. Anthony, supreme court justice Ruth Bader Ginsburg*, and a host of biblical female characters known and unknown. These women of worth stepped up to the plate when they saw a need and felt called by God to make a difference.

A *woman of worth* does not waste time complaining and saying "I can't do this." Instead, her motto is Phil 4:13, *"I can do all things through Christ Jesus who strengthens me."*

_____

3)

Our final description of a *woman of worth* is that **SHE ACCEPTS GOD'S WILL FOR HER LIFE.** Read 3:11, *"And now my daughter, do not be afraid, I will do for you all that you ask, for all the assembly of my people know that you are a woman of worth."*

It was customary for the deceased's next of kin to marry his widow. Naomi gave Ruth instructions to lie at the feet of Boaz, a distant relative, when he retired for the evening. Boaz was a much older man, and there was another relative closer in line to marry Ruth. However, seeing Boaz's kindness towards her, she chose him to be her next husband. For she believed this was God's will for her and Naomi's future.

Boaz was startled when he rolled over and found Ruth at the foot of his bed. In actuality, Ruth proposed to Boaz! She asked him to cover her with his blanket, a sign that you wanted to marry someone. At first Boaz was hesitant because he knew there was another relative closer in lineage to marry Ruth. He needed time to go and seek out this next of kin and discuss the situation with him before he could commit to marrying Ruth.

The next of kin wanted the property that came with Ruth, but did not want the marriage as he was already married with children and did not want any inheritance complications in the event of his death. So he passed on Boaz's offer to marry Ruth. This greatly pleased Boaz. Now he could marry Ruth and she would give him a son in his old age.

Accepting God's will for her life was Ruth's most outstanding quality. Often our wills do not coincide with God's will for our lives and we live to regret it. But if we are going to possess any amount of worth as human beings, and as Christians, we must learn to give in to God's will. Ruth did it; see how things turned out for her! Boaz accepted Ruth's proposal because he knew what the townsfolk were saying about Ruth's character. What is the town saying about us? Is it positive or negative?

There's a story told about a woman who was walking down the street one day and as she looked down on the ground, she saw a shiny object. She picked it up and thought it was an expensive diamond ring. Being that she was not a woman of great means, she decided to take the ring to the town jeweler and have it appraised to determine its worth.

The next day she goes to the jewelry store. As she walks in the door, she runs into the town grocer who thanks her for co-signing for his car loan. Once in the store, the town barber greeted her and thanked her for watching his children while he and his wife took a much-needed vacation. As she approached the counter, the town clerk noticed her and paid her back for the loan she gave him when he was a struggling college student.

Finally, she gets the jeweler's attention. He looked at the ring through his eyepiece and began to smile. She assumed that meant the ring was worth a lot of money. The jeweler laughed and said to the woman, *"This ring is worth nothing, but from what I heard of you today, you certainly are!"*

A *woman of worth* – her loyalty will speak for her, her excellence will cause others to praise her, and her acceptance of God's will make others emulate her. As Proverbs 31:10 says, *"Who can find a virtuous woman? She is more precious than jewels."* God bless you!

THE BOOK OF EZRA

Returning to the Scene of the Crimes

WE'RE BACK, LET THE WORK BEGIN!

EZRA 3:6-13, *"From the first day of the seventh month they began to offer burnt offerings to the Lord. But the foundation of the temple of the Lord was not yet laid... So they gave money to the masons and the carpenters, and food, drink, and oil to the Sidonians and Tyrians to bring cedar trees from Lebanon to the sea, to Joppa, according to the grant that they had from King Cyrus of Persia."*

INTRODUCTION

King Cyrus of Persia conquered Babylon in 539 B.C.E. almost 600 years before the birth of Christ. One of his first actions as their new king was to release all the political prisoners, including the Israelites, who had been captured and exiled in Babylonia by King Nebuchadrezzer for over 70 years.

Finally, the hopes and dreams of their ancestors were a reality. They were free! Not only did King Cyrus set them free, he even financed their trip back home! The book of Ezra demonstrates the many difficulties that prevailed in the postexilic community of Judah. What was once a vast nation, now has been diminished to just a small geographical area under the rule of the great Persian Empire.

Ezra was a priestly scribe who was ordered back to Judah from Persia, in order to organize the community via the laws of Moses and the Torah instructions. There was so much turmoil and chaos that somebody had to return to Judah and create a map of civilization that would organize the people. The form of the Torah that we have today is believed to be the final edition that Ezra complied in order to organize the people so they could survive as the people of God. This was not an easy task for Ezra as his first order of the day was to separate the Israelites from foreign marriages and mixed breed children.

Both Ezra and Nehemiah seemed politically stable figures to the Persian leaders to use to get the returnees under control and back on track to being God's chosen people. So now let us take a closer look at what coming back home meant to the returning exiles.

1)

So the first lesson the returnees learned is that **_WHEN YOU GO BACK HOME, THINGS MAY NOT BE THE SAME._** Read v6, *"From the first day of the seventh month they began to offer burnt offerings to the Lord. But the foundation of the temple of the Lord was not yet laid."* After 70 years of neglect and lying in ruins, Jerusalem was not the place they remembered it to be. Yes, they were back home, but now the work must begin to restore home to the grand place it was before the attack of the Babylonians.

The temple was destroyed. It had to be reconstructed on its original holy, and consecrated foundation. The walls surrounding the city had to be rebuilt for protection and security. It was not going to be easy. There were naysayers and opponents of the project. But those who felt called by God to the task of rebuilding God's house, pressed on despite the obstacles they faced.

There are times in our lives when we go away with memories of the past. But when we return we find that the memories are no longer a reality. We may have left because of a bad situation. We may have left seeking a new job or educational opportunity. Then because of a connection that lures us back home, we return and try to fit back into the past. However, we find that the past has passed us by and new and exciting things are now happening.

We then are left with two choices: either we accept the present or we try to hold on to the past and resist the newness that the present brings to our lives. The old Jerusalem was gone, destroyed, burned to the ground. Tomorrow was on the horizon. They could either fear it because of the challenges and hard work that lied ahead, or accept it as God about to do a new thing for his chosen people.

Some of the exiles resisted, complained and could not accept the situation as they found it upon their return to Jerusalem. Yet, most of them rolled up their sleeves and got right to work. They had no choice! Their survival depended on their conquering and manipulating their new reality. Houses had to be built for the returning exiles to live in. Food had to be planted so they would not starve to death. They were sent back by King Cyrus to rebuild the temple of the Lord. Now they are back home, things will never be the same again.

2)

The second lesson learned is **_HOW DO WE SUPPORT THE WORK GOD HAS ASSIGNED TO OUR HANDS?_** Read v 7, *"So they gave money to the masons and the carpenters, and food, drink, and oil to the Sidonians and the Tyrians to bring cedar trees from Lebanon to the sea, to Joppa, according to the grant that they had from King Cyrus of Persia."* King Cyrus did not send the exiles home empty handed. They were generously funded by the Persian Empire. King Cyrus commissioned them to go home and rebuild their temple. While there, they were asked to offer a sacrifice on behalf of King Cyrus, who believed that God had many names, but was one spirit.

The leaders knew the kind of materials needed to lay the foundation and collect the necessary materials to start building the new temple. The funds they received from King Cyrus were crucial to negotiating the work and hiring of skilled workers to complete the job. The cedar trees from Lebanon were known for their quality and strength as a building material. In addition, they supplied food and shelter to the workers who would stay in Jerusalem until the job was done. This was an expensive undertaking and there was only so much money available to build a structure worthy of the presence of God.

However, as anyone knows who has gone under any construction project in their home or at their place of employment, the initial budget never ends up covering the final work. All kinds of issues come up that were unexpected but had to be corrected before the real work of building can take place. So funding is a crucial component to get the work of the Lord done.

The allotted funds only covered a small rendering of the previous temple. Now that the foundation was laid, more funds were required to finish the work. Altars had to be built, seating had to be delivered and constructed, curtains and holy tapestry had to be hung. More work on the outside as well as the inside, needed attention before the temple could be open for business. However, King Cyrus did allow the holy utensils, used for sacrifice on the altar, that were stolen by King Nebuchadrezzer, to be returned with the exiles.

The funds provided by King Cyrus eventually ran out and a new leader of Persia, King Darius I, came on the scene. He too was amendable to the restoration of Israel. King Darius did not send additional funds so the people had to depend on their relatives back in Persia to provide the necessary resources to complete the project and restore their beloved city to its glory. Those who chose to stay in Persia did not hesitate to send resources in support of those who went back home. They believed in their homeland, but did not want to return because of personal reasons.

Those of this generation were born in Persia and never set foot in Jerusalem or the Holy Land. Some had established businesses and bought land to farm. Others married and intermarried and had families to support in Persia. Yet, they never neglected the work that was going on back home. They knew it was God's work and it was their responsibility to see it to its completion. Several waves of people eventually made it back to the Promised Land.

How are we to support the work God has placed in our hands to do? We are the only hands and purses God has to get his work out to the people. The songwriter asked the question: *"What shall I render to God for all his blessings?"* The Old Testament supports the tithe as God's way of covering temple costs. The prophet Malachi states in 3:10, *"Bring the full tithe into the storehouse, so that there may be food in my house, and thus put me to the test, says the Lord of hosts; see if I will not open the windows of heaven for you and pour down for you an overflowing blessing."*

God has put the ball in our court. When we are obedient in our giving, God will respond and meet our needs. So we are commanded to give to support the work of God's kingdom on earth. If we drop the ball, the church and its mission to the world will suffer greatly.

3)

The third and final lesson the returnees learned was ***YOU CANNOT PLEASE EVERYBODY!*** Read v 12, *"But many of the priests and Levites and heads of families, old people who had seen the first house on its foundations, wept with a loud voice when they saw this house..."*

Many of the captives chose to remain in the ignorance and idol worship center of Babylon. They refused to return to the holy city of Jerusalem. Some sent their money, supplies, but were not interested in returning to a city where they had no idea how bad it was. Some of them had communications from their homeland and knew that the struggles were real. Foreigners, who bordered the land near Judah, were not friendly and disputes over land issues were frequent.

Yet those who did return did not know exactly what to expect, but after 70 years, the older generation had pictured in their minds the same Jerusalem they left and had dreamed for so long to go back to. Many were carted off before the total burning of the city occurred, so they did not really know what to expect. Perhaps they thought after 70 years, repairs and restoration had been completed. Surely they did not expect to see the total devastation of their beloved and consecrated temple.

Had they chosen to look on the bright side, they were delivered and set free by King Cyrus under the arm of God. Now they were back home, although home was not what it used to be. Although they had the courage to return and leave the land of their captors, they were still not satisfied. They wept when they saw the newly laid foundation for the new temple. The older crowd remembered the beauty and expansive decoration of the old temple. Nothing could compare to what Solomon had done. That was a fact! So instead of complaining and crying over the ruins of a destroyed temple, they needed to come together and use what they had at their disposal to build God a temple that was worthy of the present generation and situation they were under. The past is always better in 20/20 vision, but never is that rear view mirror as accurate as we remember it.

Those under 20, or who were born in Babylonian Exile, only knew of a temple they had heard about from their elders. The new temple foundation was now laid and under construction. With the right attitude, tools and resources, the second temple will be pleasing to God as well! They forgot that for almost 300 years the presence of God dwelt only in a portable tent called the tabernacle.

In life you cannot please everybody. As the saying goes, *"You can please some of the people some of the time, but not all of the people all of the time."* It is more important that we spend our time trying to please God. In doing so, we will please those who are a part of God's family. Nobody else really matters. God bless you.

THE BOOK OF NEHEMIAH

A Wall of Contention

WHAT IS ON YOUR MIND?

NEHEMIAH 4:1-6, *"Now when Sanballat heard that we were building the wall, he was angry and greatly enraged, and he mocked the Jews. He said in the presence of his associates and of the army of Samaria, 'What are these feeble Jews doing? Will they restore things? Will they sacrifice? Will they finish it in a day? Will they revive the stones out of the heaps of rubbish and burned ones at that?' ...So we rebuilt the wall, and all was joined together to half its height; for the people had a mind to work."*

INTRODUCTION

Most of the book of Nehemiah consists of a first person narrative – I and We. It recounts Nehemiah's role in rebuilding the walls of Jerusalem after the Babylonians attacked and burned down the city over a hundred years earlier. At the time Nehemiah is serving in the new Persian Empire.

The Israelites found themselves in Babylonian captivity because God got tired of their sinful and evil ways. After 70 long years of captivity they were delivered and set free at the hands of King Cyrus of Persia. King Cyrus allowed the Jews to return to their city and rebuild its temple. However, after many years had passed still Jerusalem was in ruins and the temple and the walls had not been rebuilt. The people became discouraged and no longer had a mind to work on the temple's reconstruction.

The new king Artaxerxes, hired Nehemiah as his cupbearer. His job was to taste the king's food and drink to prevent his enemies from poisoning him, a common practice in the ancient world. But on this particular day in the palace, the king saw that Nehemiah was sad. So the king asked Nehemiah why he was sad. Nehemiah shared his bad news about the condition of his homeland and that he felt compelled to go home and find a way to help rebuild his city.

So the king permitted Nehemiah to go home to Jerusalem and see what he could do for his people. Nehemiah went back to Jerusalem, very aware of what he would find there. But because he prayed to God, he knew in his heart that with the cooperation of the people and the power and protection of God, everything was going to work out. For Nehemiah had a mind to work.

Yet unless we continue to have a mind to work as the people of God, we are just treading water until Jesus returns to claim his church. Those who do not know our Lord and Savior in the pardoning of their sins will be lost if we become complacent in our mission. So let us now read the text and how it relates to those of us who continue to have a mind to do the work of kingdom building.

---

1)

When we examine our text, we first learn that ***IF YOU HAVE A MIND TO WORK, GOD WILL PROVIDE THE OPPORTUNITY.*** Read chapter 2:4-5, *"Then the king said to me, 'What do you request?' So I prayed to the God of heaven. Then I said to the king, 'If it please the king, and if your servant has found favor with you, I ask that you send me to Judah, to the city of my ancestors' graves, so that I may rebuild it.'"* Back in chapter 2 we learned that Nehemiah, the king's food taster or cupbearer, grieved heavily over the slow progress of Jerusalem's restoration. The king allowed Nehemiah to leave Persia and return to Jerusalem, to spear head the revival project. He sent soldiers and letters so that Nehemiah would not encounter any obstacle or hindrance to his mission.

However, the nearby nations and peoples who escaped the wrath of the Babylonians were accustomed to coming and going as they pleased. The rebuilding of the walls would complicate what they had always done for over 100 years. Who was this man Nehemiah and how dare he try to do something different that affects our livelihood? But whenever God puts a mission, a calling, and a purpose on our lives, we have to go. It may not be comfortable, or convenient, but it is a mandatory assignment.

The work of the kingdom is never done, not until the Second Coming of Christ. The Church seems to have hit a speed bump in our society with the growing numbers of persons claiming other religions as their religion of choice, or spirituality as their preference of worship. Traditional churches are empty and struggling to keep its head above water. How we do church in the 21st century is very different from 50 years ago. Back then, belonging to a local church in your community was a symbol of status, pride and moral development.

However our minds are overwhelmed today with materialism, family, work, and other considerations, and often times supporting the church is the last thing on our minds. Yet, God has been too good to his people for us to forget about his many blessings in our lives. Every day we should wake up with our mind stayed on the Lord. When we meditate on God's word, we become absorbed by the thought that God's word needs to go forth. So many people are without a moral compass today the world is full of nonsensical violence because of it. So many people are depressed, suicidal, addicted, and we the church can be there to offer a word of encouragement and hope from the Lord.

As believers, like Nehemiah, our spirits should be grieved when we think about the work left undone for lack of willing workers to spread the good news throughout the world. Church work can only be accomplished when we have a mind to work for God, not for money or fame and fortune. For only then can we pick up and leave our current situations and allow God to use us in the ways of his kingdom building. Therefore, out of gratitude to God for all that God has done to insure our salvation through Christ, we should say in the words of Isaiah 6, *"Here I am, send me."*

_____

2)

Secondly, if we are going to have a mind to work, *"WE MUST ACCEPT THAT WE WILL FACE OBSTACLES ALONG THE WAY.* Read 4:1, *"Now when Sanballat heard that we were building the wall, he was angry and greatly enraged, and he mocked the Jews."* Nehemiah met with external forces that did not want Jerusalem to prosper, or once again become a great nation. Yet because Nehemiah was focused on his mission to restore his homeland, and because the people he inspired by his leadership had a mind to work, their enemies were defeated and no weapon formed against them prospered.

At one point in our text, the people had a sword in one hand and a brick in the other. Nothing was going to stop them from finishing the wall surrounding Jerusalem. Some were afraid, but Nehemiah kept preaching and encouraging them to keep their eyes on the prize – a completed wall. When things got worse, Nehemiah knew only one thing to do – take it to the Lord in prayer. So he prayed a powerful prayer that blocked his enemies from any further harassment and bullying.

Whenever we have goals in life that are out of the norm of our immediate family or community, there will always be the naysayers who try to discourage us and stop our progress. It's like crabs in a barrel, those at the bottom pull done those who try to rise to the top and escape their dilemma. But we cannot quit! We cannot throw in the towel! Others are depending on our success so they too may excel and finish their goals and fulfill their dreams. If we can think it, if we have a mind to do it, then God will give us the determination, the tenacity, the faith to walk in our victory. We need only continue with a mind to work no matter the obstacles that others place in our paths. Then when we are at our wits end, just take it to the Lord in prayer and leave it there. For as they use to say in the 1980s, *"Just Keep Trucking!"*

_____

3)

Then finally, if we have a mind to work, *GOD WILL BE WITH US AND LEAD US TO VICTORY.* Read v 6, *"So we rebuilt the wall, and all the wall was joined together to half its height; for the people had a mind to work."* Nehemiah never lost sight of his goal. Nehemiah prayed about his enemies, took it to the Lord and continued to work on rebuilding the walls. Sometimes he encountered opposition, but nothing would bring him down from the wall until his work was finished. Now the wall was not as high as the former wall, but it served the purpose for which it was built. They finished the job and it was a job well done!

Of course his enemies laughed at the finished wall and claimed if a fox ran across it, it would collapse. But Nehemiah was not moved by their criticism of the final product. He knew that a wall was not what actually protected Israel from her enemies, but the Lord God Almighty. The wall was a symbol and physical barrier to deter those who chose to come after Israel.

Whatever we set our minds to do, if you believe in your heart that it is what God has planned for your life, then go forward. Do not allow financial, familial, physical, health, or anything else, keep you from getting the job done that God has placed in your heart. We are here for a purpose and a mission. Until we have completed that assignment, we will continue to fall short of our calling. Instead, let us have a mind to work for the Lord in whatever capacity God needs us to perform. Then like Nehemiah, we can say, "We had a mind to work and the job got done!" God bless you!

THE BOOK OF ESTHER

(A Festival Scroll – the Festival of Purim)

When Power is Thrust upon You

ACCEPTING YOUR POSITION OF POWER

ESTHER 4:9-17; 9:5, *"Hathach went and told Esther what Mordecai had said. Then Esther spoke to Hathach and gave him a message for Mordecai saying, 'All the king's servants and the people of the provinces know that if any man or woman goes to the king inside the inner court without being called, there is but one law – all alike are to be put to death. Only if the king holds out the golden scepter to someone may that person live.'"*

INTRODUCTION

The book of Esther is a Jewish story set within the Jewish community that is now residing in the Persian Empire. These are the descendants of the Jews who were taken into Babylonian Exile in 586 B.C.E. King Nebuchadrezzer destroyed Jerusalem and captured all the upper crust of Israel. Seventy years later, King Cyrus of Persia conquered the Babylonians and released the exiles from captivity and financed their return back home.

However, because King Cyrus was not an aggressive oppressor, most of the Jews who were born in Babylonian captivity chose to remain under the leadership of the Persian Empire. Jews were allowed to come and go as they pleased. So here we are 200 years later, and once again the Jews are facing genocide, complete annihilation at the hands of their enemy. This enemy was Haman, a member of the king's cabinet.

This is where we find Esther and her people in our text. There are not a lot of religious references made in the book of Esther (the word God is not mentioned at all), but Esther's religious upbringing by her uncle Mordicai and God's presence undergirds Esther's actions through the practice of prayer and fasting. Therefore, because of her religious upbringing, and the need for a miracle to save her people from genocide, Esther had no choice but to accept her position of power.

Let us now examine our text more closely and learn how we too are positioned for a miracle.

1)

The first lesson we learn from our text is that **_RECOGNIZING YOUR POSITION OF POWER IS NEVER EASY._** Read vv 9-11, "*Hathach went and told Esther what Mordecai had said. Then Esther spoke to Hathach and gave him a message for Mordecai saying 'All the king's servants and the people of the provinces know that if any man or woman goes to the king inside the inner court without being called, there is but one law – all alike are to be put to death. Only if the king holds out the golden scepter to someone may that person live.'*"

Esther's uncle Mordecai (who adopted her when her parents died) has learned that Haman bribed the king with 375 tons of silver in order to make a decree to destroy all the Jews in the kingdom. This was Haman's way of getting back at Mordecai for refusing to bow down to him in public. You see Haman was a member of the king's court. By law whenever they were in public, everyone was to bow down to them acknowledging their authority over them.

Well Mordecai refused to bow down to any human being. He only bowed to God. Haman hated Mordecai with a passion because of this seemingly disrespect for his position of power. However, Haman got no pleasure in just killing Mordecai; that would be too easy. Instead he learned that Mordecai refused to bow because of his religious loyalty, and his commitment to the God of the Jews. So he would get great pleasure from destroying all of Mordecai's people, not just him alone.

In response to this decree to destroy his people, Mordecai dressed in ashes and sackcloth, which symbolized his distress over the situation. Wearing ashes and sackcloth was a way to get God's attention by displaying humility and total dependence on God's intervention.

Word got back to Esther about her uncle's distress. She tried to comfort him by sending clean clothes to him to wear, but he refused to take off his mourning clothes. Then he sent word back to Esther by Hathach – the eunuch servant assigned to Esther – that she needed to go to the king and tell him about this decree of genocide against her people.

At first Esther did not want to recognize her position of power. In her mind she was one of many women in the king's harem. For initially she did find favor with the king, and Esther was crowned his queen above all the other candidates for the position. But over the last 30 days, the king had not desired the pleasure of her company in his bedchamber. She felt her position of influence was slipping through her fingers.

How could she then go into the king? To enter without being summoned was punishable by death, unless the king stretched out his golden scepter allowing you to approach him. Esther realized that having a position of power is not always easy. Sometimes decisions are beyond your control and you doubt your God-given power in the face of danger or death.

I always tell people that no one can take your power; you can only relinquish it. Oftentimes we succumb to this world's temptations and ideas in order to be popular and accepted by our own family, co-workers, and friends. But to give into the pressures of this world is to forfeit our positions of power as believers in a risen Christ and an awesome God. Our positions of spiritual power come from within. *"For greater is He that is within me, than he that is within the world." (I Jn 4:4)*

It is not easy living a spiritually powerful life. People will hate you for no other reason except you have high moral standards and values. Kermit the frog from Sesame Street says, *"It's not easy being green."* That means people always expect you to be who you say you are, to act and look like who God created you to be. If we say we are Christians, then we must accept that having a position of power is not easy. You know the old saying, *"If it walks like a duck, quacks like a duck, and swims like a duck, it must be a duck."* Therefore, if you are a Christian, accept your position of power! It may not be easy, then again, God never promised you a rose garden. Instead Jesus tells us to take up our crosses daily and follow him.

_____

2)

Esther was very reluctant to do what Mordecai asked her to do – go in to see the king and stop the genocide of her people. So the second lesson we learn from the text is ***AVOIDING YOUR POSITION OF POWER LEADS TO DESTRUCTION.*** Read vv 13-14b, *"Mordecai told them to reply to Esther, 'Do not think that in the king's palace you will escape any more than all the Jews. For if you keep silence at such a time as this, relief and deliverance will rise for the Jews from another quarter, but you and your father's family will perish."* Mordecai did not hold his tongue in regards to the seriousness of the situation. Esther did not have the luxury of avoiding the situation because she was living in the king's palace! If God had to use another means to deliver the Jews, his chosen people, because Esther refused to use her position of influence with the king, she and her father's family would perish. The Jewish community, however, would be spared without her help.

This reply from her uncle Mordecai shook up Esther's world and she knew she could not avoid the problem or neglect her responsibility to her people any longer. She was not just the Queen of Persia, but a Jewish woman, one of God's chosen people, a role model for her people, and women everywhere!

But she was in a catch 22 – between a rock and a hard place! If she did nothing and ignored her position of power, her family line would die out and God would deliver her people by another means. But if she went into the king's chamber uninvited, she alone would be put to death. What could she do? What would she do? She needed to consult with a higher power, so she fasted and prayed to God for an answer. You know Jesus told his disciples on one occasion, *"Some miracles can only happen through prayer and fasting."* (Mt 17:21)

As Christians living in a world that is turning more and more secular and against Christ, we encounter situations daily that challenge our faith and loyalty to Christ. Let's face it; sometimes it is just easier not to tell people you are a Christian! This testimony seems to put people on edge. Their conscience goes into overload and they feel judged. The minute you profess your religion, Satan gets busy trying to push your buttons, getting you to defend what you believe. But we cannot take the easy way out and hide behind our religion by remaining silent. Jesus said on one occasion, if we do not acknowledge him, *"the rocks and the mountains will cry out instead." (Lk 19:40)*

Then on another occasion, Jesus declared that if you are ashamed of him down here; he will be ashamed of you before the Father. If we try to avoid witnessing to others about our faith, others will lose their lives and never know the love of God and the salvation that comes through faith in his precious Son, our Lord and Savior, Jesus the Christ. You may be the only sermon they will ever hear. You may be the only church they visit (because the church is in you, not these four walls). So stand up and be counted, even when you stand by yourself!

Then claim your position of power and authority in this world. Jesus claimed all power was in his hands when he arose from the dead. As his followers, we too have access to that same power source. But you cannot deny him! If you do, then your fate will be the same as Esther's, and you will bring eternal destruction upon your own life.

3)

The final lesson we learn from our text, teaches us that __***ACCEPTING YOUR POSITION OF POWER LEADS TO YOUR MIRACLE.***__ Read vv 14c-17; 9:5, *"Who knows? Perhaps you have come to royal dignity for just such a time as this.' Then Esther said to Mordecai, 'Go gather all the Jews to be found in Susa, and hold fast on my behalf, and neither eat nor drink for 3 days, night or day. I, and my maids, will also fast as you do. After that, I will go to the king, though it is against the law; and if I perish, I perish'."*

Esther now realized that her fate is sealed. She has no other choice but to accept her position of power and do what was best for her people. Her personal situation did not take precedence over doing the right thing. So she sends a reply to Mordecai that she is on board with the plan. She will use her position of power to bring about a miracle for her people. She will go to the king and convince him to save her people from total destruction, and if she died then so be it.

We all know how the story ends. Esther saves her people because God softened the king's heart towards Esther. When she entered the room all perfumed up and looking sexy to a tee, the king remembered why he fell in love with Esther in the first place. So he extended the golden scepter in her direction, thereby granting her permission to approach him without the consequence of death. She then exposed Haman and his plan to kill all her people.

However, the king's law could not be revoked! It was final. Yet, a miracle happened when she convinced the king to allow her people to take up weapons to defend themselves. Yes, the Jews were victorious over their enemies, because Esther was positioned for a miracle. She was at the right place at the right time. For you see, *"No weapon formed against you shall prosper."* *(Isa 54:17)* Haman was hung on the very gallows he prepared for her uncle Mordecai, and her people were saved.

The gospel singer Shirley Caesar sings a song with these words, *"You're next in line, for a miracle."* What position are you in that will bring a miracle into somebody's life? Can you become a foster parent or an adoptive parent? Can you hire some young person for a job because you are an entrepreneur? Can you tutor a child through the ACT test? Can you feed a hungry family down the street because you are a manager at a grocery store and don't want to throw away excess food?

You do not have to be royalty to be in a position of power or to function as somebody's miracle. As a Christian believer you are always in a position to be a miracle. You're next in line for a miracle. How will you respond? God bless you!

THE BOOK OF JOB

(Wisdom Literature)

Waiting for Your Change to Come

WHEN TRUSTING GOD PAYS OFF

Job 42:1-17 (1-6), *"Then Job answered the Lord: 'I know that you can do all things, and that no purpose of yours can be thwarted. Who is this that hides counsel without knowledge? Therefore I have uttered what I did not understand, things too wonderful for me, which I did not know. Hear, and I will speak; I will question you and you declare to me. I had heard of you by the hearing of the ear, but now my eye sees you; therefore I despise myself, and repent in dust and ashes.'"*

INTRODUCTION

The story of Job is an intellectual and spiritual battle that tries to explain and understand why bad things happen to good people. Now, the religious understanding of that day was *"Bad things happened to bad people."* If you suffered any kind of affliction or loss, it was because you had offended God through an unrighteous act on your part. Therefore, confession, repentance, and sacrifice were mandatory if one wanted to get right with God.

Yet we know from the prologue, the beginning of the book, that Job was a righteous man, who shunned evil at every turn and opportunity. When Job's motives for living a righteous life are questioned by a member of God's cabinet, the accuser, the Satan, a competition between God and the Satan, at Job's expense, is put into play. Poor Job is tested almost unto death. But Job refuses to give in to his friend's way of thinking about the nature of God and how God operates in the human realm.

So Job keeps on trusting God through financial loss, the death of his children, and physical illness. These are the three major challenges of life that either make you or break you. We learn in our text, as did Job, that after while trusting God pays off. Let us journey with Job as he moves from frustration to restoration.

1)

After 41 long chapters, Job learns that **_TRUSTING GOD PAYS OFF WHEN WE HUMBLE OURSELVES BEFORE HIM._** Read vv 1-6 *"I know that you can do all things, and that no* *purpose of yours can be thwarted. Who is this that hides counsel without knowledge? Therefore, I have uttered what I did not understand, things too wonderful for me, which I did not know. Hear, and I will speak; I will question you and you declare to me. I had heard of you by the hearing of the ear, but now my eye sees you; therefore I despise myself, and repent in dust and ashes."*

Job had argued all along that he was innocent and had done nothing to incur the wrath of God to the degree that he was experiencing it – loss of wealth, loss of children, loss of health, loss of integrity and credibility within his community and in the presence of his friends and wife. Job always believed that if he could just get God's attention, if he could get a meeting one on one with God, he could straighten out this mess, this misunderstanding, or perhaps a case of mistaken identity.

For Job God was his primary witness to the righteous lifestyle he had lived and required of those around him to live as well. So Job searched everywhere for God, but could not find him, and in the midst of his suffering and frustration, he said some things he should not have said. Haven't we all?

Yet in his moments of weakness and despair, God showed up and corrected Job in regards to his incorrect analysis of the situation. But Job was so happy, so delighted to see God that he gladly received the corrective teaching God provided for his own understanding.

Job learned that day that God had not abandoned him after all! What God taught him caused Job to change his mind about his situation and his circumstances. It did not matter what he had suffered, what mattered the most was his relationship with God! For Job responded to his loss in these words, *"The Lord giveth, and the Lord taketh away, blessed be the name of the Lord." (Job 1:21)* Then on another occasion Job said, *"I'm going to wait until my change comes." (Job 14:14)* Yes, Job trusted God and knew that trusting God pays off.

Now the theological position Job took against his friends caused Job to lose sight of what was really important – his fellowship with God. He now acknowledges that God can do all things. He admits that before now he was only responding to the religious ideas and teachings he had learned all his life. Job had a "hearsay religion." But now he knew God for himself. Now he heard the voice of God speaking directly to his mind and his heart.

Job realized he had been taught wrong doctrine. Suffering is not always a consequence of sin. He believed that but now he had the truth straight from the Creator's mouth. He immediately was humbled and moved to confession, repentance, and a renewed trust in this God who he had worshipped for 70 years.

What is the reason why you trust God? Do you serve God because of hearsay? Are you going to Church because of your parents and grandparents' religious experiences? Have you met God for yourself? Hearsay religion is not enough to get you through the tough times in life. Only when we humble our hearts and minds by confessing our sins before the Lord, can we truly trust God to see us through our darkest days. That is when trusting God pays off! That is why the songwriter wrote, *"When all around my soul gives way, he then is all my hope and stay. On Christ the solid rock I stand, all other ground is sinking sand."*

2)

Job did not go through his ordeal alone. As word got around about Job's situation, his so-called friends came to see about him, to bring him words of comfort, and to encourage him to confess his sins before God so that his situation would turn around. Therefore, our second less is that **_TRUSTING GOD PAYS OFF WHEN GOD GIVES YOU VICTORY OVER YOUR ENEMIES._** Read vv 7-8, *"After the Lord had spoken these words to Job, the Lord said to Eliphaz the Temanite, 'My wrath is kindled against you and against your two friends; for you have not spoken of me what is right, as my servant Job has. Now take 7 bulls and 7 rams, and go to my servant Job, and offer up for yourselves a burnt offering; and my servant Job shall pray for you, for I will accept his prayer not to deal with you according to your folly'..."*

Job's three friends kept insisting he had committed some secret sin against God. After all, that is what they truly believed! Even Job himself believed one's sins could bring about suffering, but that did not apply to him. That was not his case! He was not going to plead guilty to something he had not done, no matter what his friends believed.

Job realized he was sitting in dust and ashes but he was not dirty on the inside. He had a clean heart and a contrite spirit. His soul was innocent, pure of any charges made against him. Something else had to be going on that he was not aware of. He knew if he could just get God's attention, he would be exonerated of all charges and found not guilty.

Because Job was right and his three friends were wrong, God spoke to Job's friends and informed them of his wrath against them! He accused them of presenting him, God, in a bad light, saying untruths about his character, his nature, his mercy and his forgiveness. These friends were giving God a bad rap, a bad reputation, defaming his name before the people who knew Job's life and character before all this testing began. They were teaching lies about who God really is.

God was not going to allow their lies about him to go unpunished. They needed to first go and apologize to Job through a burnt offering. They had to seek repentance from the very man they accused of sin! Then Job must intercede on their behalf before God would even consider showing mercy on them. That is what the bible means when it says, *"He'll make your enemies your foot stool."*(Lk 20:43)

When you trust God, you do not have to worry about your enemies, your haters, the naysayers, and the backbiters. Just turn it over to the Lord and he'll work it out. You remain steadfast, unmovable, making sure that you stand on the side of righteousness. Then stand still and see the salvation of God. The songwriter said it so clearly, *"Be not dismayed whatever be tied, God will take care of you!"*

The bible gives witness over and over again of how God takes care of his own: Moses at the Red Sea – God will drown your enemies; like the 3 Hebrew boys – God will be your air conditioner; like Daniel in the lion's den – God will close their lying mouths; like Paul and Silas locked in jail – God will lose the chains that have you bound; like Jesus in the tomb for 3 days – God will raise you up with all power in your hands!

When you trust God it will pay off in God's own time.

3)

So Job finally hears the truth from God but never really is told why he was chosen for such a test. However, now that Job and God were back on track, Job was a happy man. God continued to refer to Job as "my servant." So our final lesson from the text is that ***TRUSTING GOD PAYS OFF BECAUSE IT LEADS TO RESTORATION.*** Read v 10, *"And the Lord returned the fortunes of Job when he had prayed for his friends; and the Lord gave Job twice as much as he had before."* At the end of Job's confession and God's wrath against his friends, Job was still left with nothing, even though he was cleared of all charges connected to his sufferings. So God showed up again to bless Job with twice as much as he had before. Family and friends came to honor him, bringing him gifts of silver and gold.

God gave Job 7 sons in the English translation, but in the Greek it says "2x7, which equals 14" and 3 beautiful daughters. Only the daughters' names are mentioned, not the sons. Jemimah, which means dove, represents feminine beauty, innocence, fertility, and in the New Testament, a symbol of the Holy Spirit. Keziah's name means a kind of cinnamon used in perfume as a part of anointing oil. Keren-happuch, is a kind of powered paint used like eye shadow today on the eyelashes, lids, and brows. Her name serves as a reminder that "the eyes are the windows to the soul."

Now Job's new sense of justice and fairness is extended to his three beautiful daughters as well. They were given an inheritance along with their brothers. This was unheard of if male heirs were alive. But after what Job had been through, he was in no way going to show partiality or any hint of injustice to anyone, including his own children. He loved and respected them equally. The Church and our society can take a lesson from Job's actions, Amen!

Job's life was also doubled from 70 years to 140 years. Then God doubled the number of generations he lived to see – not just two, but four generations of descendants before he died. Oh yes, trusting God paid off big for Job. He could have listened to his 3 friends and falsely admitted to a crime he did not commit (as so many have done in jail). He could have listened to his wife and cursed God and died. But because Job believed in a God who loved righteousness and hated sin, because he stood his ground until he heard a word from the Lord, not only did he meet God for himself, not only were his friends reprimanded for their false teachings about God and had to come to Job to receive mercy from God, but in the end Job got the last laugh. For Job's latter days were better than his former days, because trusting God pays off! God bless you!

THE BOOK OF THE PSALMS

Praising The Anatomy of A Worshiper

KNOWN FROM THE INSIDE OUT

PSALM 139:13-14, *"For it was you who formed my inwards parts; you knit me together in my mother's womb. I praise you, for I am fearfully and wonderfully made. Wonderful are your works; that I know very well."*

INTRODUCTION

The book of Psalms is the hymnbook of the Second Temple. Although some of the Psalms can be traced back to David and Solomon, most of them were arranged for singing in the new temple built by the returnees from the Babylonian Exile. Psalms is the only book in the bible where God does not speak to the people, but the people speak to God. They lift up praise and adoration, they cry out to God in their laments and sufferings, they invoke God's anointing on the consecration of a new king, and they encourage their audience to hold fast in the midst of their trials and tribulations.

The Psalmist in Psalm 139 is traditionally David, once a shepherd boy, then a slayer of Goliath and commander of King Saul's army, and now king over Israel. He realized in his later years and through his many adventures, that God's presence has been with him all the time. Even when he could not find God, God knew his exact location. For David knew whether he was in the heavens, or on the earth or down under in Sheol, there was no place to hide from God.

In Psalm 139 David has an "Aha moment." So he takes a pen in his hand and begins to compose in hymn format what his experience has been with God throughout his life. When we look back over our lives, we too see God's hand on the footprint of our being. We acknowledge that God knows us from the inside out, even when we try to hide from God our sins and shortcomings. God sees all and God knows all. Therefore, as we examine Ps 139 more closely, whatever you are going through today, I encourage you to let go and let God, for our Creator knows us from the inside out.

1)

David is not oblivious to the workings of God in his life. So what we must first declare is that ***TO KNOW GOD IS TO BE KNOWN BY GOD.*** Read v 13, *"For it was you who formed my inward parts; you knit me together in my mother's womb."*

The key word in Ps 139 is "Know" or "Known." It occurs 7 times, which in the bible is the number for completion. What the psalmist wants to impress upon his readers is that God knows my name, and God knows your name. There is a gospel song that says, *"I am not forgotten, I am not forgotten, God knows my name."* The biblical view that human life is not simply a biological occurrence, but is the result of the will and work of a benevolent Creator, is evident in the words of the psalmist.

The psalmist recognized that conception does not haphazardly occur. God is all in that! Ask Elkanah and Hannah, Samuel's parents. Hannah was barren, but after praying to God in the temple, in the presence of the Lord, God made sure the egg and the sperm came together at the right time, and began to grow and develop in Hannah's womb until Samuel was born. The priest Eli interceded on Hannah's behalf.

You see there were many women who were barren, infertile, and unable to conceive in the biblical period. You can call the roll: *Sarah, Rachel, Hannah, and Elizabeth.* These are just the names we know about! Therefore, unless God permits pregnancy, all the scientific knowledge today will not do what God does not allow.

God knows you and God knows me. God knows the number of years you have lived and the number of years you have left to live. It was God who took our inner parts and delicately weaved them together until he formed a human body. Like Adam on the ground, God shaped us so we are made in his image, and in his likeness. Then he breathed life into us and we became living souls.

So the psalmist understands that his conception came with a purpose. He was not created to denounce his Creator, but to praise and worship him, to represent him and fulfill the purpose of his being on earth. For while in the womb David was fearfully and wonderfully made.

Nothing we do surprises God. Yes, God is disappointed when we make bad decisions and God is rooting for us all the time to stay on the right path. Yet, when we falter and fall down, God is still there ready to catch us when we fall. Then God lovingly receives us back into the fold, as the Father does with his prodigal son, for we are fearfully and wonderfully made. To know this about God is to be known by God. For only a fool has said in his heart there is no God.

2)

The Psalmist's second acknowledgment about God declares that ***TO KNOW GOD IS TO PRAISE GOD.*** Read v 14a, *"I praise you…"* The Hebrew word "praise" is the same verb translated "give thanks." To give someone praise is to show gratitude and honor for some act committed on their part. The Psalmist praises God because of how he was created. The Psalmist is mentally and emotionally connecting his human creation to God's creation of the world.

With his eyes he can see the sun and the moon, the stars in the sky. He can smell the fragrance of the flowers. He can feel the heat of the summer and the cold of the winter. He can hear the buzzing of bees and chirping of the hummingbirds. He can taste the sweetness of honey, the oil of the olive, and the grapes in the wine. With all his five senses in tact, the Psalmist declares boldly, "*I will praise you!*"

Praise involves our entire body in order for it to be authentic. Every part of our being should be in sync with the praise that comes forth from our lips. We should not just go through the motions. If you do not want to praise God, then sit down! Do not get up on your feet because somebody told you to do it! Do not lift up holy hands if your hands are not holy! This is what the Israelites did; they just went through the rituals and liturgies required by the Torah (*first 5 books of Moses*). God said that their praise stank in his nostrils! That is not the kind of praise we want to offer up to God. One songwriter wrote, "*What if God is not happy with our praise? We must change the way we walk; we must change the way we talk; we must live a life that pleasing to our King!*"

As believers, praise is what we do; it is what we were created to do. Even when we are going through the fire and through the floods of life, praise must be upon our lips and in our hearts. Just praise him anyhow! Keep on praising him, for when sincere praise goes up, bountiful blessings come down.

Now that we know the Psalmist responds with gratitude to God's creative activity, what is your response? Can you praise God in the morning? Can you praise God at noon? Can you praise God in the evening? Let everything that has breath praise the Lord! If you really know him, as he knows you, then you cannot help but praise his holy name.

---

3)

Then finally the Psalmist teaches us that ***TO KNOW HIM IS TO ACKNOWLEDGE HIS HANDIWORK.*** Read v 14b, "*For I am fearfully and wonderfully made.*" The Psalmist uses the unusual metaphor of God as a weaver instead of a potter. Perhaps this is because when a potter is finished with his created vessel, it stands alone to be showcased for sale. However, God as the weaver gives us a more intimate connection to him. When you weave something together, something is attached to something else; it cannot stand by itself. When a woman goes to the hairdresser to get a hair weave, it is attached to the hair on her head that already exists.

So the Psalmist is relaying the message that we are connected to God through the weaving process. We are not on our own, we cannot exist apart from God, and when we try to we end up lost and vulnerable to the Evil One. Knowing who God is becomes clearer when we acknowledge his creative works. Even after all creation was completed, there was still something missing. So God created male and female as co-workers in creation. In some

African religions, Pantheism is the core belief of the faith. In Pantheism God is seen in everything – the rocks, the trees, the water, the mountain and the fire.

In Native American tradition, the Earth is our mother. She is to be treated with respect, not polluted and destroyed for capital gain. Yet, as Westerners we have lost that intimate connection to the earth. This corresponds directly in my opinion, to why we have become so disconnected from God!

So if we cannot appreciate God's handiwork, humans included, killing becomes an acceptable reaction when we feel violated, or disrespected. That is why a white man can enter a black church and shoot people he does not even know! That is why an anti-Semitic terrorist can enter a Jewish synagogue and kill people because they believe differently from him. God made us all in his image and likeness. There is no color, no gender, and no ethnicity. God is a spirit and those who worship him must worship him in spirit and truth.

To observe God's handiwork is to be fearful. Fearful can mean afraid or scared, but it can also mean in awe of, revere, hold in the highest esteem. When the Psalmist declares I am fearfully made, he is once again acknowledging that he was created to honor God, to hold God in the highest esteem, to worship God with the utmost respect. This was already stamped in our DNA. Not to worship, not to praise God, is to go against the very essence of our being.

Therefore, as we revere our Creator, it also becomes obvious that we are wonderfully made – in his image, both male and female. The word *"wonder"* is in the adverb, "wonderfully." God made us to wonder about his greatness—how great is our God. God made us to wonder about his faithfulness – God is faithful even when we are not. God made us to wonder about his majesty – King of kings and Lord of Lord. God made us to wonder about his mercy – it endures to all generations. God made us to wonder about his grace – his grace is sufficient. Yet God does not want us to ever wonder about his love – *"For God so loved the world that he gave his only begotten Son..."*

Wonder sometimes comes from a lack of understanding, or an inability to see clearly while at the same time appreciating the object of our wonder, which is God in Jesus Christ. When we look in the mirror, we should not degrade or criticize our outer appearance, for it does not yet appear what we shall be. Instead we should look beyond the flesh and try to see Christ's image in one another. Ask yourself, *"Do I look like Jesus today? Did I act like Jesus today? Did somebody see Jesus in me today?"* On one occasion in the bible, a group of Greek philosophers came looking for Jesus because of his reputation and mighty works. When they encountered the disciples instead, they said to them, *"Sir, we would see Jesus!"* (Jn 12:21)

That is what the world needs to see today, more of Jesus in our lives. For Jesus was fearfully and wonderfully made! Jesus left heaven and came down 42 generations; planted by the Holy Spirit in the womb of a virgin engaged to be married to a carpenter. Therefore, if we are his disciples, if we claim to be followers of the Lamb, who takes away the sins of the world, then we cannot be incognito. We cannot be a light hidden under a bushel. That is why the song writer wrote, *"This little light of mine, I'm gonna let it shine. Everywhere I go, I'm gonna let it shine, let it shine, let it shine."*

We are known from the inside out! David declared that God has known us from the beginning, and knows our ending. Our destiny lies in God. Without God we are nothing and we can do nothing. But to know God is to love God, and to love God is to serve God. To serve God is to be a witness for him. Why, because we are known from the inside out. God bless you!

THE BOOK OF PROVERBS

(Wisdom Literature)

In Search of a Good Woman

A WOMAN AFTER GOD'S OWN HEART

PROVERBS 31:10, *"Who can find a virtuous woman? She is worth more than rubies. The heart of her husband trusts in her, and he will have no lack of gain. She does him good, and not harm, all the days of her life"*

INTRODUCTION

The book of Proverbs belongs to the wisdom literature of Israel. The first person ever referred to as wise in the Old Testament was a woman from Tekoa, the home of the prophet Amos (2 Sam 14:1-20). Another is mentioned in 2 Sam 20:14-22. Yet in the bible, King Solomon is the epitome of wisdom in all Israel.

Wisdom was primarily a practical matter. It was that natural intelligence or shrewdness by which one performed a job skillfully and well. It was not speculative or philosophical. The wise one knew that this practical wisdom came from God. Those who were considered to be wise would sit at the town gate and give instruction both publicly and privately to anyone who sought out counsel. However, their teaching was primarily directed to the youth in the community, who would become the future rulers and wise sages of Israel.

Our passage in Proverbs is called an acrostic poem. What this means is that the first letter of each line follows the order of the Hebrew alphabet. This was a device used for memorization purposes and allowed the speaker to counsel in an orderly fashion.

Chapter 31 of the book of Proverbs is titled, *"The words of King Lemuel. An oracle that his mother taught him."* The Queen Mother was a powerful and feared position in the Ancient Near East. For a Queen Mother often times had her son's ear even more so than his closest advisors. So it was wise to please the Queen Mother before you pleased the king.

The Queen Mother used verses 10-31 as a teaching moment for young men who had reached the age of marriage. The Queen Mother used these verses as a checklist to help the naïve young men choose a virtuous woman for a wife. This wise advice was meant to prevent them from succumbing to the desires of their flesh. For beauty is only skin deep.

These verses are quite clear in describing the characteristics of a good woman, a woman after God's own heart. This model is tough to measure up to, especially with all the demands that are placed on women today. Yet every now and then, in every generation, someone spectacular steps up to the plate and perfectly fits this model. So let us now hear for ourselves the characteristics of a woman after God's own heart.

_____

1)

The first characteristic we find in a woman after God's own heart is that **_SHE IS TRUSTWORTHY AND KNOWS HOW TO GET THINGS DONE._** Read vv 10-12, *"Who can find a virtuous woman? She is far more precious than jewels because the heart of her husband trusts in her and he will have no lack of gain."* Trust is an important characteristic of a person claiming to have God in their life. As a wise person trusts in God, a wise husband can trust in his wife because she brings him good, not harm.

In trying to get her audience to understand the value of a woman after God's own heart, the author compares her to the jewels of his day that were sought after with great energy and longing. The value of jewels is priceless, and one kept their jewels close, in order to examine their beauty and worth.

According to Proverbs 31:10, this is the case when one finds a virtuous woman, a woman after God's own heart! She can be trusted in every situation to do the right thing. Her husband has complete confidence in her ability to manage the household and his money too! She always has his best interest at heart, and when he leaves the home, he knows that he has nothing to worry about.

How do we measure up to that standard as ladies living in the 21st century? Who are we, and what are the circumstances of our lives? Has our relationship with God inspired us to the point that we are trustworthy? Can family, friends, and co-workers count on us to have their backs when trouble comes their way?

Is our word our bond? Is our yes, yes, and our no, no? Ladies if we want to be called "women after God's own heart" others have to be able to depend on us – our spouses, our children, our parents, and our church. We are the driving force of all life. Remember the saying, *"The hand that rocks the cradle, rules the world."*

Those who were wise in ancient Israel understood the divine connection between virtue and trustworthiness. If we are going to be women after God's own heart, we cannot allow this world's greed and immorality to invade our spirits and dictate our lifestyles. We must read God's word daily and digest it so that it is written on our hearts. Then when we face tough times, we know who to go to.

_____

2)

The second characteristic of a woman after God's own heart is **_SHE HAS A DIVINE WORK ETHIC._** Read vv 13-18, 24, *"She seeks wool and flax, and works with willing hands. She* *is like the ships of the merchant; she brings her food from afar. She rises while it's still night and provides food for her household and tasks for her maidens..."* This is a busy sister! In the Old Testament, women worked very hard to provide for their families. Second only to childbearing, it was their major role in that society. They would go out and gather herbs and vegetables for their family to consume. They would plant gardens for food and wash clothes by hand in the faraway wells or streams. They made pottery and used it for cooking, drinking and eating. They skinned and cooked whatever their husbands brought home from hunting. Then they took the skin and made clothing for the family. While doing all of this, they had to educate the children and teach the young girls how to prepare themselves for marriage and motherhood.

This was not the end of her day! She went beyond her wifely and motherly duties. This sister had a business of her own! I guess with her husband away all day doing "manly stuff" she felt a need to exercise and explore her business sense. So she started her own business within the home. The text suggests she was a type of seamstress, making and weaving wool and flax. So you see ladies, being busy is nothing new for us. We start working from the moment we open our eyes until they close at night, then get up and repeat it all over again.

Yet, there is so much of God's work to be done. Matthew 25 tells us that there are hungry people needing to be fed, there are lonely and sick people needing to be visited, there are naked people needing clothing, hurting people needing to be comforted. For the most part it has been put in our laps, whether or not it is fair is not the question. The question Jesus will ask us on Judgment Day is whether or not we addressed the needs of those less fortunate than we are. He says it so clearly, *"The least you have done for my brethren, you have done for me."(Mt 25:40)*

----

3)

The third characteristic of a woman after God's own heart is **_SHE KNOWS HER BEAUTY IS ON THE INSIDE._** Read vv 25-31, *"Strength and dignity are her clothing, and she laughs at the time to come because she is so secure and is prepared for the future..."* What a woman! No wonder her worth is far greater than rubies. She knew what was important in life – to have dignity and strength of character, to be kind and full of wisdom. You may not find her wearing a Sasson suit, or red bottom shoes. Her clothing comes from being in a right relationship with God, for without these characteristics, all the designer clothes and shoes in the world will not help you when the troubles of life are raging against you. You better know the Lord for yourself!

Because this woman knows that wisdom begins with the fear of the Lord, and reverence for God, her future is secure, she had no need to worry. All she had to do was her best, and God would do the rest. All life is in God's hands. *"Charm is deceitful and beauty is vain, but a woman who fears the Lord is to be praised."*

What about you today? Is your beauty only skin deep? Do you spend more time in the beauty and nail salons then in God's word? Will others rise up and call you blessed? Who will come forward in a court of law and vouch for your character? Only you can insure your beauty goes beneath the skin layer and reaches the heart. As a matter of fact, how you look for the most part, is a gift from your parents (or plastic surgery).

Therefore, let God's beauty shine through you. Jesus tells us to let our lights shine so others will see our good works and glorify our Father in heaven. A woman after God's own heart is complex, complicated, and dependent on her encounter and connection to her God and the needs of others, to focus too much attention on her outer looks. Instead she knows that her inner goodness will outlast any outside make-up or fancy clothing. When we get the inside right, the outside will fall in line.

To be a woman after God's own heart takes trustworthiness, a work ethic that is in sync with God's agenda, and a sense of inner beauty that comes out in her relationship with others. Are you up for the challenge? It is a title worth more than rubies. God bless you!

THE BOOK OF ECCLESIASTES

(Wisdom Literature and Festival Scroll – celebrates the Feast of Tabernacles)

Experiencing the Seasons of Life

WHEN THE SEASONS CHANGE

ECCLESIASTES 3:1-8, *"For everything there is a season and a time for every matter under heaven; a time to be born, and a time to die; a time to plant, and a time to pluck up that which is planted..."*

INTRODUCTION

The title "Ecclesiastes" derives from the Greek word meaning "preacher", *Qohelet*. The author is aware of the world and his teachings are a combination of the theology of the day and the concerns of contemporary life. We would call him today a "practical theologian." Traditionally Solomon has been attached to the book as its writer. However, recent scholars, who have studied the book, disagree with the traditional opinion and believe that it was written after the exiles returned back home to Jerusalem.

One of the author's most familiar statements is, *"all is vanity."* Contemporary thinking in regards to the word *"vanity"* implies that it has something to do with one's pride or arrogance. However, the Hebrew meaning is *breath or vapor.* So pride is not what the author meant. But for Qohelet, this phrase means that as one cannot contain or control breath or vapor, one cannot determine the moments of life. He uses the word 38 times to consistently argue that life is just a combination of changing seasons. Jesus says something similar in the New Testament, "The wind blows and we do not know where it comes or where it goes."

Sometimes when we reflect on everything around us and all that goes on in the world, we feel like the world is in chaos and that there is no order. We are always in flux. Change is inevitable. Sometimes when things go wrong in our personal lives we feel out of control, like someone's playing a bad trick on us. But for those who have lived long enough to know, and have experienced the many directions the wind blows in our lives, say with confidence, there is nothing new under the sun – the season is just changing. This is the attitude of Qohelet, the author of Ecclesiastes. He was once young, then he was middle age, and now he is old. He looked back on his life and saw his experiences, both bad and good, merely as part of the seasons of life. Qohelet observed the world in all its contrariness in order to dispel any myths of human certainty in life. One cliché states that there are only two things in life we can be certain of, death and taxes.

Life for this author has order, it has sequence, and it has timing. We may not understand why things happen as they do because we have a limited mortal thinking capacity, nor can we see into the future. God knows just what is going on (ask Job!). The author, therefore, encourages us to be strong, trust God, but not to get too comfortable in whatever stage of life we are currently in, because before we know it, the season will change. Let us now listen to the words of Qohelet, the preacher.

---

1)

Ecclesiastes 3:1 reads, *"For everything there is a season and a time for every matter under heaven; a time to be born, and a time to die."* There is a time when we are born and we are born with a purpose. When we are born our parents and family are full of joy and love for the prospect of the future this newborn baby will have and the impact their birth will have on the family, community, country and the world.

We are born to be the best we can be. In life we can choose to be fun loving, humorous, generous, respectful, compassionate towards others, and a blessing to all we encounter on this short journey called life. The alternative is to be mean spirited, hateful, stingy, foul mouthed, lazy, fearful, seeking revenge on others, and violent.

Yet, we are born with a God given talent to use and develop for God's glory, not necessarily our own financial gain. However, most often than not, the two work together in concert. The more we bless God with our talent, the more financial blessings come our way. The book of Ephesians highlights some of the gifts God places in our DNA at birth: teaching, giving, preaching, prophesy, hospitality, and the like. Many of us have been born and blessed with skills that caused us to excel in school, on the athletic court, or on a stage. These skills we must further develop in order to bless others who may need our gifts to find their own blessings and talents.

---

2)

In the second part of v 2 the author states, *"There is a time to plant..."* We can never determine exactly when the season of life will change. There are babies in the cemetery as well as senior citizens. So what we plant between life and death reveal our purpose for being born. When that purpose has been fulfilled, we encounter the season of change known as death. Therefore, each and every day of our lives should be lived to its fullest, in preparation of the day the season shifts and we no longer inhabit a mortal body. Our ancestors use to say, *"Don't let him catch you with your work undone!"*

The author of Ecclesiastes thought that material possessions and living a life of luxury were all that mattered in this life. He planted by investing in buildings and social causes. But when he got old he realized that he these things did not give him a sense of satisfaction or that life really mattered. Qohelet realized that all that he had worked for and accumulated throughout his life, would be passed on to someone who did not work a day for it. It came from an inheritance. Therefore, he spent his whole life planting so he could reap earthly treasures and was not prepared spiritually for when the season would change.

Many people are unprepared for retirement, and have to work until their bodies say no more, or they die. Although Solomon did not have this problem because of his wealth, when he came to the end of his days, he was spiritually and emotionally broke and wondered what was the true meaning of life. Was it all for naught?

Today is the day that we are given to review and assess the accomplishments and goals that resulted from your planting. How far have we come? Are we reaching our mark? Is there a bucket list that has not been touched? One plants a seed in anticipation that something will come forth and show the fruit of our labors, so that our living is not in vain.

_____

3)

The latter part of v 2 reads, *"And a time to pluck up what was planted."* The time to "pluck up" or harvest time, comes sooner or later in our lives. God is the one who made everything right in its time. The author of Ecclesiastes does not dispute this fact. What he does question is if there is justice in the timing. The human mind cannot comprehend God's timing. Therefore, we must enjoy and celebrate whatever season we are currently experiencing. Then when it is time to *"pluck up"* what do we have to show for our years on earth? Were we a good mother or father? Were we a good daughter or son, a good sibling or relative? Were we a good co-worker, friend, church member? The evening of life moves us to reflect on things that we took for granted or said we did not have time to cultivate and the opportunity passed us by. It would be tragic to come to the last season of life and there was nothing to *"pluck up."*

When the season of life changes, and we can no longer do the things we use to do, and somebody else has to see to our well-being, will we have lived a life of joy, peace, understanding, and compassion? Will our children rise up and call us blessed? Will our spouse praise us at the city gates, or find excuses not to come home? What you plant will come out in the wash sooner or later. Will people say good things about you at your funeral, or will they stay away because their relationship with you was so toxic? These are things we need to consider before we experience our final season of life.

If you are reading this message, then your time to "pluck up" has not arrived and your final season of life has not yet happened. God has allowed you to remain planted in this world. There is still time to make a difference in this world. It does not have to be a big ripple. A little ripple goes a long way. How you spend your time now will determine where you will spend eternity. Whatever season of life you are experiencing today, soon and very soon, it will change.

Our Lord and Savior, Jesus the Christ experienced both seasons of birth and death. How he lived and how he died is our example. Jesus promised to be with us until the end of the age, so it is not too late to accept him into your heart and allow Jesus to direct your life and order your steps. Because it does not matter who you are – rich, or poor, educated or illiterate, short or tall, eventually your season will change. Funeral directors are not going out of business any time soon. Will you be ready? Can you say in the words of Paul to the Corinthian Church, "*Where, O death is your victory, where O death is your sting?*" *(I Cor 15:55)*

"*Seek the Lord while he may be found, draw to him while he is near.*" *(Isaiah 55:6-7)* Today Jesus is our Savior, but when the final season of life embraces us, Jesus will be our judge. God bless you!

THE BOOK OF THE
SONG OF SONGS

(A Festival Scroll - Passover)

Love is a Many Splendored Thing

THE COLOR OF LOVE

SONG OF SONGS 1:5-6, *"I am black and beautiful, O daughters of Jerusalem, like the tents of Kedar, like the curtains of Solomon. Do not gaze at me because I am dark, because the sun has gazed on me. My mother's sons were angry with me; they made me keeper of the vineyards, but my own vineyard I have not kept!"*

INTRODUCTION

Song of Songs (also known as Song of Solomon) is a departure from much of the religious literature found in the bible. The opening verses catapult us into a romantic and sexual relationship between two lovers. This kind of talk is usually taboo and framed in a more delicate way. It forces the reader to see this *"black and beautiful woman"* through her own eyes. She is not ashamed of her skin color although she does explain why she is so black in her own words.

Nowhere in the 8 chapters is God mentioned. This is similar to the book of Esther. Whereas Esther mentions prayer and fasting, Song of Songs takes on a more secular tone. None of Israel's sacred traditions are even alluded to.

Song of Songs is the only biblical book in which a female voice predominates. Her voice was not edited by narrators, or by later redactors. More than 56 verses are ascribed to a female voice as compared to only 36 male voices. The experience, thoughts, imagination, emotions, and words of this anonymous dark-skinned woman are central to the book's message. She is not shy, but aggressive, uninhibited and says whatever she thinks about her own sexual desires.

It appears the female leading voice tried to convince those who wanted to judge her, that there is no color in love. So let us hear her words and listen for God's message through her and to us.

---

1)

The female voice of Song of Songs wants us to know that she is ***NOT ASHAMED OF HER OUTER APPEARANCE.*** Read v 5, *"I am black and beautiful, O daughters of Jerusalem, like the tents of Kedar, like the curtains of Solomon."*

According to tradition, King Solomon composed around 3000 proverbs and 1005 songs during his lifetime. Rumor has it that he composed these poems as a legacy to his love for the Queen of Sheba. The Queen of Sheba was from the African country of Ethiopia, also known in the bible as Candace. She traveled far to meet King Solomon because his wisdom was infamous. She wanted to witness his greatness for herself.

Perhaps the Jewish daughters did not look favorably on her visit, for they knew that Solomon had a thing for beautiful women of all colors. After all, Solomon had 700 wives of his own and 300 concubines! They may have feared that she would be added to the harem. So she speaks her truth before anyone has an opportunity to judge her skin color as inferior.

Our female voice with dark skin declared boldly in 1:5, *"I am black and beautiful."* Her audience may be unable to determine why she is so dark skinned, so she compared her darkness to the color of the tents of Kedar, and the curtains in Solomon's house. The reference to Solomon's House may symbolize the temple. The Holy of Holies was the back room where the priest offered the sacrifice on behalf of the people. They went behind large black curtains to show that they were entering the presence of God. Reference to these curtains is made in the New Testament while Jesus was dying on the cross. These curtains represented the old compensation of the law and now were ripped and replaced by the new compensation, which is Jesus the Christ.

Our dark skinned female in this text is almost flaunting her sexual relationship with King Solomon, or some other powerful leader in Judah. In her eyes, love comes in all colors, shapes and sizes. Israel tried to outlaw mixed marriages in order to preserve her Hebrew blood, but it was not successful. Abraham and Moses, both took wives of dark skin. This caused tension within the Hebrew community. Later, Nehemiah and Ezra forbid mixed marriages and forced the men who married outside their culture and faith, to divorce their wives and send their half-breed children away.

But the heart wants what the heart wants! This is ever so evident in the recent marriage of Prince Harry and Megan Markle. God created us all in his image. Therefore, God's love has no color and as reflections of God, our love should not see color. Just think what a better place the world would be if love truly conquered all!

---

2)

The female voice of Song of Songs wants **_PEOPLE TO NOT JUDGE HER BECAUSE HER SKIN IS DARK._** Read v 6, *"Do not gaze at me because I am dark, because the sun has gazed on me."* The female voice addressed the daughters of Jerusalem. She appeared to be subjected to their intense scrutiny so she explains that her color is from long exposure to the sun. She seems to scold them because the daughters of Jerusalem are staring at her dark skin. Perhaps it was uncommon for women to have dark tans, although it was natural for the men who worked outside to have dark tans. For the most part, women worked inside the home, or were not confined outside in the sun for long periods of time.

If our female voice resides in Israel, why would her looks be so surprising? Why would our female character feel a need to explain her dark skin? Was working in the sun for hours and days on end a negative sign, a sign of slavery? Was she trying to argue her citizenship, or her social status? Whatever her reasons, she used a defensive tone because she is not about to let anyone snub their nose at her strictly because of her outer appearance.

Wow! Times certainly have not changed. The words of Ecclesiastes 3 rings so true here, *"There is nothing new under the sun."* Martin Luther King, Jr. said in one of his famous speeches, that he was waiting for the day when his 4 children would be judged by the content of their character and not by the color of their skin. Truly we have come so far. However, over the last 10 years, it seems as the ground that was gained during the Civil Rights Movement has been resending by every meeting of the Supreme Court.

Police brutality against people of color, shooting of unarmed African Americans, has escalated since our first African American president left office. What has happened to turn back the hands of time? The words of our dark skinned female voice rings ever so true and loud as a slogan for dark skinned children in today's society: *"I am black and I am beautiful."*

Beauty is not measured by one's skin tone or outward appearance. It is measured by one's deeds and words. Have you helped someone today? Have you called an elderly widow or widower to check on their welfare? Have you read a book to a child? What have you done to reflect the love of God in your life lately? Our world is in dire need of love, for that is the only think that there is just too little of. When we have love in our hearts, love finds a way to make a difference, to pick up the slack, to turn a bad situation around, no matter what your skin color. You see beauty is not about how you look, but it's about your service to others.

_____

3)

The third message from the voice of our female speaker in Song of Songs **ANNOUNCED THE BRUTALITY SHE SUFFERED AT THE HANDS OF HER OWN PEOPLE.** Read v 6b, *"My mother's sons were angry with me; they made me keeper of the vineyards, but my own vineyard I have not kept!"* The female voice with dark skin blamed her condition, her dark skin, on her brothers who were angry with her. Because of their anger, she was sentenced to work outside in the hot sun for long periods of time.

Now the term *"vineyard"* is not necessarily a literal reference. The vine/vineyard is a frequent symbol for both Israel and a woman. The complaint that she was forced to labor in *"vineyards"* has an erotic tone in Song of Songs. Commentators have suggested that she has been sexually violated and used as a prostitute by her brothers. This woman has not been able to safeguard her own virginity *(vineyard)*. These are the dangers single women faced in the ancient world and in many countries still today, through sex trafficking, kidnapping, brothels and porn shops. Sometimes their own family members sell them into this life of abuse. Therefore, until love has no color, no country, and no gender, atrocities and injustices of this nature will continue to thrive throughout the world.

Yet despite her unfair treatment, she continues to love the man of her dreams. Is this man King Solomon? We cannot say for sure. But whoever he is, her love for him is deep and eternal. Her lover felt the same way about her. She and her male lover try to portray to the readers the innocence of their love and to emphasize the obstacles and frustrations they had to endure in order to be together.

So let us demonstrate a color-blind love. It is the only way we can accurately reflect the love God has for his creation. God bless you!

THE BOOK OF LAMENTATIONS

(A Festival Scroll Commemorating the Temple Destruction)

SEEKING FORGIVENESS IN THE MIDST OF THE STORM

LAMENTATIONS 3:22-25, *The steadfast love of the Lord never ceases, his mercies never come to an end; they are new every morning; great is your faithfulness. 'The Lord is my portion,' says my soul, 'therefore I will hope in him.' The Lord is good to those who wait for him, to the soul that seeks him."*

INTRODUCTION

The book of Lamentations is a collection of five lament poems bewailing the fall of Jerusalem to the Babylonians in 586 B.C.E. These laments expressed the suffering and regret felt by those left behind to clean up the mess.

The book of Lamentations is one of the Festival Scrolls used by the Jews today in their annual commemoration of the destruction of Solomon's Temple. There are four primary voices in Lamentations orchestrated to portray the range of emotions and experiences encountered in the now ruins of Jerusalem. There is the funeral song, the personified Zion, the unnamed man who declared Zion's suffering, and lastly the collective voices from the community.

Tradition credits the prophet Jeremiah as the author who dictated this eyewitness report to his secretary, Baruch. However, scholars today argue this is not the case because of some later ideas presented in the book, and the fact that Jeremiah was kidnapped and taken to Egypt for refuge. Nevertheless, Lamentations provides a timeless window to that painful period of Israel's last days as an independent nation. Let us now hear the pain of God's people as they seek forgiveness in the midst of their storm. It will give hope in our time of need and despair.

1)

Our first lesson in seeking forgiveness in the midst of a storm is to ***HAVE CONFIDENCE IN GOD'S STEADFAST LOVE.*** Read v 22a, *"The steadfast love of the Lord never ceases..."* The book of Lamentations paints a dreary and painful picture of Jerusalem after the fiery attacks of the Babylonians on Judah. Judah was warned over and over again by the prophets Isaiah of Jerusalem (1-39), and Jeremiah, that unless their sinful behavior changed, God's wrath would be unleashed on God's chosen people.

The author of Lamentations acknowledged Judah deserved the wrath of God. The writer makes no excuses for the severity of the punishment. Yet the author refused to accept that God's nature had changed because of the sins of his creation. God's steadfast love *(hesed)* was who God is! Israel's relationship with God has always depended on that one aspect of God's character to forgive them because of his love for his chosen people. However, as many parents know sometimes tough love must override compassion in order for the subject to learn their lesson and change their behavior.

The people living in Jerusalem encountered hunger, thirst, cannibalism, and death. This went on for at least 18 months, until the Babylonian army finally penetrated the walls, and the people opened the gates. Their suffering was so great that the observer felt the need to record it for all posterity, the extent of God's wrath that was unleashed on Judah. The site was astonishing, shocking, and unbearable in the eyes of this witness.

In life, God promises to be with us and Jesus encourages us to ask for forgiveness when we find ourselves, "out of line" or "out of sync" with the righteousness of God. When King David sinned and his life was in utter turmoil, he sought out God's forgiveness in the midst of his storm. In Psalm 51 David prayed that God would give him *"A clean heart and renew in him a right spirit."* David knew if he humbled himself before God, God was faithful and that God's steadfast love would cover a multitude of sins.

The point here is to have confidence in God's steadfast love. God demonstrated that love on Calvary's Hill. There is no length God would not go to show his steadfast love for us. So when we mess up, let us then seek forgiveness by trusting and believing that when it seems its darkest, God's steadfast love will see us through. God's steadfast love will restore us to our initial role as his people and a light to the nations.

---

2)

Our second lesson teaches us that we seek forgiveness in the midst of a storm **_BECAUSE WE KNOW TOMORROW'S MERCIES ARE ON THE HORIZON._** Read vv 22b-23, *"...his mercies never come to an end; they are new every morning, great is your faithfulness."* Although the author has witnessed Judah's horrific conditions firsthand, he is not deterred by what he saw, but encouraged by what he believed. He believed that, as in the past, God would eventually come to Israel's defense and rescue her from her enemies.

This diehard belief stems from the teaching that every day brings new mercies into the life of the believer. These verses belong to the third voice found in Lamenta-tions. In earlier chapters, the sense of hopelessness and despair seeps through every line. Now the third voice makes a sudden reversal and becomes hopeful as if he suddenly remembered the true character of God.

God is not a man that he should lie to his people. So if God promised Abraham that his descendants would be as numerous as the stars or the sand on the beach, what is going on right now is only temporary! Tomorrow brings new mercies, new hope, new faith, new opportunities, and a new perspective. Whatever we are going through, remember it is only temporary, only for a season. Life's pendulum will swing back in your favor when and if you ask for forgiveness in the midst of your storms. We cannot always blame others for our situation and circumstances. First look in the mirror to see your participation in the drama. Eventually God will restore us and embrace us and more importantly, receive us into his eternal kingdom.

Yesterday has come and gone. Today we can receive and accept our new mercies. God forgave us of our past mistakes. There is no need to bring them into today or tomorrow. Focus instead on today's new mercies. What can I achieve with today's new mercies? Who can I help with today's new mercies? How does God want me to move forward in today's new mercies?

The definition of mercy is *"compassion or kindly behavior shown toward an offender."* We have certainly offended God! We do not deserve God's mercy yet every new morning, new mercies I see. Every morning when we rise, mercy wakes us up. Every day that we get out of bed, that same mercy gives us the strength to run on and see what the end is going to be.

Mercy is the enemy of judgment. God's judgment needs not be prematurely released on our lives. Israel's punishment and judgment was long overdue. We still have time to seek forgiveness from God. Nevertheless, this third voice has hope that *"Weeping may endure for a night, but joy comes in the morning."* For in the morning, new mercies are making my case before the court of judgment.

---

3)

Our third and final lesson teaches us that ***THROUGH IT ALL, GOD IS OUR ONLY HELP.*** Read vv 24-25, *"The Lord is my portion, says my soul, 'therefore I will hope in him.' The Lord is good to those who wait for him, to the soul that seeks him."*

The author of Lamentations remains in hope, a decision he made based on his remembrance of divine mercies in the past. For the first time in this poem, the writer addressed God directly to voice the confidence that underscored their mutual relationship – "Great is your faithfulness!"

The author knows that change will take a while. Therefore, he accepts that waiting is a part of his redemption. Taking the time to reflect on God's steadfast love, time to recognize Israel's role in her own destruction, and time to wait just 24 hours for new mercies to be realized in one's life. When we choose to wait on God we acknowledge that God's help will reestablish our relationship with him and with our neighbors. Without God we can do nothing and are left to our own devices! With God all things are possible. The old saying fits so well in this context, *"He may not come when you want him, but he is always right on time. Because he is an on time God, yes he is!"*

Yes, today God's wrath may be evident in our current physical and spiritual condition, but wait on God for tomorrow brings hope for a new experience. Our new mercies guarantee our salvation in God, if we seek forgiveness in the midst of our storms. God bless you!

THE LATTER PROPHETS

3 Major (Isaiah-Ezekiel)
12 Minor (Hosea-Malachi)
1 Apocalyptic Prediction (Daniel)

THE BOOK OF ISAIAH

Three Prophets in One

(Jerusalem, Exile, Judah)

FINDNG STRENGTH IN THE WAITING

ISAIAH 40:27-31, *"But those who wait on the Lord shall renew their strength, they shall mount up with wings like eagles, they shall run and not be weary, they shall walk and not faint."*

INTRODUCTION

Biblical scholars over the years have divided the book of Isaiah into three different prophets, prophesying during three major periods in Israel's history. Chapters 1-39 are called Isaiah of Jerusalem. The people are in Judah facing the crisis of the Assyrian Empire. Isaiah of Jerusalem, also known as First Isaiah, dates to the 8th century B.C.E. He preached a message of "doom and gloom" warning the people of God's coming wrath against them.

Chapters 40-55 are known as the Second Isaiah or Deutero-Isaiah. It covers the time period when the people are in exile awaiting their release and forgiveness by God. This dates to the 6th century B.C.E. He is known as the prophet of Comfort. His work is of an unknown prophet, whose words reflected the theological teachings of his mentor, Isaiah of Jerusalem. Then chapters 56-66 are called Third Isaiah or Trito-Isaiah. He is the prophet that encourages the returnees now back in Jerusalem to get the temple rebuilt and welcome the flood of immigrants that are about to make Jerusalem a great nation again

In chapters 40-55 the majority of Israelites are located in the city of Babylon, where they were taken into exile. The king of Babylon, Nebuchadrezzer, conquered Jerusalem, destroyed the temple and walls, and marched all the royal family, wealthy merchants and priests into exile. This is the background and location for our text.

Some believed the exile would be short and God would avenge them in some way as he had done in the past. This is what the false prophets were telling them. But Jeremiah wrote the people in exile and told them it will be a while - at least 70 years -before they would return to Jerusalem. So they were encouraged to live their lives: marry, have children, start businesses, plant vineyards. Their sins this time were too great to be ignored. However, their initial response to Jeremiah's advice is found in Psalm 137, *"How can we sing the Lord's song in a strange land?"*

So off to exile they went while their homeland lay in ruins. Where is God? Has God been defeated along with the temple? Does God not know our situation? Does God not care? These were some of the questions asked by those in exile. It is always interesting how when we get ourselves in a mess, it is always God's fault.

Now after 70 years, God's people were in a state of depression. God's people were losing faith. So God decided it was time to act. Thus the opening words of chapter 40 states, *"Comfort ye, comfort ye, my people, says your God. Speak tenderly to her. Tell her that she has paid double for her sins."* This proclamation of hope comes 70 years later! Is it too little, too late? The Second Isaiah teaches us three lessons about the character of God. These three lessons teach us how to find strength during the waiting process.

---

1)

The first lesson we learn about God's character is that ***TO KNOW GOD IS TO TRUST GOD.*** Read v 28a, *"Have you not known? Have you not heard? The Lord is the everlasting God; the Creator of the ends of the earth. He does not faint or grow weary; his understanding is unsearchable."* As the Israelites sat in exile for 70 years, a new generation was born who had not experienced the miraculous deeds God had performed on behalf of the people of Israel. Some of them forgot how God brought their ancestors out of Egyptian slavery and opened a Red Sea so that they could cross on dry land. Some of them forgot how God provided for their ancestors in the wilderness for 40 years. Some of them ignored the covenant laws they received from Moses on Mt. Sinai.

They were overshadowed with the idol gods of Babylon and the temptations of life outside the holy city of Jerusalem. They began to believe their ancestors' lies, that Marduk, the Babylonian god, had defeated the God of Israel, Yahweh. After all here they were in Babylonian captivity. Who was this God of their ancestors and what had he done for us lately?

Sometimes in the life of the Church, we lose sight of our true purpose and mission. The Israelites forgot they were God's chosen people. They allowed their current address to cause them to have amnesia about what they know God is capable of. When the Church exist in spiritual exile, we tend to go through all the right motions – have meetings, collect money, sing, pray, then go home, only to repeat the same routine next Sunday. But has anybody's life changed for the better?

Any Church can find itself in exile for many reasons. Poor leadership. Members do not know the Lord for themselves. The Holy Spirit is absent. The Church's vision is not Christ centered. The bible or what God requires of his Church is not taught. All or any of these situations can determine a Church's success or failure.

But a Church does not have to remain in exile. The key to liberation is the word of God! Only God's word can change the human heart. For in God's word we learn about God's ways. We learn how God delivers his people and how God provides for his people even when they are in the wilderness or exile of life.

Thus the key is to know God! If you know God, it does not matter what you see. For the prophet Habakkuk 2:4 says, *"We walk by faith, not by sight."* As the people of God, let us remember our yesterday in God. Let us remember our past victories and accomplishments that were the result of God's grace and mercy. Remember what God has already done for you and continues to do for you in the present. Do not get weary because of your current situation. Do not give up! Do not go after idol gods of materialism or self-medication. Instead, be like Job and say, even after he lost everything and had sores from head to toe, *"I'm going to wait until my change comes." (Job 14:14)* All we have to do is remain steadfast and we will find strength in the waiting because we are never alone in our struggles. Jesus assured us as he was ascending to heaven, *"Lo I'll be with you always, even until the end of the age." (Mt 28:20)*

———————————

2)

The second lesson Second Isaiah teaches us about God's character is **_TO KNOW GOD IS TO KNOW GOD'S POWER._** Read vv 29-30, *"He gives power to the faint and strengthens the powerless. Even youths will faint and be weary."* The Israelites felt powerless in Babylon. They longed to return to the land of their ancestors. The older generation remembered the splendor of Solomon's Temple and the rituals and elaborate ceremonies that made them feel like God's people. Now they were in a strange land. Again their mood was captured in Psalm 137, *"By the rivers of Babylon, we sat down and wept, when we remembered Zion."*

To counter this feeling, the youths compromised their faith and went along with the captor's religion. What choice did they have? Perhaps if they converted or renounced the religion of their ancestors they would earn some political positions, some prestige in the eyes of their oppressors. What did they have to lose? God turned his back on to us and now we will turn our back on him. This was a sad day for the Jewish faith and God's chosen people.

When we look at the condition of our world today, some ask, "Where is God?" When the Twin Towers in New York collapsed from 2 planes crashing into them, people felt powerless and turned to God for comfort and direction. As humans we have just so much power to bring about desired results in a situation. We raise our children right, we take them to Church, and we teach them the word of God. Then they get grown and it appears that they have lost their way and wandered off into a strange land (*The Prodigal Son story – Lk 15).* We feel powerless because we can no longer control their choices.

You work hard at your jobs, do overtime for free, and make all the deadlines early. You do not miss any meetings. Then suddenly you receive a pink slip and it sends you into a powerless spin. Where is God! Why did God let this happen to me?

To know how God works in nature is to witness firsthand God's power. God does not do what we expect God to do. God acts when and how God pleases. Yet, when all is said and done, God's plan for our lives turns out better than what we had originally planned.

Therefore, knowing this about God teaches us that God is always in control. We learn that ultimately God's will must be done. Each of us has experienced God's power in our lives in one way or another. We may not know the inner workings, but we certainly can conclude that God had a hand in it. So to know God is to know that nothing is too hard for God. Your illness, your finances, your loneliness, your unemployment, your wayward child, your situation at work; whatever you stand in need today know that God has the power to make it a reality.

Just wait on God! Put your trust in him. He is Lord! He is the everlasting God, the Creator of the ends of the earth. To know him is to plug into his magnificent power. When things in your life get messy, just recharge with Jesus for Jesus said, *"All power is given unto me."* (Mt 28:18) Then fast and pray until you receive your answer. You will find strength in the waiting.

―――――――――――――

3)

The third lesson we learn about God's character from Second Isaiah is **_TO KNOW GOD'S POWER IS TO WAIT ON HIS ARRIVAL._** Read v 31, *"But they who wait on the Lord shall renew their strength, they shall mount up on wings as eagles, they shall run and not be weary, they shall walk and not faint."* To wait for the Lord is contrasted in the prophet's mind with watching current events. The world as he knows it is about to change. King Cyrus of Persia was on the horizon, conquering nation after nation, and headed straight for Babylon, their place of exile.

The ruler of Babylon was on the outs with his people. The Babylonian priests looked forward to a new leader who would allow them the freedom of religion. Second Isaiah anticipated the effects this increase in strength would have on those in exile. He prophesied their release, their return home to Jerusalem, their victorious march across the desert, their rebuilding of the temple, and the walls, their reinstatement as God's chosen people and their new role as a light unto the nations. God was back! As if God ever really leaves us. God only looks away for a moment because he cannot look upon sin.

You see, the issue was not about where is God, but about Israel's weariness and exhaustion. So God addressed the charge that he had abandoned Israel by strengthening and encouraging Israel. Weakness and powerlessness is never an obstacle to God's grace.

Are there any witnesses? Many of us are here today not because we are so strong, or good, or rich, or pretty, or smart. We are here only because of the grace of God in our lives! Sure life has presented us with many trials and tribulations, but we are still here because we have heard a joyful sound – Jesus saves! Jesus saves! You are still here because even when others gave up or committed suicide, you believed that *"Although weeping may endure for a night, joy comes in the morning."* (Ps 30:5) You waited until your change came and made a difference in your life. Anything worth having is worth waiting for. Find your strength in the waiting. *"For they that wait on the Lord, shall renew their strength. They shall mount up on wings as eagles, they shall run and not be weary; they shall walk and not faint."* God bless you!

THE BOOK OF JEREMIAH

The Calling of a
Reluctant Prophet

TRUSTING IN THE PROMISES OF GOD

JEREMIAH 33:14-16, *"Wait, says the Lord, the days are coming when I will bestow on Israel and Judah all the blessings I have promised them. In those days, at that time, I will make a righteous branch of David spring up; he shall maintain law and justice in the land. In those days Judah shall be kept safe and Jerusalem shall live undisturbed; and this shall be her name: The Lord is our Righteousness."*

INTRODUCTION

Jeremiah is a major prophet. There were three Major Prophets in Israel: Isaiah of Jerusalem (chs 1-39), Jeremiah and Ezekiel. They are called "Prophets of Doom" because their message warned Israel of the coming wrath of God. Jeremiah prophesies during a difficult time in Israel's history. God was fed up with their sinfulness and neglect of his commandments. Jeremiah warned the people of the consequences of their sins, but they refused to listen. So they were captured and Jerusalem was destroyed. However, Jeremiah also prophesied that they would return and prosper again as the people of God.

It is during Jeremiah's life that God switched from a message of doom and gloom to one of restoration and return. This good news reminded the people to trust in God's promises. God is not man that he would lie. The promises God made to Abraham, Isaac, and Jacob are still in effect. Their sins have not cancelled these promises, or caused the covenants made with Noah, Moses, and David to become null and void.

God is aware of their pain and suffering. God has a timeline for their punishment and when that timeline has been completed, the people of God will become a light unto the other nations. Israel will be a witness to the world how God has been their Everlasting Portion. God's help is received in three promises that God has obligated himself to fulfill. Let us now read the word of God and receive the promises of God.

1)

Our first promise is the **_PROMISE OF RESTORATION._** Read vv 12-13, "*Thus says the Lord of hosts: In this place that is waste, without human beings or animals, and in all its towns there shall again be pasture for shepherds resting their flocks. In the towns of the hill country, in the Shephelah, and of the Negeb, in the land of Benjamin, the places around Jerusalem, and in the towns of Judah, flocks shall again pass under the hands of the one who counts them, says the Lord.*" Jerusalem and its surrounding cities are lying in ruins from the Babylonian attacks. Everything was burned to the ground. The temple was gone. The palace was gone. Houses were leveled to the ground. Businesses wiped off the map. It was as if hurricane Katrenia and Sandy both touched down in Israel, leaving no stone unturned.

Every family was affected. The so-called "cream of the crop" were dragged off to Babylon, leaving only the poor peasants who lived on the countryside to harvest the crops. After this catastrophe Israel was no longer the same. Life as the Israelites knew it for 200 years was gone forever (*Lamentations 1*).

Sure it looked really bad! But so did New Orleans after Hurricane Katrenia and Atlantic City after Hurricane Sandy! Yet if God can take chaos and darkness and create a new world full of light and life, God can restore the pieces of a city and the lives of his chosen people. All they needed to do was not loose hope and trust in the promises of God.

Sometimes situations and events in our personal lives feel like we have been hit by a hurricane or tornado. It has happened to many literally, emotionally and spiritually. The devil often tries to destroy what we already have in order to get us to question God's faithfulness in our lives. If we claim God as our Heavenly Father, and Jesus as our Savior, then we are covered and prepared for whatever comes our way. God's word is steadfast, unmovable.

In a moment, in the twinkling of an eye, God can restore your lost a hundred fold. Just ask Job! He received double for all the loss in his challenge with Satan. God is aware of your struggles at home, at work, and even at Church. Help is on the way, but you have to trust God and know that God will surely bring you out.

2)

Secondly, in order for this restoration to take place in an equal and fair manner, **_GOD PROMISES A RIGHTEOUS LEADER_**. Read vv 14-16, "*The days are surely coming, says the Lord, when I will fulfill the promise I made to the house of Israel and the house of Judah. In those days and at that time, I will cause a righteous Branch to spring up for David; he shall execute justice and righteousness in the land.*" The Lord is talking about the future restoration of Israel. God knows that corrupt and immoral leaders led the people down the road of destruction. The king was supposed to be "a son of God" in that he was to keep the laws and commandments and be an example, a light for the people.

Yet, the books of Kings and Chronicles record leader after leader perverting the ways of God, marrying foreign women and allowing them to worship their idol gods in God's holy temple! The religious leaders abused their powers over the illiterate, took advantage of the poor, the widow and the orphan, and interpreted the laws to their own benefit. This now had come to an end with the destruction of Jerusalem.

The future leader would be a righteous leader, one who walked in the ways and statutes of God. This leader would be from the lineage of David, and would execute justice, and righteousness throughout the land. A leader of this magnitude was experienced to some extent in the persons of Zerubbabel, Sheshbazzar, and Ezra, who all returned after the exile to help restore Israel back to a right relationship with God. But these men could only go so far! Finally, God had to come himself in the form of a baby, wrapped in swaddling clothes, found lying in a manger.

Only Jesus could fit the bill. Only Jesus could carry out the humongous task of reconciling us back to God and remain a man without sin. Jesus came, lived a sinless life, performed miracles, and taught about the kingdom of God. Then because they could not match his righteousness, nor accept his sense of justice, they killed him and buried him in a borrowed tomb.

But in the words of the songwriter, *"This is not how the story ends!"* On the third day Jesus got up from the grave, breathed the Holy Spirit into his disciples, and went back to the Father. Now Jesus sits on the right hand of God as our judge and advocate.

Jesus expects us to live a righteous life as his representatives on earth. For Jesus is coming back and he is looking for a Church without a spot or blemish.

---

3)

Just in case the audience in Babylonian captivity had any doubts about what Jeremiah was telling them, our third promise is **_GOD'S PROMISE OF FAITHFULNESS._** Read vv 19-21, *"The word of the Lord came to Jeremiah: 'Thus says the Lord: If any of you could break my covenant with the day and my covenant with the night, so that day and night would not come at their appointed time, only then could my covenant with my servant David be broken...'"* There were some doubters in the group who were exiled in Babylon. Why is God talking all big and bad now, where was he when Jerusalem was under attack? God was very much aware of the doubt and fear we carry in our hearts when life's challenges seem to overwhelm us.

God is aware that many of the Israelites lost faith in him and his power over their enemies. This is what prompted God to reach out to them through his prophet Jeremiah. Jeremiah was to remind the people of the covenant laws and that there were curses and blessings attached to them. The people's behavior determined which would be released – a blessing or a curse.

However, Jeremiah also reminded them of the promises God made with their ancestors and that God was committed to those covenants because of his faithfulness to his people. Yes, you had to be punished, but it is not forever. The Lord will return his people to their homeland because God is faithful even though we are not faithful to him.

God's faithfulness is intertwined with his steadfast love. So together these characteristics of God motivates God to forgive, forget and remain true to his original promises to Abraham and David. However, the greatest promise of all is found in John 3:16, *"For God so loved the world, that he gave his only begotten Son, and that whosoever believes on him shall not perish but have everlasting life."* That is a promise that guarantees our eternity. That is a covenant that can never be broken. God bless you!

THE BOOK OF EZEKIEL

Bone to Bone, and Flesh to Flesh

NO BONES ABOUT IT!

EZEKIEL 37:1-10, *"The hand of the Lord came upon me, and he brought me out by the Spirit of the Lord and set me down in the middle of a valley; it was full of bones. He led me all around them; there were very many lying in the valley, and they were very dry. He said to me, 'Mortal, can these bones live?' I answered, 'O Lord God, you know.'"*

INTRODUCTION

When we review the message of the 3 Major Prophets, we learn that Isaiah of Jerusalem warned the people of coming danger, but that they had time to turn things around and return to God. Jeremiah warned the people that their time was almost up and now was the time for them to make the decision to follow God's ways and laws. However, time ran out while Jeremiah was still prophesying. So we leave the book of Jeremiah with the people still in exile and Jeremiah carted off against his will, to Egypt.

The book of Ezekiel reports directly from exile. The people's faith in God has dried up like old bones and they are not interested in serving the God of their ancestors. Hundreds of miles away from Jerusalem, the people's mood is somber. It has been only a few years, since their worst nightmare came true: A foreign enemy destroyed Jerusalem. While in exile, false prophets are misrepresenting God and telling the people their captivity will be brief, two years at the most. But Jeremiah sends a letter to those in exile that it was going to be a long stay, at least 70 years.

Ezekiel was a priest in the temple before he was carted off into captivity during the second deportation. The Babylonians did not want to leave anyone who had leadership skills behind, just in case they could rally the people into a rebellion against them. Therefore, it was while in exile, as a priest, that God called Ezekiel to the role of prophet to his people. Chapter 37 is a familiar passage of scripture and it provides for us a wealth of knowledge and insight about human behavior and how we should respond to life's crises and everyday challenges. So let us read now a message from Ezekiel to help us understand that when God moves, something miraculous will happen. There are no bones about!

1)

As we read ch 37, the first lesson we learn is that ***LOOKS ARE DECEIVING.*** Read vv 1-2, *"The hand of the Lord came upon me, and he brought me out by the Spirit of the Lord and set me down in the middle of a valley; it was full of bones. He led me all around them; there were very many lying in the valley, and they were very dry."*

Now Ezekiel has been in exile for quite some time when the hand of the Lord came upon him. This hand led him to a valley and he was set down right in the middle of the valley. Now this valley was not empty. This valley was not some picturesque view of roaming grass and beautiful flowers.

No this valley appeared to be a scene of a battle that had occurred some time ago and the bodies of those killed in battle were left at the mercy of wild animals and carnivorous pecking birds. Over time, the corpses soon became merely bones, scattered throughout this valley. It was not a pretty sight.

When Ezekiel saw this valley of dry bones, he saw defeat, hopelessness, despair, death, and failure. But looks are deceiving! We must never evaluate a situation merely by what can be seen with the naked eye. Oftentimes in our lives, we tend to "judge a book by its cover." We only want to date pretty people. We drive pretty fancy cars, and we buy expensive designer clothes to parade around in. We wear shiny bling, bling. We even move into secluded and gated communities in hopes that nobody will take the time to really know what is behind the façade, no one will get close enough to see our pain.

When Ezekiel saw those dry bones, it never occurred to him that they could live again. That is because looks are deceiving. There is "no bones about it." With God it is never what it appears to be, or what it looks like on the outside. God takes what society labels as worthless, and transforms that person into a great player in life. The bible gives witness to many occasions when this happened. People today have gone to prison or been on drugs, lived as prostitutes or homeless, and had their lives changed because of the intervention of God's Spirit in their lives. God is at work and working out his own plan for your future. Do not worry about what it looks like right now, because looks are deceiving. The Holy Spirit will reveal God's plan for your life in the end.

2)

Now Ezekiel is perplexed by why he is brought to this hopeless valley of dry bones. So our second lesson is that ***GOD QUESTIONS OUR PERSPECTIVE.*** Read vv 3-4, *"He said to me, 'Mortal, can these bones live?' I answered, 'O Lord God you know.'"* As Ezekiel stood there overlooking the dry bones, his first thought was probably that God brought him there to give some kind of sacred last rites over these dry bones. After all, he was a priest!

Yet seeing the bones were very dry, not just dry, but very dry, he saw no need to perform a ritual for the dead. It would not make a difference. It is not like these bones can live again, or can they? No bones about it, in Ezekiel's mind, these bones were without hope and, therefore, the persons these bones once belonged to were lost forever.

These bones had no identity. No grave markers. No gravestone. No epitaph. No flowers. Just a bunch of hopeless bones, scattered by the wind all across, what appeared to be, this God forsaken valley. Or was it really God forsaken? Ezekiel was brought there for a purpose. His mission was determined by the question, *"Can these bones live?"*

Sometimes as Christians, life's daily blows and attacks cause our faith to waver and our spiritual power to decline. One songwriter wrote, *"I've been in the storm too long."* These words express a long period of time of suffering, disappointment, and heartache. This sentiment is uttered when we are victims of the Job syndrome. Everywhere we turn we encounter problems. Soon we become sarcastic, cynical, hopeless, unbelieving. When we reach that point, God intervenes and ask us, *"Can these bones live?"*

Are you a walking corpse, too discouraged, too frightened, too unhappy, too hurt, too fragile, too sensitive, to trust in God's promises or God's power? That is what in essence God was asking Ezekiel. Can these bones live? Has Israel lost all faith in my power to transform their situation from exile to freedom, from despair to delight, from miserable to miraculous?

Do you believe it Ezekiel? You were one of my priests back in Judah. If you do not believe, how will others believe? Stand still and know that I am God. Can these bones live? Ezekiel was too afraid to answer the question. So he put the question back to God, *"O Lord God, you know."*

God is an ever-present help. If we do not believe in God's power to transform our valley of dry bones, how can we go out and tell others about the power of God to deliver them from their valley of drugs, alcoholism, lying, stealing, debt, and spiritual emptiness? God does not want us to walk away from the valley of dry bones in our lives. Instead God wants us to trust him. For change does not come *"by power nor by might, but by my spirit says the Lord."* *(Zech 4:6)* There are no bones about it!

You see the dry bones represented Israel's spiritual condition. She no longer believed in God's power to save so their faith shriveled up and died. They lost God's Spirit and without God's Spirit we are just dry bones waiting to be scattered by the four winds.

But we must not loose faith. We cannot give up! We must take hold of God's unchanging hand and pray for the strength to hold on. When God asks us *"Can these bones live and return to the level of spirituality that keep us in God's grace and favor?"* our answer is not another question, but a declaration that says, "Nothing is too hard for God!"

We can live, we can prosper, and we can do more than just survive. We are promised a more abundant life, not a mediocre existence. Chose life over death. Then give God the praise.

---

3)

Ezekiel had not lost faith in God. He was just distracted by his temporary situation of exile. So our final lesson is that ***EZEKIEL'S OBEDIENCE BROUGHT ABOUT TRANSFORMATION***. Read v 7, *"So I prophesied as I had been commanded; and as I prophesied, suddenly there was a* *noise, a rattling, and the bones came together, bone to its bone."* God orders Ezekiel to prophesy to the dry bones. In response to Ezekiel's word, the bones are re-membered, re-connected, re-assembled, and became a great multitude of assembled corpses. Then God commanded Ezekiel again to prophesy and the Spirit, the breath of God, entered into these dead bodies and they became living souls again.

The message God gave to Ezekiel is that Israel's present situation is only temporary and that they will be transformed. God will raise them from their spiritual graves, bring them forth and return them to their homeland. Ezekiel is called to prophesy to these bones that they may hear the word of the Lord. He must speak the word even when there is no one to hear it, for God's word cannot return void. Although Ezekiel cannot see or understand why he has to prophesy to dry corpses, or how crazy he must look preaching to dry bones, he was still obedient to God's command.

Ezekiel could not abandon his mission because there seemed no hope of success. His fidelity and obedience alone released the power that brought new life to the people. Because of men and women like Ezekiel, Israel was able to rise above her calamity and be restored as the chosen people of God. They learned the lesson that with God the possibility of life after death is ever present. No bones about it!

Had Ezekiel not obeyed the inner voice of God, which told him to preach to dry bones, the Spirit would not have arrived. So let us be faithful to the tasks God has placed before us. It does not yet appear what we shall be, for the Spirit of the Lord is here! God bless you!

THE BOOK OF DANIEL

(An Apocalyptic Writing)

Friends in the Fire

EITHER BOW DOWN OR BURN UP!

Daniel 3:16-18, *"Shadrach, Meshach and Abednego replied to the king, 'O Nebuchadrezzer, we do not need to defend ourselves before you in this matter. If we are thrown into the blazing furnace, the God we serve is able to save us from it, and he will rescue us from your hand, O king. But even if he does not, we want you to know, O king, that we will not serve your gods or worship the image of gold you have set up.'"*

INTRODUCTION

There have been many who have misunderstood the book of Daniel. The book was written for a time like ours. The Book of Daniel is a call to devotion. It is a challenge to faithfulness. It is an attempt to stop the falling away from God in Daniel's day, and now in our own time.

The author of the book of Daniel believed certain things about God. First, he believed God had a moral plan for all peoples and all nations. Every act of every leader would be examined by the moral plan of God. Secondly, Daniel had faith in the Kingdom of God. He believed that it was near and with it comes God's righteousness and holiness. Thirdly, Daniel believed in absolute loyalty to God. God is a jealous God. This is the only way God deals with his people, for God it is all of nothing. Anything else is idolatry.

Our text is found in chapter 3. It is a familiar text, one that we first heard about in Sunday School, or from a preacher behind the pulpit. Chapter 3 gives us a perfect example of Daniel's belief that God expects absolute loyalty from his people. As we read the words of this chapter, let us listen and measure our own level of loyalty to the God we serve.

---

1)

The first lesson we learn from our text is ***DO NOT LET YOUR ENVIRON-MENT DICTATE YOUR RELIGION.*** Read vv 4-5, *"Then the herald loudly proclaimed, 'This is what you are commanded to do, O peoples, nations, and men of every language: As soon as you hear the sound of the horn, flute, zither, lyre, harp, pipes and all kinds of music, you must fall down* *and worship the image of gold...whoever does not will be immediately thrown into a blazing furnace.'"*

King Nebuchadrezzer made an idol that was 90 feet tall and 9 feet wide. Then he sets it up on the highest Plain of Dura for everyone to see. He chose this location for the maximum exposure he could get. He did not want anything to obstruct the people's view of his golden image. In this location the statue could be seen for miles around and in all directions.

In order for all to know the function and purpose of the statue, King Nebucha-drezzer arranged a great dedication service and sent out special messengers to invite all the chief dignitaries in the land. The satraps, who were the governors of the provinces throughout the Persian Empire; counselors, treasurers, justices, magistrates, and all the officials of the provinces. So his invitation list read like a who's who list in the Persian Empire.

Of course his three protégés were invited – Shadrach, Meshach and Abednego. These were the three Hebrew boys, along with Daniel, the king brought into his court from Judah. He saw that they had much leadership potential and counseled and trained them to serve over the Jews in his country.

Now the worship of the statue was not a voluntary option. It was mandatory, especially to those in the king's cabinet and administration. The three Hebrew boys were groomed for leadership because the king saw something special in them. You know, even your enemies know that you have a special anointing on your life. That is why they try to destroy you.

King Nebuchadrezzer was king not because the people loved him, but because he used the weapon of fear to keep his subjects in line. Fear is a terrifying weapon and to the object of the fear, it can be paralyzing, traumatic, even crippling.

King Nebuchadrezzer was aware of the other religious traditions in his kingdom, and had for the most part allowed the captives to worship their gods in addition to the gods of Babylon. But this situation was different. There was no choice or religious resistance involved in this new law. It was about either bow down to this golden image, or burn up in the fiery furnace designed especially for persons who disobeyed the new law.

At this moment King Nebuchadrezzer thought he held in his hands the power of life and death. He was convinced that everyone in his Empire would follow his every command or suffer the consequences. Often times we find ourselves in similar situations as the three Hebrew boys. At work, at leisure, at school, with friends and family, our beliefs can make them uncomfortable and for fear that we will be ostracized or overlooked for a promotion, we allow our *environment* to give us permission to compromise our faith and religious practices.

This is why Jesus says in the book of Revelation, *"You are neither hot nor cold."* When we are easily influenced by the evil around us, God is not pleased. It certainly takes courage to take a stand for what you believe. The consequences can cost you a great deal – your job, friends, family, even the community you live in can turn against you! The author of Daniel teaches us to resist all such threats and quell our fears. Let our faith in an Almighty God give us the courage to remain steadfast, and unmovable, always abounding in the love of God. When we are armed with this kind of faith it promotes absolute loyalty to the God of our salvation.

There will be times in life when we are met with two choices – either bow down or burn up. Do not allow your environment to force you to make the wrong choice. In the words of the prophet Joshua, *"As for me and my house, we will serve the Lord."* *(Josh 24:15)*

―――――――――――――

2)

The next lesson we learn from chapter 3 is that ***SOMEONE IS ALWAYS WATCHING TO SEE IF YOU PRACTICE WHAT YOU PREACH.*** Read v 12, *"But there are some Jews whom you have set over the affairs of the province of Babylon – Shadrach, Meschach and Abednego – who pay no attention to you, O king. They neither serve your gods nor worship the image of gold you have set up."* Shadrach, Meshach and Abednego were invited to the ceremony because they served in the king's cabinet. Their religion had not been a problem for the king in the past, so they were not alarmed when they heard the herald proclaim that all must bow down to the golden image when the music played. They just assumed it did not apply to them. They did not understand or give credence to the belief *"If you dance to the music, you have to pay it to the piper."* So their refusal to bow down was not intended to offend the king or his religious beliefs. They were just being true to their own religious laws and practices.

Well the text tells us that there were some Chaldeans, informants, who were colleagues of the three Hebrew men. They perhaps resented the king for having promoted these young men of a foreign ethnicity and faith, over them, true and pure Chaldeans. How dare the king overlook them! So they just waited for the right opportunity to sell out the Hebrew boys. That time was finally upon them.

These Chaldeans reported their observations to the king. They knew Shadrach, Meshach and Abednego were committed Jews and would not nor could not bow down to any other God. Perhaps on some level they admired them, but not on this day. No, today they were going to get even, rat out their co-workers and hope to see them burn like every other dissident to Babylonian policy and rules of law.

These three Hebrew men were not ashamed of their faith. So what if everybody knew that they were Jews. They were proud to be the sons of Abraham. They were even more proud to serve the Most High God. Today was no different than any other day of their adult lives.

What would you do in this kind of situation? Would you hide your faith and go along to get along? Can others see our faith in our walk, our talk, our dress, and our service to others? People are watching you, especially if you claim to be a Christian. A lot of people do not come to Church because they see our behavior and cannot tell any difference between people who go to church and believe, and those in the world who do not believe. We are the only witnesses God has to win souls to Christ! What other people do or how they act should not deter us from singing these words, *"This little light of mine, I'm gonna let it shine; everywhere I go, I'm gonna let it shine."*

3)

The final lesson from our text teaches that **_IF YOU ARE STEADFAST, GOD WILL DELIVER YOU._** Read vv 26-27, *"Nebuchadrezzer then approached the opening of the blazing furnace and shouted, 'Shadrach, Meschach and Abednego, come out, come here.' So Shadrach, Meschach and Abednego came out of the fire."* The king is enraged at such insubordination and orders the three Hebrew men brought before him at once. Actually, his feelings were probably hurt. Here he had invested so much in these three men, brought them from Jerusalem because they showed such great promise. They were his personal project. He mentored them and thought he had won their total allegiance. But he was wrong.

Responding to the king's summons, the three Hebrew men came before the king. Still angry at their open defiance of him, he asked a question that was intended to provoke fear in them, but instead increased their faith in their God. Now is that not an interesting response to a challenge from our enemies? Most of us would be mad, all puffed up, ready to fight, plotting some revenge. However, this was not so with these young men of God.

When King Nebuchadrezzer asked them this question, *"Who is the god that will deliver you out of my hands?"* the three Hebrew men must have thought in their minds about all the wondrous acts God had performed on behalf of his chosen people Israel, from the day of Abraham, to Moses, to King David. The king asked the question with such a blasphemous spirit, that the three Hebrew men could only respond in one way – the way of truth.

I can imagine they stood flatfooted, looked the king straight in his eyes and replied, *"O Nebuchadrezzer, we have no need to answer you in this matter. If it be so, our God whom we serve is able to deliver us from the burning fiery furnace; and he will deliver us out of your hand, O king. But if not, be it known to you, O king, that we will not serve your gods or worship the golden image which you have set up."*

That was all they said. There was no need for argument, or threats, or going back and forth in negotiation. Their position was clear, absolute, and steadfast. In their minds God was greater than King Nebuchadrezzer and more powerful than any circumstance that will confront their life.

When we hear the *"if not"* in their conviction statement, it is not an *"if not"* of doubt. No, no, it is an *"if not"* of supreme faith in a God who, despite all appearances to the contrary, is able to deliver them from the hands of their enemies. These three fellows trusted God not for what they would receive in return, but because God is God!

What this says is that yes, God can do all things. *Yes*, God can deliver you from a bad marriage. *Yes*, God can keep you from losing your job. *Yes*, God can pay your bills. But even if God says "no" to all these things we pray for, we must still trust in his power to do so. God is able even when God chooses not to do it.

You see religion is not an insurance policy against suffering, pain, hard times, or even death. Rather religion gives us that blessed assurance that God's purpose in our lives must be done. Jesus said it while praying in the Garden of Gethsemane, *"Not my will, but thine be done."*

So the challenge is given. The king feels he has no other choice but to accept the challenge. His whole reputation is on the line. Still angered and feeling betrayed by these three young men from Jerusalem, he ordered the fire set 7 times hotter than usual. He ordered them tied up and called his strongest soldiers to do the task. So hot was the fire that the soldiers who placed them in the furnace were struck down dead. But Shadrach, Meshach and Abednego walked right into the fire. When the news came that the soldiers were killed, the king out of curiosity, went to the furnace window and peeked inside to witness the demise of these young men.

The king may not have wanted to throw his protégés into the fiery furnace but he felt his back was up against the wall. As king he could not show compassion or emotion toward these three Hebrew men. They made their choice – to burn rather than bow down to the idol god. Then, when the king looked inside the furnace, to his surprise, and probably relief, the three Hebrew men were doing just fine. But when he looked again, he thought he saw a fourth figure that looked like a son of God!

So not only did God show up, God showed out! The Hebrew men were not burned, singed, or even smelled like smoke. God took the heat out of the fire. What a mighty God we serve! The king told the young men to either bow down or burn up. They chose the latter, because their knees only bowed to the God of their ancestors, and Jehovah is his name.

However, there is a day coming when *every knee will bow and every tongue confess that Jesus is Lord!* But until that day, our knees only bow in prayer to our God. If we bow under any other pressure, we will commit idolatry and we will be cast into an eternal fire. God bless you!

THE BOOK OF HOSEA

Pushing Love To Its Limits

WHAT'S IN A NAME?

HOSEA 1:2-9, "*When the Lord first spoke through Hosea, the Lord said to Hosea, 'Go, take for yourself a wife of whoredom and have children of whoredom, for the land commits great whoredom by forsaking the Lord.' So he went and took Gomer, daughter of Diblaim, and she conceived and bore him a son.*"

INTRODUCTION

The book of Hosea contains the prophecies of Hosea ben Beeri. He prophesied during the mid-8th century B.C.E. against the policies of the king of the northern kingdom, Jeroboam ben Joash. Hosea is the only prophet who was born in the north and prophesied to the north. He prophesied against King Jeroboam's alliance with the Assyrian Empire. This alliance reflected the king's independence from God's protection. It was viewed as a rejection of the Lord. Hosea saw Assyria and Egypt as supporters of idolatry, thereby sending a red flag that the king of Israel should stay away from these countries, less he be influenced by their practice of idolatry.

Hosea charged both Israel's monarchy and its priesthood of leading the people astray by failing to teach true knowledge of God. The religious leaders did not heed the warnings and words of the prophet Hosea. Therefore, God instructed Hosea to dramatize his message through his personal life experiences. God told Hosea to marry a woman of ill repute, a common prostitute. This was to symbolize Israel's apostasy toward God.

His new wife gave birth to three children whose names were a message of judgment from God to the people. The king's relationship with foreign nations and their worship practices broke the first commandment, "*Thou shalt have no other gods before me.*" *(Exo 20:3)* Yet the king allowed foreign idols to be placed in the temple built for the northern kingdom to worship in so they would not have to travel south to Jerusalem.

As God's word through Hosea spoke to its original audience and to its later Judean audiences, it continues to address us today. So let us now listen to the lessons from our text.

1)

The first lesson we learn from our text comes from the name of Hosea's firstborn: **_MY NAME IS JEZREEL._** Read vv 4-5, *"Then the Lord said to Hosea, 'Name him Jezreel; for in a little while I will punish the house of Jehu for the blood of Jezreel and I will put an end to the kingdom of the house of Israel. On that day I will break the bow of Israel in the valley of Jezreel."* The covenant between Israel and God was viewed as a marriage contract. When Israel went after idol gods, God viewed her behavior as adultery. God then directs Hosea to marry a woman of ill repute. Hosea responded by marrying Gomer, daughter of Diblaim. In this union three children were born. The first child was a son. Hosea was told to name him Jezreel.

Why Jezreel? Each child symbolically represented the deteriorated state of Israel. Jezreel was a place, located in a valley. The name Jezreel was chosen intentionally to bring back to the reader's memory, the horrific battle and slaughter that took place here. Jezreel was a plain nestled in the hills of the northern country of Israel. It was the site where King Jehu commanded a brutal massacre of the politically and religiously corrupt house of Omri (I Kings 21-2Kings: 9-10).

The naming of his firstborn Jezreel was God's way of telling the people that history was about to repeat itself. The same brutal massacre that occurred earlier in Jezreel, is the punishment the current administration and people were about to experience firsthand. Israel and her religious leaders refused to heed the warnings of Hosea. They misrepresented the teachings of God's word to their advantage. If they do not repent, their fate would be just as dramatic and devastating as the battle of Jezreel. Israel would be no more.

What's in a name? As a college professor, I call roll at the end of class every day. Many of the names I cannot pronounce correctly because of the alternative spelling used instead of traditional spelling. Sometimes mute letters are added and as a linguist I try to pronounce every letter in the name. However, students are quick to correct me when I mispronounce their name.

Often times their names have a history or story connected to them. Sometimes the names are handed down through generations or in memory of a family member who has passed on. Then when the child gets up in age, the parents share the meaning of their name and the child wears it as a badge of pride and loyalty.

Nevertheless, this was not the case with the naming of Hosea and Gomer's children. Their names were meant to put the fear of God in the people of Israel. Jezreel was a name meant to invoke the possibility of genocide if the people did not repent immediately and turn back to God.

Unlike Israel, we still have time to "get right with God." Now, today, we are called sons and daughters of the Most High King! This title comes with privileges, and guarantees our place in the kingdom of God and in God's last will and testament. It is all in the name!

2)

The second lesson we learn comes from the name of Hosea's second born: _**MY NAME IS LO-RUHAMAH.**_ Read v 6, _"She conceived again and bore a daughter. Then the Lord said to Hosea, 'Name her Lo-ruhamah for I will no longer have pity on the house of Israel or forgive them.'"_ Hosea's second born, a girl, is named Lo-ruhamah. This is Hebrew for _"she is not pitied."_ In the past, especially in the book of Judges, God forgave Israel of her apostasy against him over and over again. God would hear their cry, have pity and compassion for their situation, which mind you they brought on themselves, and then deliver them from the hands of their oppressor.

But no more! Their time of forgiveness was over. The idolatry and political religious corruption was too much for God to stomach any longer. No longer did the people have faith in his power to protect them from their enemies. They now trusted in foreign alliances, instead of prayer, fasting and offering sacrifices to Almighty God. They did not even cry out for help as in the days of old. Now they were self-sufficient, and blinded by what they perceived to be a powerful human alliance.

After all God had done for them, this is the thanks God got! Well if they wanted to serve idol gods, then so be it. God was through, done. Let them call on statues of stone and bronze to defend them when the approaching Assyrians rain down fire and fury upon them. God said "I will not have pity on them."

Wow! Israel really pushed God to the brink of his wrath. After Hosea prophesied the threat of complete annihilation, now God was not going to come to Israel's rescue. God had no compassion left for these stiff-necked people. They turned their backs on God, and God was reciprocating the gesture.

What would life be like without God's mercy, grace, and compassion? We, like Israel, have fallen short of God's glory so many times. God is very much aware that we are incapable of keeping his commandments. That is why he sent Jesus as our Redeemer and Advocate.

When we read God's word it should function as a _"lamp unto my feet and a light unto my path." (Ps 119:105)_ Jesus' life is our role model of how to live in a world that is hostile to our faith and belief system. But we must never stop checking ourselves to the point that we lose God's pity for us as helpless human beings.

God sends anointed leaders to serve as a blessing and to give us directions that would prevent us from getting lost or taking the wrong exit on this Christian journey. Believe that God loves you and that his love is everlasting. However, that love does not give us a license to sin and commit apostasy. Know that God is real and that God gives us a choice. We can either serve him or suffer the consequences of abandonment.

Israel made the mistake of thinking she could do her own thing as long as she wanted to. Let us not make the same mistake or display such a lack of good judgment. God's blessings are bountiful for those who diligently seek him. But the curse of punishment is just around the corner for those who continually disobey him.

3)

Our third lesson from the text comes from the name of Hosea's third child: **MY NAME IS LO-AMMI.** After weaning Lo-ruhamah, Gomer gives birth to a son, Lo-ammi. This name is Hebrew for *"not my people."* This has to be the worse pronouncement by Hosea yet! Not my people! Israel's birth occurred at Mt. Sinai when Moses read them the 10 Commandments. God agreed to be their God and they agreed to be God's people. The sins of the northern tribes were so severe that God cut them out of his covenant! The people's sins were so great that *Loammi* symbolized the nullification of the covenant contract; Israel is now on her own to do whatever she wanted to do.

Hosea's prophecies went from bad to worse. To denounce the northern kingdom and say they are no longer members of the family of God is tragic. What could Israel do? How can she turn around this declaration of destruction that came from the very mouth of God? Hosea tried to be an example by using his situation with his wife. Gomer left Hosea for another man. Hosea was not even sure if the third child was his!

However, because of his love for Gomer, he sought her out until he found her living with another man. Hosea paid the man a ransom to redeem his own wife! It is not known if she continued to be faithful to Hosea. This last effort to save his marriage to a prostitute was God showing Israel that he had done all he could to maintain a covenant relationship with Israel. But like Gomer, Israel kept whoring after foreign idols. Just as Hosea experienced infidelity in his marriage, God experienced infidelity as Israel's husband and protector.

What is the condition of your relationship with God? What is in a name? Our ancestors believed that your name held your destiny. As Christians we claim to follow the risen Christ. Are we in a covenant visible relationship that shows the world we are who we claim to be? One songwriter wrote, *"And they'll know we are Christians by our love."*

What is the name you respond to? God has many names in the Old Testament: *Elohim, Yahweh, Jehovah Jira, Jehovah Nicea, El Shaddai,* and other names that God is called according to the demonstration of his power. Therefore, as Christians, let us live up to the name and the title. The word "Christ" is not Jesus' last name, but a title meaning "anointed one." The early believers decided to make it a part of their identity. One day in the city of Antioch, they were first called "Christians" because a witness observed that the disciples were acting like the Christ. The name stuck! Before then they were called, *"Followers of the Way."*

What is in a name? Whether it is your secular birth name, or the name you were adopted into through faith in our Lord and Savior, Jesus the Christ, live up to its meaning. Be a witness for him because of the name. The songwriter said it so well, *"Precious name; O how sweet, hope of earth and joy of heaven."* God bless you!

THE BOOK OF JOEL

The Spirit is No Respecter of Persons

WHEN THE SPIRIT HITS YOU!

JOEL 2:28-29, *"Then afterward I will pour out my spirit on all flesh; your sons and your daughters shall prophesy, your old men shall dream dreams, and your young men shall see visions. Even on the male and female slaves, in those days, I will pour out my spirit."*

INTRODUCTION

The book of Joel draws on centuries of Israelite tradition in the reporting of his prophesies. Prophets that were a part of his theological understanding included the following: Amos, Isaiah of Jerusalem (1-39), Jeremiah, Ezekiel, Obadiah, Zephaniah and Malachi. His word does not focus on the past but rather is a testimony to the continual need of the prophetic word in history.

Joel hears God speaking to the current situation in Judah. Joel believes that past prophecies have not yet come to completion and extends into the present and even the future. When the book of Joel was written is debatable among many scholars. Some pre-date the book before the destruction of Israel by the Babylonians. Others date it to the post-exilic period when Judah is at home and struggling to be the people of God. The majority of scholars place it somewhere between the years 500-350 B.C.E. This covers the time period when the exiles returned home to Judah, or what's left of it, and encounter many new obstacles unanticipated and frightening.

There is no king, but the second temple is completed (515 B.C.E.). The elders and the priests are the community leaders. The walls are restored (the work of Nehemiah). There does not appear to be any external threat to Judah. Therefore, the textual evidence seems to point to the Persian period when Judah was a sub-province of the Persian Empire.

Joel is the son of Pethuel. His name means *"Yahweh is God."* He is called by an external voice, not an internal musing with his spirit. His mission is to call the people of Judah to repentance. Joel does not specify what the sins are, but one can extract them from the accusations made in the text: insincere worship, religious syncretism, excessive ritual and cultural self-sufficiency, breach of covenant, failed leadership, and reluctance to be identified with the God of their ancestors.

Israel never seems to learn her lesson. Perhaps 70 years of forced worship of idol gods while in exile converted some of the people. So they brought some of the theological and philosophical teachings back home with them and tried to combine them with the worship of their ancestors. This made them ineligible to receive the visitation of the Holy Spirit. However, the words God quoted to Joel provide a window of hope for the future generations of Israel.

Let us read what "thus says the Lord," and what to do when the Spirit hit us.

---

1)

The first lesson we learn is that when the Spirit hits you, ***IT DOES NOT MATTER WHERE YOU COME FROM.*** Read v 28a, *"Then afterwards I will pour out my spirit on all flesh;"* In chapter 2 the book of Joel informs Judah that the covenant curse that caused their near destruction as the people of God, has now changed to a covenant blessing. We hear this as well in Isaiah 40-55, where the Second Isaiah is told to speak comfort to those in exile. (40:1-2)

Joel reiterates this same sentiment to the people as they struggle to survive and restore their living conditions as well as their relationship with God. God's wrath manifested itself in the form of locust attacks and is referred to as an army. It completely devoured the landscape and people lost their vineyards, farms and animals as a result of this physical attack on Judah.

Therefore, the Lord invited Judah to return to him with all their heart, 100% loyalty to him and him alone. God is tired of the superficial worship and rituals. The Lord our God wants us to be real. Then God will turn the curse back into a blessing. Once again God will extend his protection and prosperity to his people. They need not worry about any approaching enemies. God says he will drive them far away (2:20).

This new offer of restoration is not just for the people of Israel, but is now open to all who would acknowledge the Lord as their God! The text promises that all flesh will be privy to the visitation of the Holy Spirit. Nationality is not a prerequisite. A particular ethnicity is not a requirement. No, the Holy Spirit searches for a receptive and pure heart, committed to God's ways and God's laws.

This is what God accepts and acknowledges as requirements to be called "Sons and daughters of God." The Lord first offered this opportunity of a lifetime to the Jews, but they repeatedly neglected to obey God's word and covenant laws. They refused to obey the first commandment, *"Thou shalt have no other gods before me." (Exo 20:3)* Now initially, all flesh was meant to cover all the divisions within Judah. Then later, at Pentecost, it was interpreted in a more inclusive way. Micah 6:8 sums it up best, *"What does the Lord require of you; to do justice, to love mercy, and to walk humbly with your God."*

God promises that same free grace, not cheap grace, to all who believe and trust in him. Racism has no place in God's Kingdom. When ethnic groups are mentioned in the bible, it is because of their spiritual and theological apostasy that God is offended. Never is it because of the color of their skin or their geographical location. As the kingdom of God here on earth, the church must abandon man-made divisions and barriers that pit different groups against one another. For Psalm 133 reads, *"How good and how pleasant it is when brethren dwell together in unity."* Joel teaches unity and a kind of love that runs from heart to heart, and breast to breast.

There are too many instances to count in the New Testament where the love of God supersedes the geographical location and ethnicity of believers. Paul was eventually anointed as the Apostle to the Gentiles after receiving total rejection from his own people, the Jews. God loves us no matter what we look like on the outside! Until we preach and teach that message, the church will continue to fall short in its message and ministry to "all flesh."

———————————————

2)

Our second lesson learned from this text teaches us that when the Spirit hits, ***IT IGNORES GENDER AND AGE.*** Read v 28b-d, *"...your sons and your daughters shall prophesy, your old men shall dream dreams and your young men shall see visions."* God continues to declare to Joel what mighty works he is about to do throughout his creation. God has always dealt with whomever God pleases. Age and gender have never been obstacles or limitations of the Holy Spirit.

The Holy Spirit throughout the Old Testament was given in order to empower the recipient to do a certain task on behalf of God. Now this prophecy moves the work of the Holy Spirit in a new and exciting direction. Revelation by the Holy Spirit was only through the word of the prophets. There were three means of discerning the divine will that are found in the prophetic circles: *oracles, dreams, and visions.* Joel's new prophecy tells us that the Holy Spirit will not just hit male prophets, and elderly priests, but will visit all flesh, both genders, and all ages. Individuals can now have direct communication with God.

A future outpouring of God's vital force will break all barriers separating people within society. This new reality will appear in the new age with the appearance of Jesus of Nazareth. Participation in the life of God's kingdom is now offered to all who receive the testimony that Jesus is the Promised Messiah, and that God raised him from the dead.

Unfortunately, the church has fallen short in embracing this prophecy from Joel. Yet these are God's own words and promises made to a people who were set in their ways and societal norms. The "rules" of religion have too often rejected the female gender and held back the youth until they have "grown in the knowledge and favor of God."

Humans have made this call for centuries on end. Jesus' life, death and resurrection broke the chains of gender and age. Today's church needs to allow the Holy Spirit to manifest itself in the life of all of God's people! *"The earth is the Lord's and the fullness thereof, and all that dwell therein!"* (Ps 24:1) Although some of us have been victims of racism, sexism, sexual abuse, and ageism, we continue to press forward in the prophecies of Joel and Paul in Gal 3:28 *"In Christ there is no male or female, no Jew or Greek, no slave or free."*

When the Spirit hits us, we can then declare, *"Greater is He that is within me (the Holy Spirit) then he that is within the world (patriarchal and racist institutions). (I Jn 4)*

3)

The third lesson we learn is that when the Spirit hits you, **_IT IGNORES YOUR STATUS IN THE WORLD._** Read v 29, *"Even on the male and female slaves, I will pour out my spirit."* The message of Joel is no longer limited to the Judeans. Acts 2 breaks the boundaries of Joel 2:28-29 and all persons are now offered the opportunity to become sons and daughters of the Most High King.

The pouring out of God's Holy Spirit on all flesh was meant as a definite sign pointing to the Lord's Day, and the end of time, as we know it. In the world of the Judeans, divisions of every kind were practiced. This was most obvious between master, and slave, or servant. The slave/servant had no rights. They could be terminated or beaten at will, or falsely accused of a crime and be killed. Hmm, sounds like times have not changed much.

If the slave was an immigrant or foreigner, they could not worship in the temple. Their wives and children could be sold off to pay a debt owed to the master. There were no human or religious laws that protected them from the greed and brutal treatment they encountered on a daily basis. So for slaves and servants to hear that the Holy Spirit would not overlook them, but rather include them in God's plan of salvation, this bought elation to Joel's audience. This gave them hope for the future and for their children's future.

After all, Jesus was born to a teenager who was engaged to a carpenter. They were not wealthy people, but lower class workers. His lowly birth took place among barn animals and was proclaimed by the angels in heaven. Thank God the Spirit is no respecter of persons! Thank God that where I was born does not disqualify me as a candidate to receive the Holy Spirit in my life. Thank God the chromosome that determined my gender did not cause my elimination for sanctification through the Holy Spirit.

Thank God that because my parents are not of royal blood nor do they have riches untold, my social or political status is not denounced, but embraced. The Holy Spirit still knows my name! *"For every time I feel the Spirit, moving in my heart I will pray."* The Holy Spirit hits me when my heart is in sync with God's obedience and leads me in the paths of righteousness for his name's sake. It will not matter if I live in a palace, the suburbs, the hood, a house, an apartment or in a shelter, the Holy Spirit will find me and release its power in my life. When the day of the Lord arrives all distinctions will disappear in the wake of this momentous occasion.

Then I will sing hallelujah and praises to his holy name. God bless you!

THE BOOK OF AMOS

When Worship is Broken

WORSHIPING GOD ON HIS TERMS

AMOS 5:21-24, *"I hate, I despise your festivals, and I take no delight in your solemn assemblies. Even though you offer me your burnt offerings and grain offerings, I will not accept them; and the offerings of well-being of your fatted animals, I will not look upon. Take away from me the noise of your songs; I will not listen to the melody of your harps. But let justice roll down like waters, and righteousness like an ever-flowing stream."*

INTRODUCTION

The book of Amos represents the earliest collection of the words of a prophet into a book. It is considered one of the masterpieces of Hebrew literature. He introduced himself as a sheepherder and denounces that he is a prophet or the son of a prophet. Amos is from the town of Tekoa in Judah, part of the southern kingdom, just 10 miles away from Jerusalem. The book marks the beginning of a unique tradition in the history of religion – prophecies based on God's judgment and Israel's imminent demise.

Amos is summoned from the south to go and warn the north about God's coming wrath. He is to take this message of doom and gloom to the north so they will become aware of their sins and how their behavior against their fellow citizens has raised the ire of God. The central message of Amos is the end of my people Israel (8:2). Amos speaks of death in regards to Israel's enemies, but he is the first to announce that Israel too must be punished. This is the beginning of a new act in the Old Testament's story of redemption.

Amos prophesied in the 8th century B.C.E., during a prosperous time for God's chosen people. Although the culture supported wealth and prosperity, it was on the backs of the poor, the immigrant, and the downtrodden that Israel flourished. Amos is thus called to speak out on the behalf of those who do not have a voice. His message is tough, unforgiving, and without mercy. Divine judgment announcements are his genre of choice. Amos does not bite his tongue or mix his words, because Israel has been warned over and over again about the consequences of sinful behavior.

The northern kingdom especially has broken and ignored the summary of the law, *"Love the Lord your God with all your heart, mind, body and soul, and your neighbor as yourself." (Mk*

12:28-34) Israel did not show love to God, or her neighbor. Therefore, from a religious, social, and political perspective, Amos for the first time announced the "Day of Yahweh" as not only a day of vengeance against Israel's enemies now a day against the people God called Israel.

Amos does not speak of reform or forgiveness. War dominates the thought of this book. Amos used 28 different verbs to describe how God will reveal himself as a warrior and destroyer. The new message of the book of Amos is that *exile* from the Promised Land is on the horizon and there is nothing they can do to stop it. For God has rejected their empty attempts at worship.

In light of this dismal picture painted by Amos, we must ask ourselves questions concerning our worship experience and practices. Let us now read Amos' indictment on worship and how we can avoid making the same mistakes.

---

1)

Our first lesson asks the question **WHY DO WE COME TO CHURCH?** Read v 21, *"I hate, I despise your festivals, and I take no delight in your solemn assemblies."* Amos attacks and criticizes Israel's worship practices. Israel worshiped idol gods at the countryside altars at Bethel, and Dan, then comes to the holy temple to worship the God of Israel. God knows what Israel has done before she entered the gates or the courtyard of the temple in Jerusalem. God is not pleased, but rather angered. Israel is God's chosen people and he alone is worthy of their worship, adoration, and praise. The rituals and religious festivals were elaborate displays of God's acts throughout history. Large curtains hung from the ceiling to the floor hiding the "Holy of Holies" where the priest go behind the curtains to commune with God on the people's behalf. The altar was in the center of the room, and the priests recited long prayers, read scriptures from the Torah, and preached sermons reminding Israel of her chosen status.

Eventually the worship became routine and empty, void of any heart emotion of gratitude. They were just going through the motions, because it was required of them. They gathered for many festivals to commemorate God's intervention in Israel's history: *Passover, Purim, Booths, Day of Atonement, and Yom Kippur.* Many festivals were held to honor God, and their relationship with God, in lieu of his divine protection and their deliverance from their enemies.

Now there was competition. Now idol gods were being honored and worshipped in God's holy sanctuary. Now Israel has divided its loyalty between God and the idol gods of their neighbors. Not only were their actions against God idolatrous their treatment of their own people went against the laws of God! The hearts of those in leadership were filled with anger, greed, jealousy, and injustice towards their fellow Jews. God was not pleased, nor was God going to allow this social injustice to continue. So God sent Amos to address the situation and speak judgment to power.

How we come to worship determines how we do worship. That is why David asked God to give him a clean heart. If we come to Church with malice in our hearts, gossip on our lips, and anger on the brain, our true worship will be blocked. Our prayers cannot reach heaven! Our singing will fall on deaf ears! Therefore, before we come together as the people of God, let us meet with God prior to coming to Church. In that way, you will bring the Holy Spirit with you to contribute to the worship experience. Sitting in the pew texting on your phone is not worshipping God! Whatever has your undivided attention has become your idol god. In the words of the songwriter, *"Let us lift up holy hands, gather in his name, and worship him, Christ the Lord."*

_____

2)

The second question we ask is **_WHY DO YOU GIVE YOUR OFFERING?_** Read v 22, *"Even though you offer me your burnt offerings, and grain offerings, I will not accept them; and the offerings of wellbeing of your fatted animals I will not look upon."*

Amos regards sacrifices offered to the Lord as wholly unacceptable so long as the people who offer them are morally polluted. They do not recognize the evil of their ways. The people have convinced themselves that as long as we make a substantial offering required by law, our sins are absolved and God does not care what we do.

But the purpose for the offering of sacrifices is to atone for one's sins. Different animals or grains were assigned according to the transgression. It was to be presented with a humble remorseful and repentant heart. The laws of Moses were meant to make the sinner aware of their evil and offensive act. It was to bring to mind your error so you would be aware of the consequences and not repeat the mistake again!

However, somewhere down the line, through the generations, the feelings got disconnected from the act of giving the offering and the expectation to change one's behavior. Yes they sinned against God and their neighbor, but the offering was supposed to be sufficient in eliminating any lingering negativity, and offense toward God.

So why do we give our offering today? Paul tell us to give with a cheerful heart, not grudgingly or of necessity. The offerings in the Old Testament were charged according to the crime and the person's ability to pay (grain or animal). Of course the wealthy of the tribes could afford bulls and sheep, and other large livestock as a guilt or burnt offering. The poor, on the other hand, had few large animals and needed them to survive! The law allowed them to offer grain offerings or smaller animals such as the dove. But the equalizer was the amount set - 1/10, the tithe.

Church offerings today are the most controversial topic when Church matters are discussed in a public forum (second only to female preachers). Some people do not want to give the tithe and often find excuses for their stinginess by accusing someone handling the funds of "stealing or misappropriation." Yet God requires us to give with pure motives, and let the offerings' destination be of no concern to the giver. God sees all and those who dare rob God will suffer a fate beyond our imagination. We need not worry or use it as a pretense for not giving. Let go, be generous, and let God bless you fourfold, or even 100-fold.

The people in Amos' day gave as they were mandated, but they gave with a dirty heart and dirty hands. They practiced social injustice, which caused God to reject their offerings. What in your life will cause God to reject your offering? Examine your life before you give so that your giving will not be in vain.

_____

3)

Our final question about worship asks, **_WHY DO WE SING?_** Read v 23, _"Take away from me the noise of your songs; I will not listen to the melody of your harps."_ Music was a very important part of worship in the Old Testament. The book of Psalms is comprised of 150 hymns that were sung throughout Israel's history. Yet God is declaring to the people that he would no longer listen to the noise of their songs or the melody of their harps. Wow! God called their songs "noise!" That is a very derogatory noun to apply to the hymns sung in the temple during worship.

Surely the voices were melodious and the instruments accompanying the singers were on point. But the sounds were not coming from a pure and holy place. It is like pouring clean water through a dirty pipe. The water takes on the filth from the inside of the pipe. This is what God has accused Israel of – singling beautiful songs but their insides are ugly. They play harps with cheating and abusive fingers. Their voices lie in court, and give false witness against their neighbor in order to steal their property and force them into debt slavery.

But Israel is oblivious to her predicament! She keeps going through the motions believing God is praised and they are exonerated from all guilt. God says "no!" The songwriter asked the question, _"What if God is not happy with our praise?"_ What you do from Monday through Saturday matters in the eyesight of God. God will not turn a blind eye if you refuse to acknowledge him to others, or to social injustices toward his people. Jesus tells us in the Gospel of Matthew, _"The least you have down for my brethren, you have done for me."_ (Mt 25:40)

If you ever noticed, some singers sing every note perfectly, yet nobody is moved by their performance. Then you can hear a less trained voice sing a song with emotion and conviction, and you are moved to tears. They will make you want to jump up and shout. The difference is in the connection with the words in the song and whether or not the song resonates with your life experiences and your connection to God. If you cannot sing or carry a note, do not worry about it. Jesus carried the cross and saved you and I from sin. So sing anyhow! In God's ears, you sound like one of God's angels. The songwriter said it so well, _"I sing because I'm happy, I sing because I'm free; his eyes is on the sparrow, and I know he watches me."_

_____

4)

After asking 3 questions abut worship, our final lesson tells us that **_WORSHIP IS A REFLECTION OF GOD'S JUSTICE._** Read v 24, _"But let justice roll down like waters, and_ *righteousness like an ever-flowing stream.*" Justice is probably the word most often associated with the book of Amos because of this verse. The perversion of justice is Amos' diagnosis of Israel's fatal illness. His condemnation of the oppression of the poor and the weak has been a major source of strength for many liberation theologians through the years.

So serious is Amos' accusation against those in power, that the only outcome is Israel's total destruction. He is the first prophet to prophesy that Israel will lose the Promised Land over this charge of social injustice. Israel has been charged in the divine court and found guilty! Her sentence is expulsion from the land of her ancestors.

Because Israel was once an immigrant she was mandated by God to always look out for the little guy, the wanderer. Deuteronomy 26:5 confirms her status, "*A wandering Aramean was my Father.*" Israel spent 40 years wandering in the wilderness, crossing over borders and lands that did not belong to her. However, Israel chose to go in a different direction and find ways instead to oppress the alien, a status she once held. God is a God of the oppressed and heard their prayers. Now Israel will return to the status of a stranger in a foreign land. God is done with Israel.

We learn from the prophets of old to challenge our current society and leaders who dare practice religious and social injustice against God's people of all ethnicities and religious creeds. This is why the late Martin Luther King, Jr. found strength and grounding in these words. He stood up against the powers that be with a prophetic voice as sincere and fatalistic as Amos. He warned America that her punishment was on the horizon.

Today, as Christian believers, the mantle of truth has been passed down and on to us! God insists that we come before him with clean hearts and humble spirits. We must enter into his gates with thanksgiving, and into his courts with praise. Come to worship knowing that God is God and that God is our Creator. It is all about the attitude, the mindset, a pure heart, and a receptive spirit.

To come into God's house any other way is to invite the wrath of God into your life. Let us not make the same mistakes that Israel made. Worship is about God and how we treat one another. That is why the scriptures says, "*Let your light so shine before people that they may see your good works and glorify your Father in heaven.*" *(Mt 5:16)* It is a two-edged sword. We cannot do one without the other. Worshiping God on his terms, not our own, leads us into having a true worship experience. God bless you!

THE BOOK OF OBADIAH

Short, but Not Sweet

WHAT GOES AROUND, COMES AROUND!

OBADIAH 1:12-16, *"For the day of the Lord is near against all the nations. As you have done, it shall be done to you; your deeds shall return on your own head. For as you have drunk on my holy mountain, all the nations around you shall drink; they shall drink and gulp down, and shall be as though they had never been."*

INTRODUCTION

Obadiah is the shortest book in the Old Testament. His name means *"servant of Yahweh."* He realized that God commissioned him to proclaim a message of judgment, first to Edom, then to the people of Judah. His book is called "a vision" similar to the experience the prophet Isaiah had in the 6th chapter of his book.

The primary message of the book of Obadiah is one of judgment against the people of Edom, who were the descendants of Esau. Edom was located southeast of Judah, beyond the Dead Sea (Gen 36). Esau and Jacob were the twin sons of Isaac and Rebekah. The bad blood between the two brothers started while they were still in Rebekah's womb.

Edom has been associated with Esau since the earliest times of the biblical tradition. The people of Israel and Edom displayed great mutual hostility throughout the centuries. In Numbers 20:14-21 we learn that the residents of Edom refused to allow the Israelites passage through their borders.

The bad blood continued after the Babylonian exile. Israel's relationship with Edom changed dramatically by the time of Jerusalem's destruction by the Babylonians. Then after the Babylonian exile a group of Edomites moved to the south of Palestine to get away from the Nabalaean Arab groups who they were in conflict with. This area was later known as Idumaea, a word that derives from "Edom". To connect the Edomites to the New Testament, we know that King Herod the Great was an Idumean. Thus the Jews continued to show hostility towards the Edomites and resented Herod the Great as their king.

Obadiah formulated his message in light of Jerusalem's destruction, the exile and the reaction of the Edomites when they saw their relatives were under attack by the Babylonians, yet did nothing to help them. Their response to Judah's demise is evidence that *what goes around, comes around.* Now let us learn a lesson from Obadiah's vision.

_____

1)

Our first lesson teaches that *I AM MY BROTHER'S KEEPER*. Read v v 12,

But you should not have gloated over your brother on the day of his misfortune; you should not have rejoiced over the people of Judah on the day of their ruin; you should not have boasted on the day of distress. The behavior of the Edomites against their brother Israel was unforgivable. They watched and waited while the Babylonians came into Jerusalem and literally destroyed and burned down the whole city. The Edomites should have organized and sided with their neighbor in a time such as this. But they did not lift a finger, a stone, a brick, or a sword to protect their *cousins* in need and under attack.

As if that was not bad enough, they helped the Babylonians carry out their raid on Jerusalem! What things King Nebuchadrezzer did not take or burn up, the Edomites looted for their own selfish gain. They went even further and blocked the Judeans from escaping and captured those who got away, thereby returning them to the Babylonians. As the famous cliché goes, *"With friends like these, who needs enemies?"*

When and where do we stand up for those in need in our homes, churches, places of work, communities, and beyond? Today's technology has caused us to become numb or to turn a blind eye to those who have the most needs in our society. We all walk by and try to avoid the homeless person we see on the streets. We instantly make judgments about how they became homeless. Somehow it makes us feel more blessed that we did not end up like "them."

Yet that is not God's way for how we look at others who are less fortunate than we are. *"Except for the grace of God, there go I!"* Most of us are living from paycheck to paycheck. One major illness or natural disaster, or the sudden death of the major breadwinner, and we too could end up homeless or in a shelter.

The sin of the Edomites is one we commit every day! No we are not looting or burning down cities, but is our attitude and distain towards our neighbors not the same thing? Do we harbor revenge on our enemy deep down in our hearts or at least think about it from time to time? Revenge is never the answer to human disputes. It tends to hurt the avenger more than the object of our revenge. We will not always see eye to eye with one another. This includes our family, friends, co-workers, church members and the like. However, God expects us to be a present help, a refuge, a source of comfort, and a spiritual map for anyone who stands in the need of prayer.

"Am I my brother's keeper" is a quote from the Cain and Abel story. *(Gen 4:9)* God asked Cain where was his brother, when God knew that Cain had killed Abel because Abel's blood cried out to God from the ground. Cain knew that he had allowed his anger, feelings of rejection, and jealousy, get the best of him and push him towards violence against his own

brother. His answer has become a classic response to those who feel not obligation to take care of the widow, the poor or the orphan. Bigger and more profits are the goal of big corporations. Their greed has robbed the average worker of health care and pension plans. To quote a minimum wage worker, *"the rich get richer and the poor get poorer."*

Often the argument from those who have is that the needy should pull themselves up by their bootstraps. The poor's response is that they have no boots, so they cannot pull themselves up! They need a village to lift them up until they can afford boots of their own. All they need is a hand up, not a hand out.

Support and compassion were the two main sins of Edom towards their cousins Israel. Therefore, in all we do, let us try to embrace and practice these two actions in our everyday encounters. Truly, we are our neighbors' keeper.

_____

2)

Our second lesson learned from Obadiah is that **KARMA WILL CATCH UP TO YOU EVENTUALLY.** Read v 15, *"The day of the Lord is near against all the nations. As you have done, it shall be done to you; your deeds shall return on your own head."*

Obadiah now announces God's judgment on all the nations. The coming of the Day of the Lord was a popular theology among the earlier prophets, announcing the final culmination of history through God's judgment and wrath. The final destruction of Edom served as a foretaste to the other nations that dare come up against God and God's chosen people. Yes, God can punish his people, but no one else may intervene and take advantage of the sufferings of those whom are experiencing God's wrath! Outsiders are to take heed and observe the power of God and the sovereignty of God. They are not to participate in any way to inflict additional suffering or create a greater hardship for the people.

This is what Edom chose to do. Edom saw Israel's plight as an opportunity to "stick it to Israel" for all their years of conflict and military interactions. They were not going to help Israel in any way, shape or form. As a matter of fact, they looted the burned out buildings and homes. Some even accused the Edomites of setting the temple on fire!

Then to make matters worse, they prevented Israelites from fleeing capture, by blocking all alternative exits from the city. If any were able to get to safety, the Edomites became like bounty hunters and turned them in to the Babylonian army. Wow! What hatred and malice filled the hearts and minds of the Edomites.

The Edomites did not practice Yahwehism as did their cousins the Israelites. Remember in Gen 26-27, Rebekah, the mother of Esau (the father of Edom), complained that the Gentile women Esau married caused her and her husband much grief. Perhaps this was because they did not worship the same God as the heirs of Abraham. This convinced Rebekah that Jacob was the chosen heir to the legacy of Abraham. This does not justify her actions against Esau, but it does provide some theological insight on her behavior.

The Edomites therefore, are not bound by any ancestral covenant. They are out to fend for themselves. They could gain favor with the Babylonians by capturing Israelite refugees and maybe even receive a reward. There seemed to be no moral compass in their hearts to tell them this was wrong or that one day they would reap the same havoc they were now unleashing on Israel. For we all know what goes around, comes around.

The Bible gives us a road map on how to avoid situations that will bring God's wrath full throttle on our lives. Even when we sin and fall short of God's glory, there is forgiveness through faith in Jesus the Christ. Yet, because of the nature of the universe, once we have put negative energy out in the universe, the universe has to respond. It is called "cause and effect" in science, but karma in eastern religions. Jesus also taught his disciples *"to do unto others as you would have others do unto you."*

This is why forgiveness is so important. Through the act of forgiveness, we soften the response of karma and have the strength and courage to accept the consequences for our actions. Salvation through a risen Christ does not exempt us from karma. Rather, it encourages us to try to do the right thing in all situations, thereby minimizing the amount of negative karma we have to answer for, and maximizing the positive karma that comes into our lives in the form of blessings and good relationships.

Edom wanted revenge. But the Bible teaches us that, *"Vengeance is mine, says the Lord."* (Rom 12:19) Edom took it upon herself to "get back at Israel" so now she is counted in the category of "judgment against the nations." This is because what goes around, eventually comes around.

_____

3)

Our final lesson from Obadiah teaches us that ***A DRINK FROM THE LORD'S CUP RESULTS IN DESTRUCTION.*** Read v 16, *"For as you have drunk on my holy mountain, all the nations around you shall drink; they shall drink and gulp down."* Obadiah compares the idea of divine judgment to that of a drunken person. Obadiah uses the Hebrew verb "to drink" three times in v 16 to convey the idea of drunkenness. Now drunkenness alluded to the condition of the victors after a successful conquest over their enemies. They would celebrate and get drunk from the beverages they confiscated from their enemies' camp.

In addition to this image, it also suggests the staggering level of divine judgment that Edom and the other nations are about to experience at the hand of God. But Israel is not innocent in this judgment call. Her idolatry and lack of social justice brought the same cup to her to drink. Yes, Edom made things worse, but there would have been no attack at all if Israel would remain faithful to her God. So the cup was passed to Edom as well as Israel and the other nations, for there was enough guilt and punishment to go around!

As Christians, when we think about "drinking from a cup" the first image that comes to mind is the communion meal. However, that cup is not a cup of wrath because of the sacrifice of our Lord and Savior, Jesus the Christ. Because of his shed blood, which the cup now represents, we willingly drink from the cup. This cup reminds us of the depth of God's love for us. We know God's wrath is real, but we also know that God's love is steadfast and endures to all generations. Those who accept the communion cup are safe from eternal destruction. But those who still rebel against God's word and reject God's Son, will find out what it tastes like to drink from the cup of wrath.

Are you thirsty today? What cup are you prepared to drink from? Isaiah 55:1 says, *"Ho everyone who thirsts, come to the waters; and you that have no money, come, buy and eat! Come, buy wine and milk, without money and without price."* Jesus also invites us in John 4:13-14 to come and drink from his cup, *"Everyone who drinks of this water will be thirsty again, but those who drink of the water that I will give them will never be thirsty. The water that I will give will become in them a spring of water gushing up to eternal life."*

What is in the cup makes a difference. The choice is ours. Do we choose to drink from the cup of wrath and destruction by continuing in our sinful behavior, or do we prefer to drink from the cup of salvation that quenches our thirst and calms our fears? Choose today, for what goes around, will definitely come around. God bless you!

THE BOOK OF JONAH

Gone Fishing!

MISSION IMPOSSIBLE

JONAH 1:1-3, *"Now the word of the Lord came to Jonah, the son of Amittai saying, 'Arise, go to Nineveh, that great city and cry against it; for their wickedness has come up before me.' But Jonah rose up to flee to Tarshish from the presence of the Lord."*

INTRODUCTION

Mission Impossible was one of my favorite T.V. shows of the 1960s. It focused on hiring an expert to complete a mission that was impossible for anyone else to complete. Only he had the necessary skills to bring success to the mission. If the person agreed, and accepted the challenge, the tape would then disintegrate and self-destruct.

The book of Jonah bombards the reader with a variety of actions, locations, and intrigue. Unlike most prophetic literature, the book of Jonah fails to locate itself in a particular historical setting. We have no mention of kings, cities, temple, rituals and the like. The biblical scholars are at their wits end trying to come up with a definite date, place and message of the book of Jonah. Dates have ranged from the pre-exilic period (8th century B.C.E.) to the post-exilic period (5th -2nd century B.C.E.). Jonah's name is mentioned in 2 Kings 14:23-25 which suggests the 8th century. But later in the Wisdom of ben Sira 49:10, the name Jonah is mentioned, dating to the 2nd century B.C.E.

The genre of the book of Jonah is just as confusing and complex. Is it a folktale, a parable, a myth, satire, or legend? There appear to be hints of each of these genres throughout the book of Jonah. Therefore, scholars have chosen to focus more on the content of the book rather than the academic correctness of its contents, and authenticity of its authorship.

---

1)

The first lesson we learn from our text is that ***OUR MISSION COMES FROM GOD.*** Read v 1, *"Now the word of the Lord came to Jonah, the son of Amittai saying, 'Arise, go to Nineveh,* *that great city and cry against it; for their wickedness has come up before me.' But Jonah rose up to flee to Tarshish from the presence of the Lord."*

Jonah was a prophet who lived during a difficult period in Israel's history. Many scholars place the book of Jonah during the 6th-5th centuries. This was the time when the returnees were trying to rebuild the ruin city of Jerusalem, and secure the walls around the city. But their efforts were met with much opposition and animosity. Thus they developed a spirit of bitterness and vengefulness toward other lands and peoples.

For you see, while the wealthy and upper class were in exile, their neighbors encroached upon their ancestral land, and the poor who were left and never taken into captivity, took over the wealthy land owner's property, homes, vineyards, and livestock. They claimed that they were the true elect of God.

So Jonah was called to be a prophet in the midst of all this turmoil, transition and confusion. Israel had endured so much at the hands of her enemies, that she had little vision to be the servant of God and thus reached out to other peoples. So one of the problems Jonah faced was to awaken the nation's sense of a missionary destiny to which God's people had been called (a light to the nations).

God told Jonah to go to Nineveh. God was not only preoccupied with Israel's situation, for God had a whole world full of problems! So God gives Jonah a new mission, to go to a city that in the past mistreated Israel.

But in the midst of all this drama, one can easily lose sight of the purpose of the story – which is to show the problems a missionary who has lost their sense of mission must face and endure. Jonah is a story about a man who disagreed with God about what his mission work should be about, and tried to run away from "God's presence" as if that could ever happen. For we know God is omnipresent, omnipotent and Almighty. David declared in Psalm 139: 7-10 *"Where can I go from your spirit? Or where can I flee from your presence? If I ascend to heaven, you are there; if I make my bed in Sheol, you are there; if I take the wings of the morning and settle at the farthest limits of the sea, even there your hand shall lead me, and your right hand shall lead me."*

So for Jonah to run away "from the presence of the Lord" is a shocking statement made to describe Jonah's reaction to his mission. When God calls us to a mission, there is no shirking the responsibility to carry it out. Perhaps more of the world would be committed to God if the Church would once again take up the Great Commission, but this time in our own country! The Church walls have become our place of refuge while the world is crying out for a word from the Lord. We can no longer "do Church" as we have in the last 1000 years! Unfortunately, like Jonah, it is more comfortable to remain in places and situations that do not call us to the task of evangelism or witnessing, then to go outside the box. Our mission is to go; God's mission is to grow.

Sometimes as Christians, we prepare ourselves for our life's work, and never stop to pray and ask God if this is God's mission for our lives. The Bible says, *"Many are called, but few are chosen." (Mt 20:16)* This scripture means that we have all been called to do something with our lives but only a few can God trust to send out on a mission impossible for the ordinary person to do. For the impossible mission can only be accomplished with a great deal of faith and total commitment to God's purpose for all creation. Therefore, our primary mission is to address the spiritual needs of God's people – whoever and wherever they are. This is the mission that Jonah forgot about and refused at first, to accept. Jonah learned the hard way that in all we do, we must never forget that our mission is to seek the lost and offer them salvation through Jesus the Christ.

It cannot be about "What do I want to do?" It must always be about "What does God want me to do?" How can I glorify God through my daily walk and talk and actions? This is a question we must ask ourselves daily. When we do, we stay in sync with God's mission and can avoid most of life's traps and pitfalls.

---

2)

The second message we get from our text is that **OUR MISSION IS TO SPEAK OUT AGAINST WICKEDNESS.** Read v 2, *"Arise, go to Nineveh, that great city, and cry against it; for their wickedness has come up before me."* The Babylonians had continually sinned against God and oppressed peoples all over the ancient Near East. They worshipped the idol God Marduk and other pagan idol gods. God had not yet forgotten how they treated the exiles and misused their power and authority over them.

Now was their day of reckoning for all of their past sins. This was Jonah's new mission, to go to Nineveh, the seat of Babylonian power, a great city, full of heathens and idol gods, and to preach a day of destruction to them, for *"thus says the Lord!"*

We too live in a time when wickedness is all around us and being practiced by the youngest – kids killing kids, cyber bullying, suicide packs, to the oldest – politicians trying to roll back all the gains of the Civil Rights Movement, police brutality on the rise, road rage. We find wickedness in every sector of life. Our homes, schools, churches, work places, personal lives are all infected by violence on some level. It is rampant everywhere! I would venture to say that in light of some of the gang activities across this country, that wickedness is at an epidemic level.

Therefore, what appears to be happening in our world is spiritual warfare. More guns and prisons are not the answer. Until we get out there beyond our Church walls, and touch somebody's life, wickedness will continue to be the by-product of a society that just does not care for its poor and underemployed, because it has turned its back on God's word.

As Christians, Jesus has given us our mission – *"GO YE INTO ALL THE WORLD BAPTIZING THEM IN THE NAME OF THE FATHER, SON, AND HOLY SPIRIT, TEACHING THEM TO OBSERVE ALL THAT I HAVE COMMANDED YOU..." (Mt 28:19-20)* This we must do before our fancy luncheons, pinky drinking tea parties, rubber chicken banquets, and liturgy-filled candle light services. For until we do what God has called and sent us to do, everything else is just lace and frills – pretty on the outside, but will not survive under pressure.

The Church should develop a course on how to speak out against wickedness in our communities. We need the training found in Ephesians 6, which tells us to *"Put on the whole armor of God so we can withstand the evil darts of the devil."* The early Christian Church did not take on military lingo just because it sounded good. No, no, they were very much aware of the seriousness of spiritual battle against the powers that be. They were aware that this world is Satan's realm and he will fight hard to remain in control. The status quo will not change or adjust its lifestyle easily.

Like Jonah, we are called to speak out against wickedness in all places. Do not worry about not being popular. Instead, be more concerned about fulfilling your mission.

---

3)

The third and final message we receive from our text is that ***RUNNING FROM OUR MISSION WORK ONLY DELAYS THE INEVITABLE.*** Read v 3, *"But Jonah rose up to flee to Tarshish from the presence of the Lord. He went down to Joppa and found a ship going to Tarshish; so he paid the fare, and went on board...away from the presence of the Lord."* Now Jonah was not a bad fellow. He just did not want to do what the Lord told him to do. We have all been there, and done that, Amen! Israel's mentality at this point in her theological development was that they would focus only on themselves and not reach out to anybody else. This was, of course, a reaction to their recent captivity, their identity crisis, and their complications in rebuilding the city of Jerusalem. They were also confused about what their mission was in regards to their relationship with God.

So for God to tell Jonah to go to Nineveh was out of the question! As much pleasure as he may have gotten out of hearing from God a pronouncement of destruction on his enemies, Jonah also knew that God had a mercy streak and might forgive Nineveh if she repented. So Jonah decided he would pass on this assignment, and refused to obey a direct command from God. The mission was too hard, too personal for him.

Well as many of us have learned from Sunday school, Jonah could run, but he could not hide from God's mission or spoken word. Yes, he left town going in the opposite direction of Nineveh. Yes, a mighty storm arose on the sea and the other passengers on the boat threw Jonah overboard as a last resort, once he told them that his God was angry with him. Yes, God anointed a great fish to swallow Jonah and Jonah lived and prayed inside of that fish for 3 days. And yes, when Jonah finally came to his senses, God prompted the fish to vomit him up on the beach of Nineveh's shores. You can run, but you cannot hide. Running from our mission work only delays the inevitable and causes us frustration and depression when we try to do other work to fill that void in our spiritual heart. Jonah was exactly where God told him to go in the first place. He had to learn his lesson the hard way.

Jesus gave the Church its mission through the Great Commission, as he ascended to the Father. It is not an option! To the world it is an impossible mission and seems foolish and expensive. But to those of us who are called the children of God, it is good news! It is salvation! It is our joy, our hope, and our blessed assurance.

No it will not always be easy. No, it will not necessarily make you popular. No, it will not make us rich by earthly measure (or at least it is not supposed to!). But it will give us peace to know that we are about our Father business. We will find joy in knowing that we helped bring somebody into the Ark of safety.

After ending up on the shores of Nineveh, Jonah walked 3 days to the city of Nineveh. He proclaimed the destruction of the city as God told him to do. The people repented – from the king to the maidservant. God heard their prayers and forgave them causing God to withdraw his judgment against them.

Jonah suspected this outcome. That is why he did not want to go in the first place! Yet, we do not have the right, the power or authority to determine whom God punishes, and whom God forgives. For if the truth is told, we are living on grace every day of our lives. Every morning new mercies we see. God's forgiveness in our lives moves us to forgive others of their transgressions towards us. Jesus taught this principle in the Lord's Prayer: *"Forgive us our trespasses as we forgive those who trespass against us."* (Mt 6:9-14) God said in his word that if we do not forgive one another, he would not forgive us. Thank God for mercy!

To the believer, there is nothing too hard for God. There is no mission impossible for God's power to overcome the challenges you face from day to day. Just trust God! Just be obedient to God's commands through his word. Then stand still and see the salvation of God work miracles on your behalf. God bless you!

THE BOOK OF MICAH

What Does God Require of You?

MEETING THE QUALIFICATIONS

MICAH 6:8, *"With what shall I come before the Lord and bow down before the exalted God? Shall I come before him with burnt offerings, with calves a year old? Will the Lord be pleased with thousands of rams, with ten thousand rivers of oil? Shall I offer my firstborn for my transgression, the fruit of my body for the sin of my soul? He has showed you, O mortal, what is good. And what does the Lord require of you? To act justly and to love mercy and to walk humbly with your God."*

INTRODUCTION

Micah was a prophet in the 8th century B.C.E. His name means, *"Who is like Yahweh?"* Micah lived in Moresheth, a small village lying southwest of Judah's capital city, Jerusalem. Micah's contemporaries were Isaiah of Jerusalem, Amos and Hosea. By profession, Micah was a craftsman who had a deep sympathy for the poor and the underprivileged. Micah was responsible for bringing about a major repentance among the people of Judah. As a matter of fact, it was Micah and Amos who were the first to defend in an active way the cause of the oppressed people of God.

Therefore we can understand the motivation behind Micah's words in 6:8. In his lifetime, he had witnessed the destruction of Samaria and the northern kingdom of Israel, witnessed the destruction of Syria, and Judah became a buffer zone between Assyria and Egypt. In other words, political and international threats were the stimuli for Micah's prophetic career.

The key to understanding this text and the difficulty that Micah was up against is in defining what true religion is all about. For you see, the oppressors of the poor, usually the rich, were the biggest hot shots in the synagogue! Their understanding and practice of religion was one sided –to their advantage. And if by any chance they found themselves out of line with God, they would present burnt offerings and have long rituals of worship to show penance for their sinful deeds. But Micah calls their acts of repentance bogus! He knew that it was not a true repentance of the soul, but rather a superficial symbol to ease their own guilt. There was a serious misunderstanding in regards to what true religion was all about and what God required of them.

The situation of ordinary citizens was of great concern to Micah. He felt compassion for the poor and dispossessed, and held the leaders responsible for their suffering. The poor were forced to contribute to the armament and fortification efforts of the city due to threat of war. In a treaty with Assyria, great tribute had to be paid to secure Israel's freedom and position as a vassal state. Where did the money come from? The poor of course! Additional immigrants fled from the northern city of Samaria because of Assyria's destruction of the city, to Judah in the south. Again, this placed great financial and physical strain on the people already struggling to survive on meager means.

The book of Micah consists primarily of poetry. The literary genres he uses include judgment and salvation oracles, lament, lawsuit, disputation speech, prayer and hymns. Micah recruited whatever language or communication tools necessary to get his message across to his audience. Through these genres, Micah tries to provide insights into the nature of God and to the way humans relate to God and to each other. We find both hope and judgment in the pages of Micah, but his message is meant to stir up the hearts of the leaders so they would obey the commandments of God and recognize that social justice is a priority for daily living.

Micah's message is timeless. His words can easily fit into our worldly issues today, as people are continually being oppressed, ostracized because of their ethnicity, class, and gender. Genocide is occurring throughout the world and the Church is silent. So let us now read the words of Micah and adjust our religious thinking to a new level that sees God's face in all that God has created.

---

1)

The first lesson we learn from our text is that ***GOD REQUIRES JUSTICE.*** Read v 8a, *"He has told you O mortal, what is good; and what does the Lord require of you but to do justice..."* The people asked the question, *"With what shall I come before the Lord, and bow myself before God on high?"* Micah has preached against the leaders, accusing them of all kinds of social injustices. So now the people are asking what can they do to better their image in the presence of the Lord. God has blessed Israel more than any other people he has created, as they are his chosen people. Nations and lands have been conquered on behalf of Israel so that she may serve her God in peace and prosperity.

Yet due to bad leadership and teaching, greed and idolatry, Israel has lost her way. She has even convinced herself that she is in the right. It is not until a prophet of God comes to the people, denounces their behavior, accuses them of breaking the covenant laws made between them and God, that they even see a problem with their worship! They are oblivious to their own sin, but readily acknowledge the sins of the poor and downtrodden.

So in her ignorance to her crimes, Israel as worshiper, asks what offering is needed to placate the Lord. She proposes extravagant gifts, even child sacrifice. Yet none of these suggestions fit the bill for her insensitivity to the poor, the widow and the orphan. Micah declares that only God's justice will erase Israel's past sins towards one group in society. Justice in Micah's prophecy entails equal treatment for all according to the covenant laws. Filling false claims against the poor as a way to steal their ancestral lands is unacceptable in the sight of God. Keeping people in debt slavery longer than the law requires is unjust and takes advantage of the less fortunate. The leaders know better, but they refused to do better.

Micah's answer changes the question. The people's questions were about how to please God through worship only. However, Micah, along with other prophets, taught that worship was not the end all in regards to their relationship with God. God is more interested in the way people live their everyday lives than in their religious practices only on the Sabbath. Amos states that God hates superficial piety displayed only on Sundays, and are not accompanied by lives dedicated to justice and righteousness throughout the rest of the week (5:21-24). For Micah, justice is something people do, an action against evil, greed, and injustice. There may be a law that exists on the books stating a certain behavior unlawful, but not until someone enforces that law, can justice become a reality.

A summary of the biblical interpretation of justice is, *"Do unto others as you would have them do unto you." (Mt 7:12)* That is the Golden Rule we have all grown up hearing. It is a simple theological and practical statement, yet so hard for believers to adhere to, not to mention unbelievers. When a person believes that a wrong can be made right by an empty ritual, something is wrong with that person's religion. When one ethnic group can support the slavery of another ethnic group and use the biblical texts to support it, there is something wrong with that banner of religion.

When a Church can cater to the needs of the powerful members, and neglect the poor and lowly, something is wrong with its religion. When a Christian can despise another person because they do not like something about their looks, something is wrong with that person's religion. This was the problem Micah had to deal with in the 8th century B.C.E. and it is still a problem in the Church and religion as a whole, today. Micah screams at us that God requires justice!

_____

2)

Our second lesson on what true religion really looks like according to Micah is that **_GOD REQUIRES US TO BE MERCIFUL._** Read vs 8, *"...and to love mercy."* The Revised Standard Version of the Bible uses the word *"kindness"* instead of *"mercy."* I think that waters down the impact that mercy has on our everyday lives. Kindness brings to mind a smiling face, a firm handshake, a good ole boys pat on the back. But mercy says I have to get involved in my neighbor's life. How do I help make their lives more livable, sustainable, and less stressful? Mercy means I have to stand up for the God-given rights of others, no matter the cost to me.

The word used in the Hebrew *"hesed"* describes God's unconditional love for his creation. It has to do with love, loyalty, commitment and faithfulness. To practice mercy is to be like God! God has been merciful towards his creation since the Garden of Eden fiasco. Israel enjoyed God's mercy every day. God promised new mercies each morning. So mercy from

God is taken for granted, without the understanding that mercy is a two way street. God shows mercy and we as his children, are obligated to show mercy towards one another.

But now God's mercy has run out. Micah responds to their question about how to worship God by smacking them in the face with accusations that they have not shown mercy! Why then should God continue to show mercy to them! They have tried God's patience for the last time, and now God will allow their enemies to destroy them.

God would be untrue to God's own self if God allowed evil to continue to rule with no response. God is acting justly. God has shown mercy. The verdict of the heavenly jury is *GUILTY AS CHARGED*!

_____

3)

Our third lesson on the requirements of God's worship is **_WE WALK HUMBLY WITH OUR GOD._** Read v 8d, "*...and to walk humbly with your God?*" Some scholars point out that the Hebrew word for humbly "*sn*" is better translated as "carefully." The key word in this verse is "walk" or "*halak*" in the Hebrew. Therefore, the two words together suggest that we are to "walk carefully" with God by not allowing outside worldly concerns and issues to penetrate or affect our relationship with God. Walking with God conjures up images of pilgrimages made to the holy city of Jerusalem with God as their constant companion. This same sentiment is carried over into the New Testament when Jesus promised to be with us always, even until the end of the world. The word "always" means "all the days." So it does not matter what kind of day you are having, Jesus is walking right by your side. You are never alone.

The threefold summary of Israel's behavior towards God and others is stated here so plainly: *do justice, love mercy, and walk humbly with your God.* Why then could she not get it right? Why did Israel repeatedly disobey God's commandments? Why did Israel worship idol gods and succumb to the abominable practices of her neighboring nations? Why do God's blessings and mercies not engender Israel's complete loyalty and praise?

We can ask the same questions of us today. Has God not blessed us as a country, as a nation, beyond any other nation? Has God protected America from its enemies time after time? Then what happened to cause us to turn away from God? Why have we become such a secular nation? Have our leaders led us astray? Have our idol gods become materialism and commercialism? Where are the prophets? Why is no one answering the question, "*Is there a word from the Lord?*"

Yes, there is a word. The word says, "*He has told you, O mortal, what is good; and what does the Lord require of you but to do justice, and to love mercy, and to walk humbly with your God.*" The ball is in our court. God bless you!

THE BOOK OF NAHUM

The Lord is Slow to Anger, but Great in Power

REVENGE IS BETTER SERVED COLD!

NAHUM 1:6-8, *"Who can stand before his indignation? Who can endure the heat of his anger? His wrath is poured out like fire, and by him the rocks are broken in pieces. The Lord is good, a stronghold in a day of trouble; he protects those who take refuge in him, even in a rushing flood. He will make a full end of his adversaries, and will pursue his enemies into darkness."*

INTRODUCTION

There is an old saying, *"Revenge is better served up cold."* This implies that one should cool off before taking action against someone because you feel betrayed, or threatened in some way. Unfortunately, God has served his vengeance cold too many times and Israel has taken advantage of God's mercy and grace. The book of Nahum lets us know that God's vengeance is hotter than ever.

Nothing is known about the prophet Nahum as an individual. His name means *"comfort"* or *"consolation."* Nahum's hometown is Elkosh. It appears to have been located in southwest Judah. The book begins with the superscription, *"An oracle concerning Nineveh. The book of the vision of Nahum the Elkoshite."* The topic of the book is the imminent fall of Nineveh, the capital city of the Assyrians.

The fall of Nineveh in 612 B.C.E. was one of the most infamous downfalls of that day. The Nineveh of Nahum's time was the premier city of the Late Assyrian Empire. The Late Assyrian Empire comprised the reigns of six kings and lasted for over 130 years (744-609 B.C.E.). Judah had been under Assyrian threat since the reign of Tiglath-pileser III in 744 B.C.E. His successors conquered and destroyed most of the Northern Kingdom of Israel, and started to infiltrate the Southern Kingdom of Judah.

Therefore, Judah's consciousness in regards to Nahum's prophecies, fit perfectly within the mindset of celebrating the final destruction of Nineveh and the demise of the Late Assyrian Empire. The theme of Nahum's poetry is the avenging wrath of God redressing Assyrian oppression and the abuse of power by Nineveh. Due to the theme of "vengeance" and "payback" both the books of Obadiah and Nahum have been pretty much ignored by the Christian Church. The Church of Jesus Christ prefers to promote forgiveness and restitution. However, the Old Testament scholar Elizabeth Achtemier states in her book *Nahum-Malachi* that the book is best summed up in this way, *"Evil introduced and evil done away"* (Achtemier, p 5). Most scholars agree that the book was written in Judah, before the fall of Nineveh in 612 B.C.E.

The message for today's reader is that God's vengeance is better served up cold. When God's wrath is hot, the consequences are far beyond the human comprehension and control, and there is no turning back. So let us now read about Nahum's message of God's revenge against Nineveh and how we can avoid the same situation in our relationship with God.

———————————

1)

Our first lesson teaches us to **BEWARE OF GOD'S VENGEANCE WHEN IT IS SERVED UP HOT.** Read v 6, *"Who can stand before his indignation? Who can endure the heat of his anger? His wrath is poured out like fire, and by him the rocks are broken in pieces."* Wow! God's wrath is this verse is all consuming, frightening, and overwhelming to the human mind. Nahum's depiction of God's vengeance against Nineveh falls in line with the Ancient Near East understanding of God as a divine warrior, emerging to do battle against his enemies. The object of God's vengeance in the book of Nahum vacillates between Nineveh and Israel. However, the primary target is Nineveh.

Although the Assyrians and the Babylonians functioned as God's arm of wrath against his people because of their constant sinful behavior against him, Assyria took her treatment of Israel to a level that did not please God nor did it serve God's agenda. The people of God were punished because of their adultery against their husband, the Lord God of Hosts. Israel continuously sinned against God and her own people. God warned the political and religious leaders of his coming wrath by sending the prophets of "doom and gloom" (Amos, Hosea, Isaiah of Jerusalem, and Jeremiah). But their warnings fell on deaf ears. They left God no other choice but to act on his word.

God's creation shook and trembled at the prediction of God's vengeance. Nahum asked the question, *"Who can stand before his indignation? Who can endure the heat of his anger?"* The people of Israel were so use to God "changing his mind" or forgiving their "trespasses," that they heard the warnings and it was like water on a duck's back. There was no effort to change at all. Even though the Northern Kingdom's capital city of Samaria was destroyed in 722 B.C.E. and never to rise again, still the Southern Kingdom of Judah refused to heed to the words of the prophets and their call to repentance.

However, now the intended target is Nineveh herself. Nineveh's demise was a long time coming. Many nations suffered at the hands of the Assyrian army's brutal tactics and vicious killings of both women and children. Israel may be under her control now, but what God was about to do to Nineveh would be epic. Nineveh was a polytheistic country, serving many idol gods. So perhaps the Assyrian people tried to appease some of the idol gods with tributes and burnt offerings. Yet, this would not have appeased God's anger. God is slow to anger, but when

God has reached his point of no return, when God's anger is hotter than a 500-degree oven, watch out, you do not want to be in the line of fire.

This is where Nineveh found herself. This is her destiny as prophesied by Nahum. You had time to back off your aggression towards God's people when God's vengeance was cold, negotiable, and mercy and forgiveness were still options. You had time to repent, restore, and comfort God's chosen people. But Nineveh failed to change her strategy towards her prisoners of war. So now God's vengeance was too hot for Nineveh to stand before the pressure. God's vengeance was too fierce to endure like the hot furnace of the three Hebrew men in the book of Daniel. This fire was all consuming and hot as the red spots on a burning coal.

The fierceness of God's vengeance would shatter the rocks, cause earthquakes, avalanches, and tsunamis. Nature was participating in the vengeance aimed at Nineveh. Truly she had no recourse, no one to come to her aide.

In this life, we should never allow God's wrath to reach this level of no return in our lives. Prayer and fasting, praise and worship, acts of repentance and restitution, are all avenues to bring calm before the storm of God's vengeance can form. God reveals to us through his word and his servants, when we have offended him so severely that we will become victims of his vengeance. The only way we can survive is to encounter God's vengeance when it is still cold. Then we can seek his presence after we have sinned.

Our punishment is still coming, but its impact will be much less abrasive, and our survival rate much higher, if we come to God with a clean heart and a right spirit. There was a movie in the 1960s called, *"Some Like It Hot!"* I assure you that you do not want to encounter the wrath of God in that state.

———————————

2)

Our second lesson teaches us that **GOD'S VENGEANCE PROTECTS HIS OWN.** Read v 7, *"The Lord is good, a stronghold in a day of trouble; He protects those who take refuge in him, even in a rushing flood."* Verse 7 introduces God as a stronghold for those who are seeking refuge from their enemies. Nineveh is Israel's enemy and has now become an enemy of God. God cares about those who come to him for protection and safety. God gathers them under his wing as a hen does with her baby chicks.

There is comfort in serving a retributive God who will one day in his own time, settle the score and set things straight between you and your enemies. Knowing that God has the power to annihilate evil, and at the same time offer comfort to his people, is mind-boggling! Israel was well aware of God's *two-edged sword*. It was to Israel's advantage to try and stay on the side of God's comfort and to avoid the side of God's judgment. She knew both sides of God through her many encounters with God over the centuries.

Nahum's God is a divine warrior, but also a great comforter to those who earnestly repent of their wrong doings and seek transformation for their lives (remember Jonah?). Nineveh did not repeat her act of repentance this time, so she felt the intense heat of God's vengeance.

Judah, who is also an audience of this message, still has time to turn away from her evil ways and find comfort in the arms of a loving God.

Whenever life throws us a curve ball, we have the peace and comfort in knowing God's got our back and that there is nothing too hard for God. Trying to live in God's presence and walk in the ways of God oftentimes attracts Satan's demons, who will try to confuse us, tempt us, oppress us, and destroy our peace.

We need only remain in the refuge of God's Holy Word. These words provide us with the armor we need to stand strong until our help comes. That help brings us comfort and dishes out vengeance on our enemies. Even when Job experienced his life test, his comfort was always in knowing that God was his refuge, no matter what the Satan threw at him. The overwhelming floodwaters of Noah's day did not destroy Noah and his family for they were found guiltless in the eyes of God. Noah trusted God and knew God would care and provide for him, his family, and at least two of every animal in order to procreate and recreate a new world. The Hebrews walked through the floodwaters of the Red Sea, but Moses knew his God was a good God and a refuge in times of trouble.

Therefore, stay close to God so you can avoid God's vengeance and its release upon your life.

————————————

3)

The third lesson we find in our text teaches us that ***GOD'S VENGEANCE IS PERMANENT.*** Read v 8, *"He will make a full end of his adversaries and will pursue his enemies into darkness."* There is great comfort in the conviction that evil will be brought to a final reckoning. The Assyrians had oppressed Israel for almost 130 years. The people prayed for that glorious day when the Assyrian yoke would be removed from their necks. Nahum announced that it was coming sooner then they realized. God's vengeance against the city of Nineveh was representative of the vengeance God was about to release on all of Israel's enemies. However, the underlying message to Israel was this could happen to you just as it will happen to her enemies. Amos included Israel on the list of nations that will be utterly destroyed on the Day of Yahweh, which traditionally is a day in the future when God finally destroys all his enemies. Israel will suffer the same fate if she is not careful.

Nahum reassures us that God will put an end to our opposition and pursue our enemies into darkness. We need not fear them, nor compromise our faith practices to get along with them. Our lights will continue to shine and God will be glorified while our enemies descend into utter darkness.

So let us hold our heads up high in our service to the Lord. Let us avoid becoming objects of God's hot vengeance by keeping our faith in him strong through the reading of God's word, prayer and fasting. Let us receive God's refuge and protection, which is extended to those who trust in him through his precious Son, our Lord and Savior, Jesus the Christ. Then let us be rest assured God will put a full end to our enemies and drive them into utter darkness. God bless you!

THE BOOK OF HABAKKUK

Living by Faith

WHEN FAITH IS ALL THAT'S LEFT

HABAKKUK 2:2-4, *"...Then the Lord answered me and said: 'Write down the vision; make it plain on tablets, so that a runner may read it. For there is still a vision for the appointed time, it speaks of the end, and does not lie. If it seems to tarry, wait for it, it will surely come, it will not delay. Look at the proud! Their spirit is not right in them, but the righteous live by their faith.'"*

INTRODUCTION

The book of Habakkuk deals with the problem of evil in the world. Habakkuk questions God's justice and mercy because from where he sat, the world was in a mess; violence was everywhere; nation fought against nation; politicians were crooked; there seemed to be no justice, no compassion for the poor; even the worship experience had become corrupt. To read Habakkuk's complaints you would think he just looked at the morning news today! Nothing has changed! As the book of Ecclesiastes 3 says, *"There is nothing new under the sun."*

Habakkuk's major concern for justice places him among the prophets in Israel's tradition. He calls attention to and criticizes the miscarriage of justice in the political, judicial, economic and religious arenas of his day. Justice is nowhere to be found. Habakkuk predicts that God will punish this unjust society and reestablish equity and proper order.

Habakkuk differs from his predecessors and contemporaries in that he confronts the issue of a just God and an unjust world head on. Versions of this can be seen in Job's search for God, in the psalms of lament, in his contemporary Jeremiah, and now in Habakkuk. Habakkuk presents two arguments to God in his complaint against injustice in his world. In his first argument, Habakkuk complains to God about the lack of justice in Judean society and God's failure to move against evil in the world. Then in his second argument, he questions God's plan to eliminate Judean corruption by allowing a Gentile nation, Babylon, to come in and destroy his chosen people. To Habakkuk, one does not equal the other. There needs to be a different plan! Good people will be hurt because of the evil deeds of bad people. How is that fair?

Habakkuk puts people into two categories – the wicked and the righteous. The wicked are the unrestrained oppressors and the righteous ones are the helpless victims of their oppression. Although he wants God to intercede on behalf of the righteous people, God's plan to use the

Babylonians is unacceptable. So God and Habakkuk are in a conundrum and Habakkuk is directed to trust God and live by faith.

---

1)

The first lesson we learn from our text is that when faith is all that's left, **_WE HAVE TO WRITE THE VISION DOWN_**. Read v 2, *"Then the Lord answered me and said: 'Write the vision; make it plain on tablets, so that a runner may read it.'"* God's second response to Habakkuk is found in verses 2-4. This response promises a resolution to the problem of corrupt leaders. This text is the shortest speech in Habakkuk and the first thing Habakkuk is told to do is to write down the vision, so that it is available and clear for all who pass by to read God's plan for the people.

Habakkuk does not use the traditional prophetic judgment speech that presents the sins of the people, which convicts them, then pronounces judgment on them. Instead Habakkuk uses a lament genre and assumes the role of a victim whose case has not been redressed by divine intervention. As he complains, God told him to write.

There was so much confusion during this time. The city was under siege, politicians and religious leaders were jockeying for position and power. Other prophets were speaking their own truth. So Habakkuk was told to write his vision down. His vision attacks the status quo and pleads with God for a return to a time of peace and loyalty, a time when the covenant laws were practiced and festivals celebrated their relationship with God and with one another.

Habakkuk saw tension between the traditional prophetic theology and his actual experience with God and the people. For Habakkuk God is holy, God is eternal, so why God is tolerating this behavior is beyond his comprehension. Habakkuk lodges a religious complaint against God! Like Job, he felt the need to take his case directly to the Lord. But also like Job, Habakkuk was not privy to the total plan of God's salvation and redemption for the righteous.

When I write something down, it is usually to remember my plans for the day. It is for my own perusal and no one else. As my day progresses, I check off each line item I successfully complete. Habakkuk writes the vision for his day and for all posterity. Now we can look back and read how God punished the wicked, and how the righteous are preserved to serve God as a remnant. Writing the vision also serves as a contract between Habakkuk and God.

Writing down our visions help to make them more real and help to bring them to fruition. We can pace ourselves, measure our progress, alter the vision, or eliminate it all together. But what is important here is that we write the vision down. For God's word cannot return void.

---

2)

The second lesson learned from our text is **_WE HAVE TO WAIT FOR THE VISION TO COME TO PASS._** Read v 3, *"For there is still a vision for the appointed time; it speaks of the end,* *and does not lie. If it seems to tarry, wait for it; it will surely come, it will not delay."* One of the tests to prove a person is a true prophet was whether or not their prophecy came true. When a prophet spoke on behalf of the Lord, he or she was anxious about how soon the prophecy would reveal itself. They knew the penalty for false prophecies was death by stoning.

This also caused some persons to be reluctant to accept the call to prophesy. Some of the "doom and gloom" prophets did not live to see their predictions come true. However, their disciples, and school of prophets, were able to preserve their prophecies: some wrote them down and some committed them to memory. Then when the time of the prophecy came to pass, they remembered the words of the prophets. For some it was almost 200 years before their predictions came true.

God tells Habakkuk not to be concerned if the vision takes a while, just wait on it. It is on the way. For one day is like a 1000 years in the eyesight of God. Delay does not mean denial. God guarantees the vision will come to pass. In its written form it will serve as an affidavit to verify the trustworthiness of the vision's content. The vision is a reliable pledge that God will act on it at the appropriate time in history.

As believers we pray and wait, pray and fast, and pray and worship, yet our requests are not answered to our satisfaction or on our schedule. Perhaps the vision is not what God has planned for our lives. Perhaps the vision is too shortsighted and will take us down the wrong path. Or just maybe, God is working it out, moving things around and making room for you in the universe, setting up the scene so when the time is right, we can just take the stage and be blessed. Whatever God is doing, do not lose faith in the vision. For in everything there is a season.

---

3)

Our third lesson teaches us that **_PRIDE COMES BEFORE A FALL._** Read v 4, *"Look at the proud! Their spirit is not right in them, but the righteous live by faith."* In this verse, Habakkuk contrasts the proud with the righteous person. Another reading of this verse comes from the Old Testament scholar J.J. Roberts, *"Now the fainthearted his soul will not walk in the visions"* (Roberts, J.J. *Nahum, Habakkuk, and Zephaniah,* p 106). In this translation, the so-called "proud" is described as *"fainthearted"* for they cannot accept what they cannot see. All they see is the destruction and devastation left by the Babylonian invasion. They walked by sight and fell into despair.

But God tells Habakkuk that those who trust in him, they live and walk by faith. Habakkuk struggles with an appeal for more faith because his current assessment of the situation puts God on trial. The wicked will have their day. The wicked live lives of luxury and plenty now, because they walk by sight. Yet when all they see is gone, they will not be able to survive the challenges they are about to face.

Whereas, the righteous put their faith in God, not people or possessions, they will stand firm. Because when everything fails and all you have left is your faith; that is enough for the righteous. Your faith will take you through and hold you up until your season of life changes. That is what God was trying to get across to Habakkuk. Habakkuk needed to reach down deep into his religious teaching and experiences for in the words of his successor Isaiah 40:31: *"But they that wait on the Lord, they shall renew their strength; they shall mount up on wings as eagles, they shall run and not get weary, they shall walk and not faint."*

Habakkuk's struggle challenges us even today to remain committed to God's vision for the world, not just our little corner of it. Every trial and every tribulation we encounter in our personal lives can be met with faith. For it is through our faith in God that we are able to rise up to any occasion that might cause us to despair. Therefore, let us respond with the words of Psalm 121:1-2, *"I lift my eyes to the hills - from where will my help come? My help comes from the Lord, who made heaven and earth."*

THE BOOK OF ZEPHANIAH

Singing Songs of Victory from an African Prophet

LET EVERY VOICE AND SING!

ZEPHANIAH 3:14-17, *"Sing aloud, O daughter of Zion; shout, O Israel! Rejoice and exult with all your heart, O daughter Jerusalem! The Lord has taken away the judgments against you; he has turned away your enemies. The King of Israel, the Lord is in your midst; you shall fear disaster no more. On the day it shall be said to Jerusalem: Do not fear, O Zion; do not let your hands grow weak. The Lord, your God, is in your midst, a warrior who gives victory; he will rejoice over you with gladness, he will renew you in his love; he will exult over you with loud singing as on a day of festival."*

INTRODUCTION

The book of Zephaniah is the ninth book of the 12 Minor Prophets of the Old Testament. His 3 chapters of collected oracles date to the seventh century B.C.E. In the superscription he is identified as "Zephaniah ben Cushi," which means, "son of Cushi" in English. The word Cushi means *African* in the biblical tradition. The name "Zephaniah" is a combination of divine names meaning, "*hide*" or "*protect*" in Hebrew. To put the names together one reads, "*Yahweh protects.*"

Based on the content of his preaching it appears that Zephaniah must have been a Jerusalemite with connections to the royal family. His message focused primarily on the "Day of the Lord" which brings both judgment and salvation. The book of Zephaniah was composed to be read aloud, in order to accommodate the illiterate members of the community (which were the majority). The sins of the community vary and the list is long: idolatry, syncretism, adoption of foreign dress and customs, etc. etc. These are repudiated in the Reform Movement of King Josiah (2 Kings 23:4-14; Deut 12-26).

Zephaniah encouraged his readers and listeners, to do what is right and shun all manners of evil. Scholars place the prophecy during the time of King Josiah's reign (640-609 B.C.E.). When King Josiah discovered the lost book of Deuteronomy, hidden in the walls of the temple during a renovation, he immediately embarked on a major religious revival as a way to inform the people of their religious and social responsibilities, and how far off they were because of the corrupt practices of his father, and earlier kings. Zephaniah's prophecies were read between 630-620 B.C.E. very close to the time of Nahum.

Zephaniah begins with a dire message of doom and ends with a melodious message of hope and restoration. Zephaniah's voice was the first raised against the people's sins since the time of his predecessor, Isaiah of Jerusalem, 70 years earlier. In line with his predecessors, Zephaniah's work form is called the "oracle." An oracle is the vehicle through which the prophet proclaims, *"What thus says the Lord"* to God's covenanted people, Israel.

Zephaniah's sermons are set in Jerusalem on a festival day at the temple. He gets the peoples' attention by prophesying complete and total destruction of the whole earth. Israel's judgment is so profound because they are God's covenanted people. They know the law! They know the history! They know what God requires of them. Yet they turn away and embrace the religious and societal norms of their neighbors.

Nevertheless, after all his ranting and raving against them, Zephaniah's message ends on a note of hope. God has not given up on his chosen people Israel. God has not forgotten his promises to his friend Abraham. Let us now read the words of Zephaniah and embrace his message of hope.

---

1)

The first lesson we learn from our text is that ***WE SHOULD SING BECAUSE OF GOD'S FORGIVENESS.*** Read vv 14-15a, *"Sing aloud, O daughter Zion; shout, O Israel! Rejoice and exalt with all your heart, O daughter Jerusalem! The Lord has taken away the judgments against you, he has turned away your enemies."* The concluding oracle in Zephaniah calls on Jerusalem, to sing aloud, rejoice and exalt praises with all their hearts. Finally, all the messages of "doom and gloom" are coming to an end and a new beginning is on the horizon. The unidentified voice calls for a change in attitude from lamentation to joyous confidence.

Zephaniah reads the verdict of a heavenly jury to his audience, "Sing, rejoice," God has forgiven us once again. Those who led Israel into sin are now destroyed, gone to offend God no more. God is now their only king, as he was before the final days of the prophet Samuel. The jury's verdict is *"forgiven"* instead of *"not guilty."* For Israel was very guilty of the crimes brought against her. She was guilty and her guilt made her unclean in the eyes of her God.

So in priestly language, a blessing of forgiveness is pronounced thereby determining Israel "clean," again to become what God intended her to be all along – his chosen people and now a light unto the nations. Her enemies are turned away, no longer God's arm of wrath. Now they can find protection and solace under God's care.

Protection comes with forgiveness. Protection was one of the conditions in the covenant laws. *"If you will be my people, I will be your God."* (Exo 19:5) This included protection, land, many descendants, and blessings too numerous to count. For a moment Israel had lost her way and it seemed her judgment was too great for her to survive. Yet, God was always waiting in the wings for Israel's punishment to be over, to follow its course. Now that day has come and forgiveness has replaced judgment.

This is a reason to sing! God is exalted again king over Israel, not a human with flaws and shortcomings, prone to leave the God they love, and subject to idolatry and betrayal. Now God is back and that is a reason to sing praises to his holy name.

To be forgiven is always a reason to sing and shout. Just recently when a mother, who was arrested and sentence to life in prison for a drug bust in her home was released, because the sentence was too harsh, the whole world rejoiced with her. Her family sang praises to God and rejoiced with those who fought so hard for her release. That mother learned on that day a great lesson about forgiveness.

What has God forgiven you for in the past, even today? The Bible says we sin by thought, word and deed. So there is no escaping the DNA we inherited from Adam and Eve. Job tried to minimize the consequences of his sin, and that of his family, by praying everyday asking for forgiveness for the past sins, the present sins, and any future sins that may occur.

The Bible teaches us that if we come to God, God is faithful and will forgive us of our sin. But we also have to go to those whom we have sinned against seeking their forgiveness as well. Then we have to forgive others because they too are the victims of original sin. The hymn writer put it so succinctly in these words, *"I sing because I'm happy. I sing because I'm free. God's eye is on the sparrow, and I know God watches me."* So let us sing, even when our lives are in a mess and we do not know what the future holds. For singing denotes forgiveness, singing acknowledges hope, singing invokes restoration, and when we sing our confidence and faith in God takes us to a new level of grace.

So when life knocks you down, get up and sing these words, *"Up above my head, I hear music in the air, there must be a God somewhere."* Know and believe that God is there even when we cannot feel his presence.

_____

2)

Our second lesson from the text teaches us that **_WE SHOULD SING BECAUSE THERE IS NOTHING TO FEAR!_** Read v 16, *"On that day it shall be said to Jerusalem: Do not fear, O Zion, do not let your hands grow weak."* After all the prophecies against Judah threatening her demise at the hands of her enemies, no wonder Judah was in a fearful place, physically, emotionally, and spiritually. Her enemies were nations she shared borders with, who could easily attack her at any moment. Judah's fear radar was up because of the words of the prophets! Thus fear was an emotion that she lived with every day as the people of God, now under God's judgment.

Again the priestly word of blessing states, *"The Lord your God is in your midst, a warrior who gives victory; he will rejoice over you with gladness, he will renew you in his love." (vv 17-18)* It is God who authorized curses for those who are disobedient to his commands, and blessings for those who are faithful and steadfast. Israel's sentence has been commuted from a death sentence, to a life of singing and rejoicing over their new beginning in God. Fear was no longer an emotion that was part of their repertoire.

We live in a time when technology is over the top. Yet new fears have come attached with modernity. Job security is no more. Healthcare is no longer a given in a job. Privacy and identity theft is violated. Millennials do not appear to have the same value system as the Baby Boomers. A person's word is not their bond. Sexual assault and human trafficking are on the rise. Road rage can end your life in an instant. Churches are closing their doors for lack of attendance. Our educational system is broken. Ethnic groups are pitted against one another for a slice of the economic pie of our society. The world many of us grew up in no longer exists and our hearts are full of fear of the unknown.

The world today is a more fearful place to live in than it was 20 years ago. All the security systems, monitors and passwords do not seem to dissuade hackers from trying to invade our financial portfolios and bank accounts. Many of us own guns for protection out of fear that a thief will break into our homes and assault us, robbing us of our most precious possessions. Where does it all stop!

God's word serves as a source of peace because it causes us to depend on God while at the same time taking the necessary precautions to not be a victim in today's world. We cannot allow fear to consume us or control our every move and thought. A song that the late Doris Day made famous in one of her movies in the 1960s says, *"Que Sera, Sera, whatever will be will be. The future's not ours to see, Que sera, sera."* We can only plan and prepare within our limitations. The rest is left in God's hands.

Therefore, the opposite of fear is faith and trust in a sovereign God. When we turn our lives over to God, our anointing will block most of Satan's arrows aimed at us, but the few that get through can be dealt with through prayer, fasting, worship, and the reading of God's word. God never promised us a rose garden, but Jesus did promise to be with us always. God did promise that *"no weapon formed against me shall prosper."* So let go of your fear and receive the peace of God, which passes all understanding.

Why does it pass all human understanding? *Because* we know that no matter what we face and encounter in this life, we are more than conquerors. *Because* we walk by faith and not by sight. *Because* the Lord is our Shepherd and we shall not want. *Because* the Lord is my light and salvation, in whom shall I fear, whom shall I be afraid? This songwriter sums it up Oh so well, *"Because he lives, I can face tomorrow. Because he lives, all fear is gone. Because I know who holds the future, and life is worth the living just because he lives."*

_____

3)

Our third lesson learned from this passage of scripture teaches us that ***WE SHOULD SING BECAUSE GOD IS IN OUR MIDST.*** Read v 17, *"The Lord, your God, is in your midst, a warrior who gives victory; he will rejoice over you with gladness, he will renew you in his love; he will exult over you with loud singing as on a day of festival."* God has returned and resumed his rightful place on the throne of their hearts as their mighty king. His presence will fill the new temple as it did in Solomon's temple. The kings of the Ancient Near East were also warriors and led their army into battle. That is how King Josiah lost his life.

So Zephaniah now preaches that God will take on the military role of warrior as well as king, and they have the victory merely because of his presence in their midst. Zephaniah predicts that God will rejoice over their joy and he will renew Israel in his love. The NRSV version of the Bible reads, *"He will renew you in his love."* But the NIV reads, *"He will quiet you with his love."* The Hebrew in this verse is controversial and complicated by the Septuagint (*Greek translation of the Bible*) reading of this verse. Yet, when you think about all Israel has gone through with the judgment sentence placed on her for centuries, the translation of *"quiet"* might fit the sentiment better.

Although the period of judgment is now over, loud cries of suffering and lament were heard throughout the community and the temple in years gone by. Jeremiah predicted that Rachel was weeping for her children because they were no more. Lam 2:18b reads, *"Let tears stream down like a torrent day and night! Give yourself no rest, your eyes no respite!"* Now God responds to that sad scenario. As Rev 21:4 states, *"And he shall wipe all your tears away."* This will occur through God's love, which covers a multitude of sins. God's love will restore Israel as his chosen people. God's love will reinstate the covenant promises God made to their ancestor, Abraham. When Israel sees her plight has changed for the better, her tears and cries of lament will be quieted. They will be replaced with shouts of joy, with singing as boisterous as that heard on the festival days Israel celebrates throughout the calendar year.

Their fear is quieted by God's love for them. Their feelings of abandonment are quieted by God's return. This all came about because of God's love! He could not remain angry at Israel forever. God's love is always stronger than his judgment.

When God is in our midst, there is nothing to fear, and everything to sing about. We hear that sentiment in the words of the hymn writer, *"I was sinking deep in sin, far from the peaceful shore; Very deeply stained within, sinking to rise no more. But the Master of the sea heard my despairing cry from the waters lifted me now safe am I! Love lifted me, when nothing else could help, love lifted me."*

God used every avenue to reach his chosen people and maintain them as his chosen people. But they could not keep God's commandments. Therefore, God decided that the only way to accept his people with all their flaws was to accept them in love. *"For there is faith, hope, love, these three, but the greatest of these is love."* (I Cor 13:13)

We celebrate God's presence in our midst during the worship service. We feel God through our prayers, the read word, the preached word, and in our singing. We realize that God rejoices with us and that God's love was shown to us in his greatest gift to humankind – the sending of his Son, Jesus the Christ, our Lord and Savior.

Now through faith in his Son, we can become sons and daughters of God! Then, through our acts of love on God's behalf, they will know we are Christians. Therefore, along with the angels on high, let us *"Lift every voice and sing, till earth and heaven ring, ring with the harmonies of liberty. Let our rejoicing rise, high as the listening skies; let it resound loud as the rolling sea."* Keep singing! God bless you!

THE BOOK OF HAGGAI

Rebuilding God's House

REMEMBERING THE ASSIGNMENT

HAGGAI 1: 2-6, "*Thus says the Lord of hosts: 'These people say the time has not yet come to rebuild the Lord's house.' Then the word of the Lord came by the prophet Haggai, saying: 'Is it a time for you yourselves to live in your paneled houses, while this house lies in ruins?' Now therefore thus says the Lord of hosts: 'Consider how you have fared. You have sown much, and harvested little; you eat, but you never have enough; you drink, but you never have your fill; you clothe yourselves, but no one is warm; and you that earn wages earn wages to put them into a bag with holes.'"*

INTRODUCTION

The book of Haggai is rare in how it records the events that occurred in these short 2 chapters. We are given the dates – August 29, 520 B.C.E. to December 7, 518 B.C.E. – when Haggai prophesied to the exiles returning from Babylon. He mentions important names of prominent figures that are crucial to the dating of this material as well as providing insight on the work (King Darius I, Zerubbabel, and Joshua the High Priest – not the successor to Moses). Some scholars believe Haggai belongs with Zechariah 1-8 as a composite work. His work places focus on the beginning and the refoundation work of the temple. This proposed date is probably December 18, 520 B.C.E.

Haggai's name stems from the Hebrew word which means, "*make a pilgrimage*" or "*observe a pilgrimage feast.*" It was a popular name in the post-exilic period and can also be found in extra-biblical writings. Haggai's family name is not mentioned which is peculiar seeing that the names following his name, all have family connections. The absence of a family name has been discussed, but no consensus has been reached among the scholars.

Haggai has been defined as a Judahite farmer who never left Palestine and did not experience the exile. Others suggest he was one of the early returnees eager to help in the rebuilding of the temple. However, his style has convinced most scholars that he was not a cult prophet. Yet, Haggai is remembered as a prophet with authority. He uses the messenger formula, "*Thus says the Lord*" five times. His is a message of hope grounded in the reality that his beloved homeland now lays in ruins. Haggai is very much aware of the mandate to rebuild the temple given by King Cyrus the Great to the first group that left Babylon, now Persia, to return to Jerusalem. Now it has been almost 18 years, 3 kings later, and still the temple is not rebuilt.

So Haggai's message concentrates on getting the assignment to rebuild the temple completed. The urgency lies in the consequences for not completing the work, thereby once again stirring up God's wrath against them. The book is really about Haggai's involvement in the restoration of the temple and Judah as a whole. Let us now hear the concerns of the prophet Haggai and how he motivated his people to complete their assignment.

_____

1)

The first lesson we learn is that it's hard to complete an assignment **_WHEN NOBODY IS IN CHARGE!_** Read v 12, *"Thus says the Lord of hosts: These people say the time has not yet come to rebuild the Lord's hours."* King Cyrus the Great conquered Babylon and released the Israelite exiles in 538 B.C.E. They were sent back home with a mandate to rebuild their temple. Only a small remnant returned. Numbers range from 2000-5000 people. They were in exile for 70 years, a period of time where almost 2 new generations were born into captivity. The flip side would be that most of those who were taken captive have now died in Babylon or were too old to travel and remember Jerusalem in its glory days.

The younger crowd only knew the lifestyle they experienced while captive in Babylon. They were settled there. Some married, started businesses, and birthed children. So Babylon was all they knew. No one was in a hurry to go to a land in ruins and start from scratch. Their parents and grandparents told stories about their homeland, but for the new generation, home is where the heart is and their hearts were now in Persia.

So those who returned came with a mission, an assignment, to rebuild the temple and offer a sacrifice on behalf of their benefactor, King Cyrus the Great. However, King Cyrus passed on and his son as well. His nephew Darius I was now the new ruler of Persia. There was some confusion over the Edict of King Cyrus when Nehemiah wanted to rebuild the wall. Eventually the original document mandating the building project was located. So Nehemiah got busy and the returnees finished the wall.

Yet the temple was still unfinished. Perhaps the project was too much for the few who returned. The Lord says, *"These people say the time has not yet come to rebuild the Lord's house."* Who are *"these people?"* Are they the leaders of the returned community? Who is in charge? Where are the prophets, the priests, the Elders?

Haggai speaks to the leaders because *"these people"* deny that the time has come to rebuild the temple. But it has been 18 years since their return! *"These people"* found time to plant olive trees, grow food, establish vineyards, and build places for them to live. Some even had relatives that took them in who remained in the countryside. So what was the problem? The identity of *"these people"* is unknown, but their decision to hold up the building project suggests the community was in agreement with this decision and behind the vote 100%.

Whoever *"these people"* were, they have caused God's ire to rise up against them. God then sends his spokesman, Haggai, with a message, *"Build the temple or the drought will continue indefinitely.* That will be the consequence for ignoring the Lord's House. Since nobody seemed to be "in charge" the punishment will fall on the whole community.

Who is in charge of finding a solution when our communities appear to be out of control and bad decisions bring the ire of God upon us: The Church, the police, the school system, the politicians, the business sector? Violence is rampant and innocent people are dying every day in the crossfire. We are all responsible for our own village. If we come together in the spirit of love, growth, and prosperity for all, each community can address the needs of the whole. But somebody has to be in charge! Somebody has to take the bull by the horns and develop a life survival plan for our young people. Our young people feel hopeless and left behind. They feel acceptance from gangs and pimps, more so then they do in the Church and our society as a whole.

It is time for us to step up to the plate and everybody take a turn to be in charge. In that way all ideas and leadership styles can be embraced and incorporated into a resolution to the problem. Bringing children into the world or just having them under our care is an assignment from God that we as a society and village, must see through to fruition, from birth to adolescences, to teen-age years, young adulthood, and finally adulthood if they need our support. Otherwise we will continue to see and experience the consequences of dropping the ball at any of these stages of life too soon, thus leaving the work unfinished. Enough is enough! Let's get the work completed.

―――――――――――――――

2)

The second lesson we learn from the text is that it is hard to complete the assignment ***IF YOU PUT YOUR NEEDS FIRST!*** Read vv 3-4, *"Then the word of the Lord came by the prophet Haggai saying: 'Is it a time for you yourselves to live in your paneled houses, while this house lies in ruins?'"* *"These people"* did not have the time to complete God's House, an assignment they received 18 years ago, but they found the time to build new houses for themselves. They had no guilt about God's House lying in ruins. Where were they having worship? Where were they offering sacrifices to God? Had these practices become defunct while they lived as exiles in Babylon? Did *"these people"* create a new way to worship God that excluded the need for a temple? Did they think they left God back in Babylon? Did they run out of funds because they used them to build their own homes? So many questions for *"these people."*

Haggai places emphasis on the state of completion. The people have finished their personal homes, while God's House is unfinished! Have they even started the task? If Haggai remained in Jerusalem after the Babylonian attack, the memories shared by others would have affected him greatly. Haggai's age is thought to be around 70 years old, so he would have just been born when his people were carted off into exile. His mother would have been pregnant with him, and that may support the notion why he was not in Babylon.

So rebuilding the temple may have meant even more to him since he was too young to experience Solomon's magnificent temple. God used Haggai as his messenger in order to get the temple completed and quickly. The prophet's task was to assist in the early stages of rebuilding the temple by pressing the people to move forward and complete their assignment. Haggai did not disappoint God.

When I was growing up, people seemed more giving and selfless than they are today. The 1990s focused on the promotion of self and becoming a millionaire before the age of 30. This feat was accomplished no matter whom you had to step on or over to win. But when we put ourselves first, and not God's plan for our lives, we tend to make more mistakes and bad choices that ultimately contribute to our downfall. Eventually, the setbacks become more frequent and loneliness creeps into our lives because we ignore or neglect the needs of others.

God is not pleased when we put anything before him. The first commandment is very clear on that point. The returnees chose to put their needs above rebuilding God's House. God was not pleased by their behavior or selfish choices. And when God is not happy, there will be a divine response to address the situation.

Where does God place in your life? Is God first place? Is God second place? Is God third place? No place? Then the question Haggai asked the returnees, now applies to us: *"How are you faring in your life?"*

_____

3)

The third lesson we learn from the text of Haggai is that ***THERE ARE CONSEQUENCES FOR NOT COMPLETING THE WORK.*** Read vv 5-6, *"Now therefore thus says the Lord of hosts: Consider how you have fared. You have sown much, and harvested little; you eat, but never have enough; you drink, but never have your fill; you clothe yourselves, but no one is warm; and you that earn wages earn wages to put them into a bag with holes."* The returnees are struggling to survive in the land of their ancestors. They are farmers from way back and farming is their major skill and trade. It is not just a career it is their only source of food and financial support. Yet no matter how hard and how long they work, nothing seems to come together for the returnees. They cannot seem to get ahead or even break even.

The land of the people and all living things now suffer from the effect of a long-term drought. The Hebrew word for "devastated" is *"hareb"* and the Hebrew word for "drought" is *"horeb."* The two are very similar in spelling and the play on the words is no accident. In other words, for God's House to be devastated and lie in ruins directly connects and causes a drought for the people - both spiritually and physically. The two words play off of each other as the editor's way of showing that the God of Israel must be honored and glorified.

For the unfinished temple is a sign that Israel's faith lies in ruins as well. The fact that she can ignore it for 18 years symbolized a spiritual drought in her relationship with God. So God equates the two and allows the *"cause and effect"* rule of the universe to respond to their neglect of the temple and unfinished business.

Haggai informs the people it does not have to be this way. All they have to do to end the drought is complete God's House! Stop procrastinating! Get the assignment done now before the drought is so devastating that the land cannot come back to its fertile status for decades to come.

They are commanded to do for their God as their neighbors had done for Baal, the idol god of storm and rain. The Baal worshipers built a house of worship for their idol god, yet Israel could not complete her assignment and do the same. Haggai calls God the Lord of Hosts, establishing his sovereignty over Egypt, Babylon and Palestine as well. God can only be honored when we take charge of the work and fulfill our commitment to him. For the returnees this meant completing the task of rebuilding God's House. This is evidence that God is real and present in a very tangible way. Although a temple will never again limit God's presence or power, the temple's very presence is a reminder of God's power over Israel's enemies.

To be obedient is to honor God in whatever task God has assigned to our hands. When we allow ourselves to become side tracked, or distracted by worldly comforts, we dishonor God in our witness and our behavior. Matthew 6:33 says it so well, in the New Testament, *"Seek ye first the kingdom of God and his righteousness, and all other things will be added unto you."* That is advice that will help us avoid the consequences of leaving God's work undone. God bless you!

THE BOOK OF ZECHARIAH

Extending an Open Invitation

ALLOWING THE SPIRIT TO MOVE MOUNTAINS IN YOUR LIFE

Zechariah 4:5-7, *"The angel who talked with me came again, and wakened me, as one is wakened from sleep. He said to me, 'What do you see?' And I said, 'I see a lampstand all of gold, with a bowl on the top of it; there are seven lamps on it, with seven lips on each of the lamps that are on top of it. And by it there are two olive trees, one on the right of the bowl and the other on its left. I said to the angel who talked with me, 'What are these, my lord?' Then the angel who talked with me answered me, 'Do you not know what these are?' I said, 'No, my lord.' He said to me, 'This is the word of the Lord to Zerubbabel: Not by might, nor by power, but by my spirit,' says the Lord of Hosts. 'What are you O great mountain? Before Zerubbabel you shall become a plain; and shouts of 'Grace, grace to it!'"*

INTRODUCTION

Zechariah is identified as the son of Berechiah and the grandson of Iddo. He is a close colleague of the prophet Haggai. His message addresses many subjects ranging from reversal of the nations, the sovereignty of Israel's God, God's dwelling place is in Zion, a branch of David will rule over Israel – but not as its king, and moral transformation that will come as a result of God's return.

Zechariah 1-8 is a series of visions framed by a pair of sermons. At the heart of First Zechariah (1-8) are the visions. They appear to be dated in the 11 month of the second year of the reign of King Darius of Persia. That would place his writing from 520 B.C.E.- 518 B.C.E. The Persian policy towards the exiles was benevolent. Its purpose was to establish loyalty throughout the Empire while at the same time providing imperial control.

According to Ezra 2-3, Zerubbabel and Joshua, the High priest, led a group of Jewish exiles from Babylon to Judah and two years later, initiated the rebuilding of the temple. Zechariah, on the other hand, does not urge the community to continue building the temple. In Zechariah's prophecies the temple's completion occurs during the inauguration of the "New World Order" by the "branch," or Promised Messiah.

The visions of Zechariah are interpreted differently by many of its readers. The message it holds for us today is that we should know that God can and will change his mind when his people turn back to him. There is hope for the future no matter what the scenario looks like at this moment, for we are a people who walk by faith, not by sight.

Let us take a closer look at the message of hope we find in the Book of Zechariah and his visions, as we learn how to allow the Spirit to move the mountains in our lives.

_____

1)

Our first lesson teaches us that if we want the Holy Spirit to move mountains in our lives **_WE HAVE TO ASK THE RIGHT QUESTIONS?_** Read vv 1-4, "*The angel who talked with me came again, and wakened me, as one is wakened from sleep. He said to me, 'What do you see?' And I said, 'I see a lampstand all of gold, with a bowl on the top of it; there are seven lamps on it, with seven lips on each of the lamps that are on top of it. And by it there are two olive trees, one on the right of the bowl and the other on its left. I said to the angel who talked with me, 'What are these, my lord?'…'*" The angel of the Lord awakened Zechariah again from his sleep. Zechariah is now having a fifth vision. In this vision Zechariah describes a scene. He sees a golden lampstand, 7 lamps with 7 lips on them, a bowl, and two olive trees. Totally unaware of what these items in this vision mean, he asked the angel "What are these?"

By the fifth vision, Zechariah is aware that the visions mean something beyond his understanding. As a prophet, Zechariah wants to know what is the message he is to proclaim to the people because of the vision. What is God saying to him through this angel? Why is God talking in riddles that confused him and caused him to ask the angel of the Lord for an interpretation?

Zechariah did not have a temple experience because at this time in Israel's history, there was no temple standing! So the presence of a golden lampstand and a bowl on top of it boggled his mind, not to mention that he was asleep or in a trance-like state when the vision appeared. So he says to the angel of the Lord, "What are these my lord?"

Things sometimes happen in life that throw us into a tailspin. We become confused about consequences we suffer after trying to help someone in a bad situation. We work and get along with our co-workers, but are continually passed up for a promotion we are in a marriage for 20 years and one day our partner wants out of the relationship. So we ask the question -Why? Why are we being treated in this manner? Can anyone explain what is going on and why no one cares that this scenario makes no sense or is unfair?

If we get the run around, which is usually the case, we go to God in prayer and pose the question to God as did Job. God is omniscient so God is the one we should address our questions to. Zechariah was dealing with an angel of the Lord, so it was natural that Zechariah would address the question to the angel. Since the angel represented the Lord, the interpretation of the vision must have been revealed to him beforehand!

Like Zechariah when God speaks to us in a dream we do not always understand what it means. Therefore, rather than remain in the dark, ask God to shed his light on the situation.

Then wait on his answer. In the words of the songwriter wrote, *"We'll understand it better, by and by."*

_____

2)

Our second lesson teaches us that if we want the Holy Spirit to move mountains in our lives, ***WE HAVE TO DO IT GOD'S WAY***. Read vv 5-6, *"Then the angel who talked with me answered me, 'Do you not know what these are?' I said, 'No my lord.' He said to me, 'This is the word of the Lord to Zerubbabel: Not by might, nor by power, but by my spirit, says the Lord of hosts.'"* There is nothing more annoying than for someone to answer a question with a question. But that is exactly what the angel of the Lord did. After Zechariah posed his question, in a surprising response, the angel of the Lord asked Zechariah a question, *"Do you not know what these are?"*

Now if Zechariah knew what the vision meant, he would not have asked the angel what does it mean! So again he responds to the angel, "No, my lord." Then the angel tells Zechariah that the vision represents the message God sent to Zerubbabel, the governor of Judah. Zerubbabel was to know that God was not going to use conventional military strategy to defeat Israel's enemies. No, the new weapon against Israel's enemies is summed up in verse 6, *"Not by might, nor by power, but by my spirit, says the Lord of hosts."*

This time, God was using only the Holy Spirit to get the temple completed. The Spirit would move upon the hearts and wills of the people to get the work done. They will come together as one people, under the influence of one Spirit. Once the temple is completed God will again take up residency in Zion.

After the confrontation Nehemiah experienced with the neighboring peoples when he was rebuilding the wall, God refused to use force or power in the rebuilding of his Holy Temple. As the Psalmist said, *"The Lord is in his Holy Temple, let all the earth keep silence, before him."* (Hab 2:20) Perhaps because of the sacred nature of the temple's existence, using the Holy Spirit will consecrate the building project and keep it holy for God's return. Remember King David wanted to build God a house, but because he was a man of war and had blood on his hands, God allowed his son Solomon to build it instead.

Zerubbabel is credited for completing the temple in the book of Haggai, and strongly suggested in the book of Zechariah. Unfortunately, he suddenly disappears from the biblical record. Yet God's Spirit was now under contract. Just as the Spirit participated in creation, now its role and function was to bring Israel back into the fold of God, through her worship of God in God's House.

We sometimes out of frustration want God to just zap our enemies and make them disappear. But remember Jesus teaches us to *"Love our enemies, pray for those who despitefully use you."* (Mt 5:43) Might and power are no longer the tools for revenge we are to use when dealing with our mountains. God has now instructed us to allow the presence of the Holy Spirit in our lives and that the Holy Spirit will take on and defeat any mountain that would dare block our vision of God, or try to stop us from succeeding in our service to God. Isaiah teaches us that, *"No weapon formed against us shall prosper!" (Isa 54:17)*

God's Spirit is enough for us to continue to move forward in whatever God has put our hands to do. We just need to trust God and know that *"All things work together for good for those who love God, who are called according to his purpose." (Rom 8:28)*

At first the angel did not give the interpretation that Zechariah asked for. Instead we have the repeat of the words God said to Zerubbabel. Then after Zechariah understands how God plans to restore Israel, not by power, war, pestilence, drought, but through his Spirit, the angel of the Lord explains the meaning of the vision in verses 10-14. Yet, there is still one more reference to Zerubbabel's leadership that encouraged Zechariah to move forward in his prophecy. We read this in our next lesson.

---

3)

Our third and final lesson teaches us that if we want the Holy Spirit to move mountains in our lives, **_WE HAVE TO REMOVE THE MOUNTAIN ONE STONE AT A TIME._** Read v 7, *"What are you, O great mountain? Before Zerubbabel you shall become a plain, and he shall bring out the top stone amid shouts of 'Grace, grace to it!'"* The reference to a mountain here is believed to describe the remaining debris of the destroyed temple. The rubble would have been massive as the temple was a magnificent structure designed by King David, but built by his son Solomon. The height and width and breadth of the temple was grand and included the best of everything in its design, from sapphires and rubies to diamonds, gold and silver, and cedar for Lebanon.

So it is not hard to image the amount of debris left behind on the site after the Babylonians (with some help from the Edomites) burned it to the ground. Zechariah looked at what could be perceived as a monumental task, but instead approached it as an accumulation of many smaller stones (it's all in how you look at it), half-full, half-empty. Zechariah records Governor Zerubbabel taking on the task of removing this *"great mountain"* of rubble in stride. He is not conflicted or overwhelmed by what he sees before him.

Governor Zerubbael knew what he was sent to Judah to do – rebuild God's House – and no amount of burned stone was going to stop him from accomplishing his task. He had no bulldozer, no dynamite to facilitate the work. No, his strategy was to start from the top stone, and work his way down. One stone at a time until the foundation was cleared and prepped to rebuild the new temple. The temple had to be built on the same sacred ground in order to honor the Lord God of Hosts. Otherwise, they could have chosen a different space and place to rebuild. In this way, every person could participate by removing some debris, and see the finished product as the work of the whole community, inspired by God's Holy Spirit.

The attitude and perhaps a symbolic gesture to remove one stone at a time sent the crowds into a state of jubilation and celebration. It represented the new reality that Israel and God were back in business together. Israel's enemies better watch out! The terminator is back!

In life we often encounter obstacles that on face value, appear to us as great mountains, too surmountable for us to take on by ourselves. However, that is the key word, "by ourselves." We can never take on the challenges of life alone, without God's Holy Spirit leading us, empowering us and guiding us to the destination God intended for our lives.

Whenever we face an obstacle that is when we immediately have to go to God in prayer. Mountains cannot be avoided if we live in this world. Our strategy and how we approach that mountain, is the key to our successfully removing the mountain and bringing it down to size. That strategy has to include the Holy Trinity – *God the Father, God the Son, and God the Holy Spirit*. Therefore, it is *"Not by might nor by power, but by God's spirit"* that any and every mountain will be climbed over or destroyed.

An old gospel song from the 1960s used these words, *Lord don't move my mountain, just give me the strength to climb it. And Lord, don't take away my stumbling blocks, just lead me all around."* There is no life without mountains to face. It does not matter if you are rich or poor, black or white or yellow or red, educated or uneducated, the universe will present you with a mountain from time to time. Some mountains will feel like a molehill and easily conquered, while others will feel like Mt. Everest and cause us to fall into utter despair. But do not ever give up. Just remember with God, all things are possible.

Are you allowing the Holy Spirit to move your mountains, or are you trying to use your human might, political connections, and power? Mountains are moved when you are in a relationship with God and are filled with the Holy Spirit. *"Not by might, nor by power, but by my spirit, says the Lord of Hosts."* God bless you!

THE BOOK OF MALACHI

Giving God His Due!

WHEN A MINISTER LOOSES THEIR WAY

MALACHI 2:7-9, *"For the lips of a priest ought to preserve knowledge, and from his mouth men should seek instruction – because he is the messenger of the Lord Almighty. But you have turned from the way and by your teaching have caused many to stumble; you have violated the covenant with Levi, says the Lord Almighty. So I have caused you to be despised and humiliated before all the people, because you have not followed my ways but have shown partiality in matters of the law."*

INTRODUCTION

The book of Malachi consists of only four chapters and 55 verses. It is the final book of prophecy we find in the Old Testament. The book does not belong to a time when Israel was a great power in the world. Most scholars place it during the post-exilic period, when Judah (also called *Yehud*) was under the tutelage of the vast Persian Empire.

The Book of Malachi addresses issues such as: animal sacrifice, payment of tithes, bored priests, unfaithful husbands, and a dissatisfied community. He also has a passion for justice, concern for the widow, the orphan and the common laborer. His name means *"my messenger"* in Hebrew. This has caused some to think it is a title rather than his personal name. Since we have no mention of a specific person or events, the book is considered "ahistorical" meaning it could easily fit anywhere within the time frame of prophetic literature. However, the general consensus is that it was written during the time when the returnees were living in Judah.

Some of the abuses listed in the book of Malachi are also found in the Ezra-Nehemiah saga. This connection helps the reader place the context within the framework of the Ezra-Nehemiah portfolio. Like his predecessors, Malachi condemns specific abuses that are in violation of the Mosaic covenant. The returnees are ignoring the Law and behaving in ways that only please themselves and oppress others in the community who have no voice.

So Malachi organizes his book by using a set of accusatory questions that God asks and the priests respond to by asking for proof of these abuses. When God accuses them of breaking the covenant law, they ask God for an example and God gives them one. It comes off as a dialogue of contention between God and the religious leaders.

Malachi uses the prophetic formula *"Thus says the Lord of Hosts"* over 22 times thereby verifying that his message comes from God Almighty. In addition, he asked 22 questions in only 55 verses! This appears to be a new prophetic style that is evident in Malachi's composition. Yet, the genres he employs include prophetic disputation, discussion, and lawsuit, all mixed in together in a way that speaks to his audience. It is more dialogical and argumentative than literature we find in the earlier prophetic material. It is meant to bring accusations against God's religious leaders, the priests, who were supposed to be the guardians of God's word and commandments. Instead they led the people away from God's justice and righteousness with their false teachings.

This text is a good reminder to all religious leaders that they must remain in sync with God's purpose and plan for his people and not become arrogant, greedy, self-serving, and oppressive towards God's called community of believers. It is never about us, it is always about God. So let us read Malachi's words as he blames the priests for the peoples' spiritual, moral, and social decline.

_____

1)

Our first lesson takes the form of a question ***WHAT IS THE ROLE OF A RELIGIOUS LEADER?*** Read v. 7, *"For the lips of a priest should guard knowledge, and people should seek instruction from his mouth, for he is the messenger of the Lord of hosts."* There was a struggle for power between the Aaronite priest (appointed by Moses) and the Levites who on occasion performed priestly duties. Is Malachi taking sides in condemning these priests while at the same time praising the Levites? This may be an underlying grudge, but the essence of the question is not which priests come from which lineage. The question is concerned about who's teaching has become so corrupt that the people are behaving in ways that are contrary to God's word.

The text reads, *"The lips of the priest should guard knowledge..."* What knowledge? The knowledge of God's relationship with Israel and the commandments she was given to uphold as grounds for the covenant relationship to continue. This knowledge is used as a guard against social injustice and spiritual idolatry. The book of Proverbs is filled with wisdom teachings to prevent Israel from invoking God's wrath as well as social instruction about everyday life.

The priest' role was to guard and protect this knowledge so that it did not become watered down, or infiltrated with bad teaching or syncretized with foreign habits of behavior. How did they allow their teachings to become in opposition to God's laws? There seems to have been a shift after the return to Judah. Survival became the primary concern, not instituting or enforcing the Torah laws. That is why Ezra was asked to return to Judah from Persia because the people did what they thought was right in their own eyes.

Malachi holds the priests accountable because the people seek instruction from them. The religious leaders have the knowledge and the answers to the people's questions about life as it pertains to living under the obedience of God's word. If the religious leaders are corrupt or mislead the people for their own selfish gain, how can the people know God's truth? Many were illiterate and depended on the priests to read and interpret God's word to them. The question of the day was, *"Is there a word from the Lord?"*

It was God's word that settled disputes between families and neighbors. If the religious leaders were susceptible to bribes and intimidation by those in power, then they failed both God and the people they were called to protect! Justice was not administered and lives were negatively affected. This behavior was stench in God's nostrils. The minister is the messenger of the Lord. One cannot take that role lightly for God will hold them accountable. The New Testament says that it is better for that person not be born, then to mislead people away from God's word by altering the message. To fail to give right instruction and disseminate correct knowledge based on God's holy word is equivalent to a false prophet.

We have many places of worship today all around the world. People tend to "church hop" when they become unhappy at their current place of worship. Every sermon does not guard the knowledge in God's word. Therefore, it is imperative that we read and know the word for ourselves in times such as these. False prophets are everywhere, trying to claim your dollars and loyalty. Yet before you make a commitment ask the Holy Spirit for guidance, then fast and pray. Measure what you hear from the pulpit against God's written world. If they do not match up, it is time to move on.

_____

2)

Our second lesson asks the question, ***WHAT HAPPENS WHEN THE LEADERSHIP GOES AWRY?*** Read v 8, *"But you have turned aside from the way; you have caused many to stumble by your instructions; you have corrupted the covenant of Levi, says the Lord of hosts..."* The crimes against the priests are serious accusations. The priests themselves have turned away from God's ways and commandments. Their behavior has a "cause and effect" that I will refer to as *"follow the leader."* The priests were supposed to lead by a holy example. The people looked to them for instruction as well as correction. The different sacrifices made at the altar of the temple categorized the level and kinds of sin made against God and the offerings necessary to appease God's wrath and receive God's forgiveness. But the priests have corrupted the covenant laws. Now the people only know the punishment for their sins according to the word of the priests – right or wrong!

Other prophets, such as Jeremiah, also shed a negative light on the ministers and religious leaders in his day. That is why Jeremiah 33:31 says that God will write his laws upon our hearts so we will not have to depend on others to teach us God's way. But Malachi puts special emphasis on the Levites as having remained faithful to the law. Malachi traces his position before the line of Zadoc and the Aaronite priesthood. He determined that Levi was the founder of the priestly line. This may come from the influence of the authors of the book of Deuteronomy, who were the final redactors of the Old Testament prophetic literature.

By comparing different lines of the priesthood, Malachi places judgment on the current acting priesthood. Who else has caused the people to wander so far from God? Who else has the opportunity to expose the people to heretical teachings over and over again? According to Malachi, it is the priest fault! They know better! They intentionally broke God's covenant either because of their own ignorance, or neglect. Either way, the people ended up in the same spiritually deprived state of mind and heart.

When the religious leaders lose their way, Satan's teachings are able to co-exist alongside of God's truth, which makes them more palatable to the hearer. Based on the personality and charisma of the leader, sometimes the unadulterated word of God is overshadowed by the hearing of smooth words that do not convict, accuse, or cause one to repent. When the religious leaders lose their way, chaos and oppressive tactics masquerade as God's rule. This causes people to stumble and fall short of God's glory. People can only do better, when they are taught better.

This is why we cannot look to human leaders to sustain our faith and commitment to God. Instead, like the words of the Psalmist, *"I lift my eyes unto the hills - from whence comes my help? My help comes from the Lord, who made heaven and earth."* (121:1-2) Religious leaders are human and prone to error. Just look at the biblical characters and how they fell short and did not always fare well. So that teaches us to not depend on flesh and blood for the cultivation of our souls, but in the words of 2 Timothy 2:15, *"Study to show thyself approved, a workman who need not be ashamed, rightly explaining the word of truth."*

When we become knowledgeable of God's word, then our steps will be ordered by the Lord and not by human intelligence. Nothing and nobody will be able to turn us around.

---

3)

Our third lesson from this text asks the question, ***WHAT ARE THE CONSEQUENCES OF BREAKING BAD WITH GOD?*** Read v 9, *"And so I make you despised and abased before all the people, inasmuch as you have not kept my ways but have shown partiality in your instruction."* God draws the contrast between the priests of Levitic descent, and the current priesthood, in order to show how far the priests have fallen away from God's justice. Their behavior and false teachings can no longer be tolerated in the House of God.

So now their day of reckoning has come to pass. God is threatening to publicly embarrass them and expose them for the liars and frauds that they have become. No longer will they be able to justify and promote their evil deeds through God's instruction. They will now be punished for accepting maimed, deformed and blind animals as sacrifices to God. This is a blatant disobedience to the laws of sacrifice found in the book of Leviticus!

They can no longer cheat and rob God of the tithe that is due him in order to live luxurious and comfortable lifestyles, while the poor sleep on the cold ground. They can no longer be in agreement with unfaithful husbands, nor can they silence the complaints of the people they are called to serve. No longer will justice be sold to the highest bidder. God says enough is enough! The buck stops here! God is going to shut down this illegal organization that operates in his name. The people will now see them for who they really are and God will see that his divine justice is mediated and made a reality so that reform can take place.

It is the priests' role to speak from the knowledge of accumulated tradition and professional learning. They were supposed to be the *"Custodians of God's truth,"* not the perpetrators of Satan's lies! God says, *"Vengeance is mine!" (Rom 12:19)* It is now time for the priests to be held accountable for what they have done to contribute to the spiritual and moral demise of the community of faith.

There are so many similarities between the words of Malachi and what is currently going on within the Christian community today. Cases of sexual abuse, oppression of a woman's right to be ordained and or serve as pastors, and racial tensions between people of color serving in leadership positions. These are disagreements and heresies promoted by God's religious leaders, not by God's Holy Spirit!

Just as God was disgusted in Malachi's day, his disgust continues to loom over the 21st century Church. The world looks on the Church and accuses it of hypocrisy and injustice. Paul tried to set the record straight and promote equality across the board, by noting that God is no respecter of persons when he wrote Gal 3:28, *"In Christ there is no male or female, no Jew or Greek, no slave or free."*

Yet, the Church in an effort to assimilate allowed the social customs and culture of its environment to overrule God's word. This has caused much harm to peoples who come to Christ under the pretext that they can be free – socially, financially, and spiritually. Yes, the Church for centuries made great strides to fulfill the *"Great Commission"* but somewhere along the way, the leadership shifted gears and became a more secular organism by using the world as its model, instead of depending on God's word to survive.

The clergy of today must read and learn from the book of Malachi so that God's Church can get back on a spiritual track before Christ's Second Coming *(the Parousia)*. For Christ is looking for a Church without a spot or blemish. God is a God of his word and will do to the present clergy as he promised to do to the priests of Malachi's day if we do not heed his word and teach it to our congregations. So let the Church move forward in the love and knowledge of our Lord and Savior Jesus the Christ. For he gave us the one commandment that turned the world upside down 2000 years ago, *"Love ye one another, as I have loved you." (Jn 13:34)* When we get that commandment right, everything in God's kingdom on earth will fall into place.

Yes, as clergy we sometimes make mistakes. People in powerful positions may offer us promotions to turn a blind eye or support a position that we know is not of God. Sometimes they may try to influence our decisions by offering to make substantial financial contributions to our church treasuries, without God's interest at heart. The sins and needs of the flesh sometime overrule the demands of the spirit. However, there is still time to repent, time for forgiveness because mercy is still our primary defense. It is mercy that pulls at God's heart and overrules his justice. God is a benevolent God and hears a repentant sinner's prayer. Mercy for the priests in Malachi's time ran out; we do not want that to be the case today.

There is still time to turn the Church of business and politics, back into the Church of restoration and salvation for all peoples. We just need the courage and faith to do it! We have to disengage from the demands of this world, and embrace the spiritual blessings from God's kingdom. For the word says that if we are obedient, God will open a window from heaven and pour out a blessing. The last question we ask is, *"What does God require of us? "Do justice, love mercy, and walk humbly with our God."(Micah 6;8)* God bless you!

REFERENCES

The Holy Bible. KJV and NRSV

The Interpreter's Bible. Vols 1-12, Abingdon Press: New York, 1953

Interpreter's Dictionary of the Bible. Vols 1-5, Abingdon Press: Nashville, 1976

The Anchor Bible Dictionary. Freedman, David Noel, editior-in-chief. Doubleday: New York

The New Century Bible Commenary. Marshal, Morgan and Scott, Ltd: London, 1971

The New Interpreter's Bible. Vols 1-12. Abingdon: Nashville, 1995

The New Interpreter's Study Bible. NRSV with the Apocrypha. Abingdon Press: Nashville, 2003

The New Testament Study Bible. Vols 1-20, The Complete Biblical Library: Springfield, 1986

The World Biblical Commentary. Word Books: Waco, 1988

LIST OF HYMNS AND SONGS QUOTED

1. You're Next in Line for a Miracle
2. He's an On Time God
3. Because he lives
4. Many things I don't know about Tomorrow
5. And they'll Know we are Christians by our Love
6. Any ole Way you bless me Lord, I'll Be Satisfied
7. Every Time I Feel the Spirit
8. There is a Balm in Gilead
9. What Shall I Render?
10. Precious Name, O How Sweet
11. This Little Light of Mine
12. The Battle Is Not Yours, it's the Lord's
13. At the Cross
14. Jesus Dropped the Charges
15. What If God is not Happy with our Praise?
16. Courage My Soul, and Let Us Journey On
17. Be Not Dismayed
18. I Trust in God
19. How did You Feel when You Come Out of the Wilderness?
20. Up Above My Head I Hear Music in the Air
21. His Eye is on the Sparrow
22. Because He Lives
23. Lord Don't Move my Mountains
24. Lift Every Voice and Sing
25. My Hope Is Built

Printed in the United States
By Bookmasters